THE POLITICS OF ICONOCLASM

Religion, Violence and the Culture of
Image-Breaking in Christianity and Islam

JAMES NOYES

For Elodie

New paperback edition published in 2016 by
I.B.Tauris & Co. Ltd
London • New York
www.ibtauris.com

First published in hardback in 2013 by I.B.Tauris & Co. Ltd

Copyright © 2013, 2016 James Noyes

The right of James Noyes to be identified as the author of this work has been asserted by the author in accordance with the Copyright, Designs and Patents Act 1988.

All rights reserved. Except for brief quotations in a review, this book, or any part thereof, may not be reproduced, stored in or introduced into a retrieval system, or transmitted, in any form or by any means, electronic, mechanical, photocopying, recording or otherwise, without the prior written permission of the publisher.

Every attempt has been made to gain permission for the use of the images in this book. Any omissions will be rectified in future editions.

References to websites were correct at the time of writing.

ISBN: 978 1 78453 479 0
eISBN: 978 0 85773 431 0

A full CIP record for this book is available from the British Library
A full CIP record is available from the Library of Congress

Library of Congress Catalog Card Number: available

Typeset by Mach 3 Solutions Ltd, Stroud, GL6 8JY

Contents

List of Illustrations	vi
Note on Transliteration	vii
Acknowledgements	viii
Preface to the Paperback Edition	x
Introduction	1

PART I: THE PROTOTYPES

1	Calvinism and Iconoclasm	23
2	Wahhabism and Iconoclasm	60

PART II: THE CASES

3	The French Revolution and Iconoclasm	97
4	The Bourgeois City and Iconoclasm: Venice	114
5	World War II and Iconoclasm	127
6	The Balkan Wars and Iconoclasm	147
7	Islamic Iconoclasm Today	166
	Conclusion	180
	Notes	187
	Bibliography	221
	Index of Key Names	234

List of Illustrations

Page 5:   Follower of Filippino Lippi, 'The Worship of the Egyptian Bull God, Apis' (c. 1500). © National Gallery, London (NG 4905).

Page 14:   Unknown Artist, 'King Edward VI and the Pope (includes John Russell, 1st Earl of Bedford; Thomas Cranmer; King Edward VI; King Henry VIII; John Dudley, Duke of Northumberland; Edward Seymour, 1st Duke of Somerset)' (c. 1570). © National Portrait Gallery, London (NPG 4165).

Page 57:   The 'Monument International de la Réformation' in Geneva, featuring Farel, Calvin, de Bèze, and Knox (1909). Photograph taken by Daniel Fernandez (2008).

Page 107:   Hubert Robert, 'La violation des caveaux des rois dans la basilique Saint-Denis' (1793). Musée Carnavalet, Paris (P 1477).

Page 118:   Still from Nicolas Roeg, *Don't Look Now* (1973). By kind permission of Nicolas Roeg.

Page 140:   Cologne in Ruins: Cologne Cathedral, Central Station, and the destroyed Hohenzollernbrücke over the River Rhine during B-24 VE 'Trolley Missions' (1945). Photograph taken by James Beadling, co-pilot of the 'Wazzle Dazzle'.

Page 141:   Part of the model prepared to the plans of Donald Gibson (Coventry City Architect) for the post-war rebuilding of Coventry's bomb-damaged city centre (1945). © Imperial War Museums, London (D 15515).

Page 164:   Graves at Hadum Mosque in Gjakova, Kosovo (2011). Photograph taken by Kristine Lunde-Tellefsen.

Page 174:   Abraj al-Bait, with the Kaaba in foreground, Mecca (2011). Unknown Author.

Note on Transliteration

For Arabic words, I have followed the American Library Association – Library of Congress (ALA-LC) Romanization standard and have removed accents (for example, on the letters ض or ص) in order not to alienate the reader with no knowledge of the Arabic alphabet. Seeking also to maintain consistency around the three Arabic vowels of A, I, and U, I have at times adapted the spelling used by other authors. For example, another author might refer to Mahomet (common in French), Mohammed (common in English), or Muḥammad (following the ALA-LC method of transliteration). Following ALA-LC but removing accents, I refer to Muhammad, and adapt most references to the name accordingly. Likewise, Hejaz becomes Hijaz, al-Sa'ud becomes al-Saud, and Muḥammad ibn 'Abd al-Wahhāb becomes Muhammad ibn Abd al-Wahhab. There are two exceptions to this rule. First, when I cite older European texts describing 'Musulmen' and 'Mahomet', I retain such terms for the sake of achieving a sense of historical context. Second, I follow contemporary standard practice by referring to the Islamic holy book as the Qur'an.

For Arabic theological terms, I have often kept the original words without translating them into English. For example, while 'associationism' is not a perfect translation of *shirk*, I consider it to be theologically clearer in the Islamic context than 'idolatry'. If I can, I prefer to use English terms; however, when the meaning of a concept like *shirk* is not readily translatable I keep the original in parentheses. I have used English versions of Arabic names when they are common – for example in the cases of Cairo and Egypt, Damascus and Syria, Mecca and Saudi Arabia, and Jerusalem and Palestine.

Finally, I have retained accents in European languages like French and Serbo-Croat, as their letters are not open to the same range of transliterative interpretation and possible confusion as in Arabic.

Acknowledgements

A number of people have been influential during the evolution of this book, from its first steps as a doctoral thesis to its later sprint through a political history of iconoclasm since the sixteenth century. In particular, I would like to take this opportunity to acknowledge three scholars: without the encouragement and the ideas of Richard Clay at the University of Newcastle, Timothy Jenkins at the University of Cambridge, and Adrian Pabst at the University of Kent, this book could not have been written. I am immensely grateful to each one of them for their time and support.

I have also been helped, at different times and in different ways, by the feedback, conversations, financial assistance, and the moral and institutional support of the following people: Patricia Aske at Pembroke College, Cambridge; Dario Gamboni at the University of Geneva; Bruno Latour at Sciences Po; Simon Cane at University College London; John Milbank at the University of Nottingham; Richard Westerman at the University of Alberta; Alan Winter at Christ's College, Cambridge; and Timothy Winter at the University of Cambridge. Without the financial support during my doctorate of both the Faculty of Divinity at the University of Cambridge and the fellows of Christ's College, Cambridge, much of the research for this book could not have been achieved. Over the years, Christ's College funded many of my travels, including visits to the Balkans and the Middle East. I have also benefited enormously from my interaction with the 'Iconoclasms Network' led by Leslie Brubaker at the University of Birmingham, and the exchanges with the curatorial team at Tate Britain. On a practical level, I am grateful to those who enabled me to use certain images, especially Charles Collier and Kristine Lunde-Tellefsen, and to those who lent me their quiet corners of countryside in which to write, in particular my family-in-law and John and Liz Downing.

Finally, I would like to thank both my family and friends for their loyalty and support. I am above all blessed by the love and encouragement of my wife, and it is to her that these pages are dedicated.

With the increasing productivity and division of labour, the formation of a large surplus, and the building of states with hierarchies and elites, large-scale destructiveness and cruelty came into existence and grew as civilization and the role of power grew.

> Erich Fromm, *The Anatomy of Human Destructiveness*

Ideas do, at times, develop lives and powers of their own and, like Frankenstein's monster, act in ways wholly unforeseen by their begetters, and, it may be, directed against their will, and sometimes turn on them to destroy them.

> Isaiah Berlin, 'Kant as an Unfamiliar Source of Nationalism'

Preface to the Paperback Edition

The Arab Spring has turned into a Summer of Destruction.

Old regimes have been destroyed by the uprisings, but so too have ancient places. Destruction extends across borders: in Libya, Sufi shrines have been bulldozed; in Egypt, Coptic churches have been firebombed; in Iraq, Catholic monasteries have had their crosses dismantled, their buildings emptied, the images of their saints scratched out.

Non-religious sites have also been targeted. Some of these are of such historical significance that their destruction has led to a storm of worldwide condemnation. The Assyrian city of Nimrud exists no more. Its famous winged lamassu have had their faces chipped away by electric drills, and its walls have been detonated. In March 2015, the Parthian city of Hatra was attacked. William Friedkin used Hatra in 1973 as the setting for a scene in *The Exorcist*. Now his film must serve as a historical document as well as Hollywood blockbuster. In Mosul, a city renowned for the pluralism of its religious communities and its heritage, the museum's collection has been smashed into fragments by sledgehammers. Its destruction was captured on video and broadcast through the internet into our homes.

These events shocked people around the world. An uncomfortable debate began: how could the promise of democracy in the Middle East have descended into this orgy of devastation? Why are Islamists destroying statues and archaeological artefacts in Syria and Iraq? What is the reason for this apparent battle between religion, art and cultural heritage? And how can we justify our anxiety, our anger about the value of that heritage, when so many innocent lives are being oppressed and lost?

When I began writing this book, the word 'iconoclasm' seemed to many people to be an obscure concern: something scholarly, antiquarian, slightly exotic. If the word had any common currency, it was connected to the Protestant Reformation, and the popularity of books like Eamon Duffy's *The Stripping of the Altars*. Indeed, my own interest in the subject stemmed from growing up surrounded by the ruins of English abbeys and churches. Ruins are a common feature of the Norfolk landscape where I spent my days: broken portions of priories and friaries, solitary arches standing unsteadily in fields, stumps of church towers no longer attached to chancels and naves. From afar, these flinty structures look like rubble, buried under ivy and bird nests. And, of course, there are the well-known ruins of St. Benet, Castle Acre, and Walsingham - monuments to the Dissolution of the Monasteries and the new order struck between Church and State.

My first sense that the word 'iconoclasm' extended beyond the borders of that world was in 2001. Two major events happened in that year. In March, the Taliban destroyed the famous Bamiyan Buddhas. Chapter 7 of this book describes the event, and the beginning of a debate over universal heritage which is so familiar to us today. As Afghan antiquities were being attacked, the director of New York's Metropolitan Museum of Art pleaded to the Taliban, 'let us remove them so that they are in the context of an art museum, where they are cultural objects, works of art not cult images'. In the weeks following the destruction of the Buddhas, a Taliban spokesman responded by condemning the importance that international museums placed on stone objects while tens of thousands of Afghan children were dying from the effects of drought, conflict and economic sanctions. During a meeting at the United Nations, one delegate called the destruction of the statues 'barbarism', a word which has since been used to describe the actions of the self-proclaimed 'Islamic State'. Injustice or barbarism. Art or idol. Heritage or human life. These are the questions which now frame the debate over iconoclasm.

The other major event of 2001 was, of course, al-Qaida's destruction of the World Trade Center. Few commentators at the time made the iconoclastic connection, with some exceptions: *Der Spiegel* called the World Trade Center 'the ultimate icon of capitalism', and Jürgen Habermas described it as 'an icon in the household imagery of the American nation'. In the years that followed 9/11, this kind of language became increasingly common when used to describe the events and actions of al-Qaida, the 'War on Terror', and the sectarian conflict that had begun to take hold in parts of the Muslim World. The famous toppling of Saddam Hussein's statue in Baghdad's Firdos Square was described as an act of 'iconoclasm' and broadcast on television; following the fall of Saddam, important Shiite shrines in Karbala, Najaf, and Samarra were attacked by Sunni militants; at the same time, riots erupted in Arab cities in protest at the depiction of Muhammad in European papers like *Jyllands-Posten* and *Charlie Hebdo*. By 2007, the word iconoclasm was no longer an obscure or antiquarian concern. It was rapidly becoming a key to understanding conflict in the modern world.

This was the context to my time spent researching and writing *The Politics of Iconoclasm*. I wanted to take the events following the destruction of the Bamiyan Buddhas and the World Trade Center, and to trace them back to their historical, theological and political origins - in doing so, I wanted to examine the relationship not only between image-breaking in Christianity and Islam, but also the relationship between the destruction of images and the construction of political order and control.

I finished the book in 2012, just as the Gaddafi regime had fallen to a coalition of Libyan revolutionaries, NATO jets, and Qatari special forces. Two moments from that chapter of history stick in my mind: first, the sight of Gaddafi's Bab al-Aziziyah compound, and its iconic sculpture of a golden fist crushing an American fighter jet being scaled by rebels, graffitied with slogans, and removed. Second, the sight of Bernard Henri-Lévy, in snappy white shirt and fancy tan, flanked in Tripoli by Mustafa Abdel Jalil, David Cameron and Nicolas Sarkozy. To see Henri-Lévy proclaim the 'fair wind of democracy' in Libya, alongside the two men who commanded Europe's heaviest guns, seemed to me to reiterate the theme contained in the Conclusion of this book: namely, that despite its claim to represent universal and enlightened values, the practice of building modern states operates in the shadow of violence. The fact that Gaddafi had been welcomed into the palaces of London and Paris just a few years before his demise serves to underline the absurdity as well as the awkwardness of that theme.

In the years that have followed these events, and with the changing fortunes of the Arab Spring, the relationship between religious iconoclasm and political revolution has become increasingly destructive. Many commentators predicted that conflict between regime loyalists, Islamists and rebels of different stripes would define the direction that countries like Libya, Egypt and Syria were taking. Few anticipated the extent of the explosion of ISIS on the world stage. As a result, the iconoclasm at the heart of that explosion has often been described as something new: a culture of destruction which we have not witnessed since the darkest days of World War II.

In this book, written over a year before the emergence of ISIS as a recognisable group, I argued that there is nothing new about iconoclasm. Describing al-Qaida attacks on Shiite shrines in Iraq between 2003 and 2007, as well as earlier attacks on those same shrines by Wahhabi forces at the beginning of the nineteenth century, I contended that while these events might represent an unfamiliar phenomenon to many in the media, they are part of a long-standing tradition of image-breaking in Christianity, Islam, and certain structures of state formation. These structures are not cast-iron rules. But they are patterns nonetheless - sometimes clear, sometimes opaque - which can be discerned throughout history and today. My book provides something of a context to these patterns, and anticipates the destruction we have seen unleashed since the turning of the Arab Spring.

One of the key patterns in the history of iconoclasm is the way in which it is used as a means of bridging the principles of theological and political unity. Theologically, iconoclasm upholds the absolute unity of the 'One God' against polytheism. Politically, it destroys the objects of polytheism, of superstition, of pluralism, and draws into itself those diverse cultures and communities which created such objects. My book argues that throughout history iconoclasm has tended to take place alongside political centralisation. This is, in a sense, inevitable: after all, localism is messy, and the aim of iconoclasm is purity.

It is for this reason that we should not be surprised to see ISIS attack non-religious sites like Nimrud and Hatra. In the mind of the iconoclasts, religious and territorial purity cannot be separated, because the unity of worship (*tawhid*) and the unity of God's people (the *Ummah*) are one and the same thing.

This type of thinking is particularly apparent in the *mujahideen's* use of the word for polytheism: *shirk*. Typically, *shirk* is used by ISIS militants to describe the statues and shrines which they destroy. But the word has been expanded to include other targets: for example, when demolishing a checkpoint marking the frontier between Syria and Iraq, they declare that they are fighting the 'imaginary borders of Sykes-Picot' in order to make the world whole for Allah. Thus the demolished checkpoint, as well as the discarded flags and badges of the border police, are all described with the same word as that for 'idol': these things are called *shirk*. The word has become something of a catch-all phrase used by ISIS fighters: they target the *shirk* of Shiite shrines, the *shirk* of Bashar al-Assad, the *shirk* of museums, the *shirk* of passports.

The pursuit of purity is inevitably doomed to depend on impure methods and means. ISIS is no exception in this respect, and there are numerous reports of the group operating an illicit smuggling trade of looted Syrian artefacts across the Turkish border. Indeed, many commentators have suggested that the broadcasting of spectacular attacks on famous archaeological sites over the internet is designed to serve as an advertisement for this trade as much as a religious statement. Stories have emerged of ISIS militants digging for treasures in places like Mosul, Dura-Europos and Palmyra - an accusation of looting which has also been levelled at the Assad regime and the Free Syrian Army.

The extent of this trade is unclear, as is the final destination of the looted objects. Nevertheless, while many of the reports of a 100-million dollar black market involving European dealers are probably exaggerated, there remains a general consensus that the destruction of heritage in Syria and Iraq operates within the established structures of political economy: not just the mechanics of supply and demand, but also the different layers of official and unofficial consent, acquiescence and permission.

These structures not only undermine ISIS's claim to purity, they also highlight the problematic relationship between destructive looting and European codes of heritage, ownership and value. Some of Europe's most famous museum collections are products of this relationship. In Syria and Iraq, sites like Nimrud and Palmyra were excavated by Europeans during colonial rule, and many of their most precious artefacts were shipped to the new national museums of London, Paris and Berlin. Chapter 3 of this book touches on some of the questions underlying that process.

It would be remiss of me not to conclude by mentioning the attack on *Charlie Hebdo*, when Islamists massacred a team of cartoonists who had repeatedly produced derogatory depictions of Muhammad. In the Western media, this episode was presented as part of a struggle between religion and the freedom of speech. As my book shows, there is a different story at play: the story of a struggle between systems of consent, value and imagery at the heart of the politics of iconoclasm.

The depiction of Muhammad is forbidden in much of Islam, but it has also been blackballed by the Western press. What we see instead is the proliferation of *permitted* images such as the '*Je Suis Charlie*' slogan: as banners on newspaper websites, as avatars on social media, as badges on the lapels of politicians and celebrities. This is the work of art in the age of digital reproduction, and I am reminded of John Berger's words on its manufacturing: such images have become ubiquitous, available, valueless and free. Thus the symbol of '*Je Suis Charlie*' performs in exactly the same way as iconoclasm. It is permitted; it conflates; it draws the messiness of the world into itself. That is why it is so politically powerful.

Permitting and producing one type of image over another is at the heart of the politics of iconoclasm. That is why the value of cultural heritage, and its destruction, is so closely tied to the power of the modern state. If there is a main message to my book, then, it is this: the breaking of images belongs not only to militants with hammers and soldiers with guns, but also to administrators and officials wielding pens in the quietude of their offices.

Introduction

In 1919, as part of a further move against religion, the coffins of mediaeval 'saints' were opened up and exposed to scientific scrutiny. The sweet-smelling, tear-shedding, eternally fresh dead bodies of church doctrine were revealed as little bundles of bone and dust. 'The cult of dead bodies and of these dolls must end', read the Justice Department's instruction. The policy ceased to apply when, in January 1924, Lenin had his last stroke. A powerful refrigerator was imported from Germany, and the Immortalization Commission worked flat out for six months, anxiously monitoring the mould on Lenin's nose and fingers. The corpse was rendered incorruptible, by science, and enshrined as an icon.

Martin Amis, *Koba the Dread: Laughter and the Twenty Million*[1]

The premise of this book is that the destruction of religious and cultural icons has gone hand in hand with the political construction of the modern State. By State, I refer to a type of Weberian 'officialdom' that administrated into extinction those communities and rituals which were deemed traditional, superstitious, and idolatrous. Weber argued that this fusion of administration and destruction was peculiar to the Christian West, particularly the Protestant territories of Germany, Great Britain, and the United States of America. The history of iconoclasm, however, shows that the destruction of shrines, tombs, and sacred objects has also shaped the Islamic world and the development of territories such as Bosnia Herzegovina, Iraq, and Saudi Arabia. Iconoclasm has been a formative feature of both Christian and Islamic history, crossing the boundaries of religion, culture, and politics. This book will examine those boundaries: through a comparative account of iconoclasm in Christian and Islamic history, it will connect the culture of image-breaking to the political system within which many Christians and Muslims live today.

With such a focus on modern politics, the reader will understand why this book begins with the European Reformation and not with the Byzantine iconoclastic controversies of the eighth and ninth centuries. The wave of so-called Calvinist attacks on religious images and buildings during the sixteenth century has been described by historians as occurring alongside – and, at times, precipitating – the emergence of a set of terms to describe a new political class operating within the 'State'. This political account of Reformation iconoclasm is not in itself original. Nor is the account of so-called Wahhabi attacks in cities like Mecca and Karbala during the eighteenth and nineteenth centuries which links iconoclasm to the construction of new Arab territories in the twentieth century. However, the task of translating these accounts into a comparative study of Christian and Islamic iconoclasm in relation to the modern State has been avoided by historians, for understandable historiographical reasons. Those who have written wide-ranging comparative studies of iconoclasm – scholars like Besançon, Gamboni, and Latour – have provided primarily philosophical and art historical narratives. They have stopped short of presenting an explicitly political account of the subject. This book will therefore attempt to make that step: beginning with the Calvinist Reformation, comparing it to Wahhabism, and connecting acts of image-breaking to versions of modern state-building, it seeks to identify a coherent politics of iconoclasm.

Drawing on the examples of Calvinism and Wahhabism as the two prototypes of a modern politics of iconoclasm, this book looks for wider historical connections between Christian and Islamic image-breaking that can be traced from the eighteenth century to the present day. As such, the examples of Calvinism and Wahhabism represent half of the book: Part I. Part II provides a series of shorter case studies in broadly chronological order with which the terms of the Calvinist and Wahhabi prototypes might be tested: iconoclasm during the French Revolution; iconoclastic rhetoric against the nineteenth-century bourgeois city; iconoclasm during World War II; iconoclasm during the Balkan conflicts of the 1990s; and, bringing these cases to the present day, iconoclasm in the twenty-first-century Muslim World. With each of these case studies, beginning with the attack on Geneva's St. Pierre Cathedral in 1535 and ending with the construction of a shopping mall next to the Kaaba in Mecca today, this book will ask whether it is possible to trace a historically coherent account of iconoclasm in different Christian and Islamic traditions and, by extension, will examine the nature of the relationship between religious violence and politics.

Before introducing these historical examples, it is necessary to outline the theoretical context within which a study of iconoclasm takes shape: namely, an introduction to the scriptural basis for iconoclasm shared by both Christians and Muslims; an account of the icon itself, and the theology of images; and an examination of how the theology connects to issues of political authority and the organization of society. Central to this context is the scriptural prohibition, influential on both Christianity and Islam, and with which the book will begin: the story of the golden calf.

THE GOLDEN CALF

Iconoclasm is a contested term[2] with complex theological, cultural, and political significance. From its scriptural origins, the term has been a matter of debate. The English word *iconoclast*, recorded in 1595, was taken from the Greek *eikon* and *klastes* via the French *iconoclaste*: the word is defined therefore as a 'breaker or destroyer of images' (the *eikon* being translated as 'image', not 'icon'). In the *Oxford English Dictionary*, the word is defined as 'one who took part in or supported the movement in the eighth and ninth centuries, to put down the use of images or pictures in religious worship, in the Christian churches of the East; hence, applied analogously to those Protestants of the sixteenth and seventeenth centuries who countenanced a similar destruction of the churches'. This conflation of meanings has resulted in a definition of the term 'iconoclasm' where the breaking of idols, the breaking of icons, and the breaking of images is typically considered to mean the same thing. It has led to a source of semantic confusion, most apparent in the question of why the word *idoloclasm* did not emerge in response to idol-worship or *eidolon latria*, and further complicated by the fact that while 'iconoclasm' is used to describe Islamic image-breaking, the word does not exist in Arabic. Despite these questions, Besançon states that, while its etymology is complex, 'the word "idol" acquired a stable and precise meaning through usage: it is the image, statue, or symbol of a false god'.[3] Following this meaning, the term 'iconoclasm' can be understood in a 'stable' sense too: it describes an attack against and often the destruction of a physical object, be it a statue, a painting, a tomb, a building, or a natural object like a tree that is believed to have some kind of spiritual power or sacred significance and which is worshipped in the place of the 'true' God. That is, iconoclasm is the destruction of the idol. Within the Abrahamic tradition, for Jews, Christians, and Muslims alike, the defining scriptural moment of this broadly understood rejection of the idol is found in the story of the golden calf.

For Christians, the story of the golden calf is given in the Book of Exodus. Having being brought out of slavery in Egypt by Moses, escaping across the Red Sea, the Jews are described as enduring the trials of crossing the desert in hope of reaching a Promised Land. It is in these circumstances that Moses receives the Covenant Code, and the following Commandment:

> Thou shalt have no other gods before me. Thou shalt not make unto thee any graven image, or any likeness of any thing that is in heaven above, or that is in the earth beneath, or that is in the water under the earth: Thou shalt not bow down thyself to them, for I the Lord thy God am a jealous God.[4]

Moses receives this Commandment on the Mountain of God, separated from the others in the desert by cloud and by fire – the unknowable God thus remaining invisible – for forty days. Yet in his absence the Israelites, with Aaron, turn to worship a golden statue of a calf:

> And the Lord said unto Moses ... They have turned aside quickly out of the way which I commanded them: they have made them a molten calf, and have worshipped it, and have sacrificed thereunto, and said, These be thy gods, O Israel, which have brought thee up out of the land of Egypt.[5]

This statue of a golden calf is generally assumed to be Apis, an Egyptian god associated with fertility and the protection of the dead. The Israelite worship of such an object signifies not only a lack of faith during Moses' absence and disobedience of the Commandment over graven images, but also a return to the religious practices of their oppressors. In the words of Thomas Hobbes: the Israelites 'relapse' into the idolatry of the Egyptians, and in doing so they 'revolt' against the 'True God'.[6] This relapse is described in Exodus as putting into jeopardy the very Covenant with God; in the context of the Promised Land, then, it represents a territorial-political as much as a religious

Follower of Filippino Lippi, 'The Worship of the Egyptian Bull God, Apis' (c. 1500)

error. So fundamental is the revolt of idolatry, that it is seen as apostasy and is met with violence: the 'jealous' God threatens to exterminate His people as punishment, but Moses intercedes; as a concession, three thousand of those who worshipped the golden calf are killed instead. Moses' moment of intercession is at the heart of the difference between Muslim and Jew. For the Jew, it marks the continued journey towards the Promised Land; for the Muslim, it marks the collapse of the Covenant. This difference, a tribal variation of the same story, is central to understanding the political significance of the golden calf. As Besançon notes, it is part of 'the history of a people whom God "chose" and set apart from other nations. Between these nations and that people stood the hurdle of the Torah'.[7]

For Islam, the prohibition against images recounts the same story as Exodus:

And indeed Musa [Moses] came to you with clear proofs, yet you worshipped the calf after he left, and you were [polytheists and wrong-doers].

And [remember] when We took your covenant and We raised above you the Mount [saying], 'Hold firmly to what We have given you, and hear [Our Word]'. They said, 'We have heard and disobeyed'. And their hearts absorbed [the worship of] the calf because of their disbelief. [8]

Like the Jewish and Christian Bible, the Qur'an describes the Israelites worshipping the golden calf in defiance of Moses; however, rather than this act representing a chapter in their journey as the chosen people of God, the Qur'an depicts the idolatry of the Israelites (their 'absorption' of the calf) as the breaking of the Abrahamic Covenant:

> The people of the Scripture [Jews] ask you to cause a book to descend upon them from heaven. Indeed they asked Musa for even greater than that, when they said: 'Show us Allah in public', but they were struck with thunderclap and lightning for their wickedness. Then they worshipped the calf even after clear proofs, evidences, and signs had come to them. [Even] so We forgave them. And We gave Musa a clear proof of authority.
>
> And for their covenant, We raised over them the Mount and [on the other occasion] We said: 'Enter the gate prostrating with humility'; and We commanded them: 'Transgress not [by doing worldly works] on the Sabbath'. And We took from them a firm covenant.
>
> Because of their breaking the covenant, and of their rejecting the *Ayat* [proofs, evidences, signs] of Allah, and of their killing the Prophets [Jesus] unjustly, and of their saying: 'our hearts are wrapped' – nay, Allah has set a seal upon their hearts because of their disbelief, so they believe not but a little.[9]

These Quranic verses thus share the same prohibition of idolatry as those of Exodus in the Bible, albeit with different tribal consequences. They also introduce the first pillar of Islam: the *Shahada*, the declaration that 'there is no god but one God, and Muhammad is his messenger' adopted from Surah al-Baqarah ('And your God [*wa ilahukum*] is One God [*il-Lahun* – Allah] ... there is no God but Him [*la ilaha illa Huwa*])'.[10] The *Shahada* is mentioned twenty-nine times in the Qur'an, and Allah is described as the 'sole divinity' thirteen times,[11] typically in reference to the Covenant between God and Ibrahim (Abraham), connected with the building of the Kaaba, being broken by his 'offspring' the Israelites. Surah al-Baqarah describes how 'this [submission to Allah (Islam)] was enjoined by Ibrahim upon his sons and by Yaqub [Jacob], saying "O my sons! Allah has chosen for you the [true] religion, then die not except as Muslims"', but that this was not heeded by the Jews, 'a nation who has passed away'. The Arabic word used to describe the Jews, and ultimately the Christians, is *mushrikun*, those who commit *shirk* or associationism (a word which is usually translated as 'idolatry'): 'they say, "Be Jews or Christians, then you will be guided." Say "Nay, [we follow] only the religion of Ibrahim, *Hanif* [Islamic Monotheism], and he was not of *al-Mushrikun*'.[12] As such, the Muslims are described as fulfilling the 'true religion' of the Covenant between God and Ibrahim because of the associationism or idolatry of the Jews and Christians, linking 'those who disbelieve [*kufr*] among the people of the Scripture' with *shirk*[13] and asserting that 'Ibrahim was a true Muslim and he was not of al-*Mushrikun*'.[14]

In the Qur'an, the idol which leads would-be Muslims to worship false gods represents an ontological corruption. The *Shahada* of 2:163 is followed by a description of God's creation, the argument that creation is proof of God's nature in itself, and finally the claim that idolatry is a corruption of the relationship between Creator and created:

> Verily, in the creation of the heavens and the earth, and in the alternation of night and day, and the ships which sail through the sea with that which is of use to mankind, and the water which Allah sends down from the sky and makes the earth alive therewith after its death, and the moving creatures of all kinds that He has scattered therein, and in the veering of winds and clouds which are held between the sky and the earth, are indeed *Ayat* [signs] for people of understanding.
>
> And of mankind are some who take [for worship] others besides Allah as rivals. They love them as they love Allah. But those who believe, love Allah more.[15]

This denouncement of the worship of rivals to Allah is made against later indigenous Arabian traditions in addition to the Jews. As well as describing the incident of the golden calf and the breaking of Abraham's Covenant in 4:153, the issuing of certain laws in 5:3 and 5:90 also prohibits the Arabian practice of using arrows to seek luck, and 53:19 refers to the worship of al-Lat, Al-Uzza, and Manat,[16] examples of pre-Islamic Arabian (*jahiliyyah*) deities. Additionally, the Qur'an condemns the Christians, who are described as associating Isa (Jesus) with God, as 'Allah will say [on the day of Resurrection]: "O Isa, son of Maryam! Did you say unto men: 'Worship me and my mother as two gods besides Allah?'" He will say: "Glory is to You! It was not for me to say what I had no right [to say]. Had I said such a thing, You would surely have known it. You know what is in my inner self, though I do not know what is in Yours"'.[17] In this way, Islam is presented as the fulfillment of God's Covenant with Abraham as it alone preserves God's unity, and the Qur'an is structured around a distinction between the 'believer', the *Muslim*, and the 'unbeliever', synonymous with the 'associators' or the *mushrikun*, including the pagans, the Christians, and the Jews – a division which in turn explains why non-Muslims are forbidden from visiting Mecca, as the Qur'an states '*al-Mushrikun* are impure. So let them not come near the mosque at Mecca [*al-masjid al-haram*]'.[18]

The story of the golden calf shows that a significant part of the scriptural understanding of the 'True God' is shared by Jews, Christians, and Muslims, despite their differing interpretations of the Abrahamic Covenant and consequent divisions of religious identity. As such, Christian and Islamic approaches to notions of worship, the forbidden object, and idolatry can be compared and contrasted. The scripture also shows a division of tribal identity based around differences between these religious interpretations. From tribal division, the first signs of social organization are made apparent, for example in the belief in a Promised Land or in the separation of the mosque at Mecca from *al-Mushrikun*. This is not an insignificant detail. The idea that a tribal identity – that is, a delimitation of a law, a definition of a territory, a belief in sacred ground, and a notion of communal destiny – is built on the basis of idol destruction as much as territorial construction makes a connection between its religious and political existence. This is the dialectic at the heart of the politics of iconoclasm: from its first articulation in the story of the golden calf, it has continued through a range of Christian and Islamic traditions to the present day.

THE IMAGE-ICON-IDOL

Before examining in more detail these points of religious and political exchange, it is necessary first to give an outline of the target of destruction itself: the image-icon-idol. As I have taken Calvinism as my first historical prototype for a study of iconoclasm, it follows that the target for destruction should correlate: it is a Catholic object. This is not to relegate the iconoclastic controversies of the Byzantine Church. Both the Orthodox Catholic Church and Roman Catholicism have historically shared much of a common discourse concerning religious imagery, where the icon can be described as having five key attributes. First, it exists as an emblem of *orthodoxy*. Second, this emblem is intimately associated with the incarnation, giving the icon *miraculous* properties in the eyes of its advocates. Third, the icon as an emblem of Christ's incarnation is considered to maintain the *traditions* of the Church. Fourth, this belief has been expressed in practices involving relics and acts of *pilgrimage*. And fifth: as with the relic and the pilgrimage, the icon's role as an emblem of the incarnation and the traditions of orthodoxy serves to strengthen the *authority* of the Church.

The following story goes some way to illustrating these five attributes. In April 1994, after fourteen years of restoration, Michelangelo's depiction of 'The Last Judgement' was unveiled in Rome. Several centuries' worth of candle smoke and varnish had dirtied the walls of the Sistine Chapel, giving the fresco its reputation as the 'shadowy masterpiece' of the Vatican. By removing the patina, some critics argued, the original work could be damaged. To others, however, it was being reinvigorated.[19] Pope John Paul II was of this latter opinion. At the Mass that followed the fresco's unveiling, he explained why the Vatican had invested in the project. These restored images, he began, should be celebrated as they stimulate 'us to reassert our adherence to the risen Christ' and represent, therefore, a matter not solely for art history but 'the centre of the theological question' concerning the depiction and worship of God.[20] Referring to both the Old Testament and Islam, John Paul reiterated the Catholic rejection of the worship of graven images. At the same time, however, he presented a question: what of the 'soul's gratitude to the invisible God who grants man the power to represent him in a visible way?':

> The icon is not only a work of pictorial art. It is, in a certain sense, like a sacrament of Christian life, since in it the mystery of the incarnation becomes present. In it the Mystery of the Word made flesh is reflected in a way that is ever new, and man – the author and at the same time participant – is gladdened by the sight of the Invisible.

Defined in this way, the icon represents to the Catholic the unity of God, described by Augustine as 'the Supreme Artist',[21] with a Christ who declared that 'whoever has seen me has seen the Father'[22] and an Adam created in the image and 'likeness' of his creator.[23] Michelangelo's fresco is anthropomorphic inasmuch as 'the Sistine Chapel is precisely – if one may say so – the sanctuary of the theology of the human body'.[24] Thus the terms of the icon take shape: the 'theology of the human body', professed by John Paul II, encapsulates a tradition linking the image, creation, and creativity.

This example illustrates the five different attributes I have suggested are of central importance to the historical depiction of the icon. First among these is its association with orthodoxy. Although controversial, the term remains a coherent pointer towards those religious traditions, whether within the Orthodox Catholic Church or Roman Catholicism, which have retained the use of images in their worship according to the practice, so they claim, of some of the earliest Christian traditions. Since the seventh-century orthodox apologist John of Damascus, this position has been distinguished from iconolatry (the worship of the images themselves). For example, one nineteenth-century historian of John, associating the symbols of fish found in Rome's catacombs with a 'natural instinct' to preserve the Church's tradition, made the distinction by quoting the sixth-century Pope Gregory the Great: 'neither do we ... prostrate ourselves before the image as before a Deity; but we adore Him, whom the symbol represents to our memory'.[25] Thus the icon operates as a tool of orthodox tradition as much as devotion, considered by its advocates to be an emblem of the Church's continuity.

Orthodoxy claims an unbroken line connecting scripture with tradition. To an advocate like John of Damascus, scriptural justification of images could be found throughout the Bible. Even within the context of the Second Commandment and the golden calf, certain passages describe the Ark of the Covenant ornamented with golden cherubs;[26] furthermore, God instructs Moses to make an effigy to cure the Israelites in the desert: 'Moses made a serpent of brass, and put it upon a pole, and it came to pass, that if a serpent had bitten any man, when he beheld the serpent of brass, he lived'.[27] Passages like these were taken by John to connect the icon to both the Torah and the New Testament's description of the incarnation as 'the Word made flesh'.[28] In the three *Apologetic Treatises against those Decrying the Holy Images*, he stated that 'to reject the icon is to reject the incarnation'[29] and that he would 'never cease honouring the earthly material by means of which his salvation has been affected'.[30] This argument, presented against Manichean concepts of Christ's corporality, promoted a belief that the physical presence of Christ not only superseded the Mosaic prohibition against 'false gods' but also provided his followers with a sacred image which they might adore.[31]

As the early Church used images to shape scripture into the traditions of orthodoxy, a belief in their miraculous properties was asserted. For example, St. Luke is held by many Catholics to be the author of a portrait of Christ that hangs above the Santa Scala in Rome. The image is considered to be *acheiropoieta* (not made by human hands), of which famous examples include the Veil of Veronica, the Image of Edessa, and the Shroud of Turin. Edessa was of particular importance to John of Damascus. It involved the story of King Abgarus asking Christ to visit his kingdom; Christ declined, instead pressing his face against a handkerchief and sending its imprint to Edessa. The image is regarded by some to be the original Shroud of Turin, recorded in its first location before the crusade that brought it to Savoy.[32] This story illustrates a way in which miraculous properties were often attached to images, icons, and *acheiropoieta* to support claims of political authority. Such images became the emblems of kingdoms. The kingdom stood or fell with the emblem – a declaration of orthodoxy which explains the story of a governor of Damascus who, when faced in 624 with the attacking Muslim army, raised above the city gate a giant crucifix and laid at its feet the New Testament and an image of Jesus Christ.[33]

The association of the icon with miracles encouraged the designation of certain sites for veneration. By associating the thaumaturgic object – whether the severed limb of a saint, *acheiropoieta*, or an image on a handkerchief – with a specific place, the orthodox argument for the icon became the same as that for both relics and pilgrimage, as the theological issues of God's physicality, depiction, and mediation with man were connected. To the historian of iconoclasm, then, the question of sacred territory and pilgrimage is relevant to the theology of the image. The sociologist of religion Simon Coleman describes pilgrimage thus:

> On their return, pilgrims frequently bring back a token of the place, both a proof that the journey has been completed and as a physical manifestation of the charisma of a sacred centre. In this way, the sacred landscape becomes diffused, permeating even the everyday lives of those who have never been to, say, Mecca or Jerusalem.[34]

This 'sacred landscape' which, according to Coleman in Weberian terms, makes tangible its charisma, is one perceived 'not only in permanently fixed locations like temples and shrines, but also in movable objects such as amulets, relics and even holy persons',[35] objects described by Aquinas as being the 'limbs of God'.[36] It follows that the more concentrated are the clusters of relics, saints, and myths within a particular site, the more holy that site will be considered as a target for pilgrimage. To the orthodox advocate, the site contains holiness in the way that the icon depicts it – both exist as physical pointers for worship. For many sites, a miracle does not even have to have occurred, the presence of a limb that had once been part of a holy and miracle-performing body often being enough to enhance the site's status. After the crusades, parts of saints, pieces of the true cross, and garments of Mary and the disciples furnished the churches and monasteries[37] of cities, towns, and villages throughout Europe. With these objects came migrating pilgrims, trade, and claims of political supremacy. Local hagiographies were constructed; around them, societies were shaped by conflicting claims to authority. The individual religious experience became codified, not only in the regulation of the taxes and trade around a pilgrimage, but also in the use of relics and icons as objects with which to consecrate a church[38] and in the fabric of the architecture itself – a tradition set in stone by the mediaeval Gothic cruciform form of churches with nave as body, transepts as arms, and apse as Christ's head.[39]

This brief introduction to the Christian theology of the icon can therefore be summarized: located within churches, tombs, and sites of pilgrimage, and representing the unity of God with man as artist, creator and created, it made emblematic the orthodox Church. In the words of Léonide Ouspensky, 'the Church affirms that the icon is a consequence of the divine incarnation, that she was founded on this incarnation'.[40] Thus the final attribute associated with the icon has been that of its political *authority*. This attribute can be illustrated by considering again the example of the Michelangelo fresco. In addition to outlining a theology of the icon, John Paul's 1994 homily also contained a political message, concluding with the reminder that 'the Sistine Chapel became for the entire Catholic community the place for the action of the Holy Spirit who appoints the Bishops in the Church, and in particular the one who is to become Bishop of Rome and Successor of Peter'.[41] This expands the perceived power of the icon: as well as being an emblem of the Church's unity, it also operates as a component of Church order. To grasp the icon's message is to understand the succession of such an order. To tear it down is to challenge not only orthodox worship but, crucially, orthodox authority. The social and political events that have expressed this — namely, the acts of coronation, pilgrimage and the miracles with which the icon is associated — have each served to strengthen this authority. In short, icons enable private or popular devotion to be brought within the tradition and under the authority of the orthodox Church. To understand iconoclasm — to understand, that is, why Calvinists stripped their buildings of these forms, or why the Wahhabi mosque prohibited the ornamentation of its Ottoman counterpart — a study of iconoclasm must examine such acts as political statements against authority as much as theological statements against the mediation of divine beauty.

THE POLITICS OF ICONOCLASM

Having introduced the image-icon-idol, it is necessary to outline the theological and political basis of its destruction, before this is examined in more detail in the historical prototypes of Calvinism and Wahhabism in Part I of this book. To many sixteenth-century Protestants, the Old Testament Commandment against image-veneration undermined later ecclesiastical traditions involving the incarnation. Rejecting Catholicism's connection between the incarnation and artistry, these reformers looked to scripture to support their iconoclastic theology. For example, Paul's statements in 2 Corinthians 5 concerning the body and heaven configure the material world as God's 'house': 'we know that if our earthly house of this tabernacle were dissolved, we have a building of God, a house not made with hands, eternal in the heavens'.[42] To Andreas Karlstadt in 1522, writing a decade before Calvin's *Institutes*, this 'house' provided the location for a theological debate on idols. Christ said that 'my house shall be called the house of prayer; but you have made it a den of thieves';[43] for Karlstadt, 'only God's name should be invoked here ... Christ says: My sheep listen to my voice (John 10: 27). He does not say: They see my image or images of the saints'.[44] This importance of the 'voice' reflected a wider reformist emphasis on the Word of God over the images of the Church. It also opposed orthodoxy's association of icons with an unbroken tradition. By positioning scripture *against* both Pope and Church, the reformers were making a claim for greater authority. In this way, they inverted the logic of orthodoxy — iconoclasm rather than the icon reflecting the bridge between divine and temporal order.

This theological framework for destruction, linking ideas of image-breaking with political authority, was codified in a new set of terms that emerged during the sixteenth century, partly in response to the French wars of religion, including the English vocabulary of the 'State', the 'iconoclast', the 'Calvinist', the 'modernist', and, twenty years later, the 'rationalist'. Under these terms, it is clear that a study of the politics of iconoclasm must begin with an account of sixteenth-century Calvinism (itself a label), for although its theological origins are shared by Islam and its predecessors were Byzantine, the etymological and political context for image-breaking stems from sixteenth-century Geneva's particular combination of a rejection of idolatry with a rebellion against Rome. Following the etymology of the word 'iconoclasm', then, the destruction of images is analysed within the post-sixteenth-century lexicon of the modern State.

Unknown Artist, 'King Edward VI and the Pope (includes John Russell, 1st Earl of Bedford; Thomas Cranmer; King Edward VI; King Henry VIII; John Dudley, Duke of Northumberland; Edward Seymour, 1st Duke of Somerset)' (c. 1570).

Historical opinion divides over whether Calvinist iconoclasm had primarily religious or political motives. This is in part due to the partisanship of many Catholic and Protestant accounts, and in part to the reformers' own changing priorities. In the 1530s, Calvin's *Institutes of the Christian Religion* denounced images within the context of scriptural exegesis; however, the attacks on Genevan churches were as much a declaration of autonomy from the rule of Savoy as they were an adherence to the Second Commandment.[45] Calvin's move to Geneva in 1536 combined these forces of religious and political rebellion within the walls of one city and, eventually, under the formal auspice of a government. Accordingly, iconoclasm is considered by some of its advocates to have been a central factor in the development of Genevan civil society. Throughout the city today, plaques still celebrate how image-breaking and rationalized democracy worked in parallel. This brand of Protestantism was also exported from Switzerland to the Low Countries, England, and eventually America, promoting an idea of reform that was associated with the new words 'Calvinism' and 'iconoclasm' and within which, according to Skinner, 'by the end of the sixteenth century, at least in England and France, we find the words "State" and "*l'État*" beginning to be used for the first time in their modern sense'.[46] These –isms, now codified as labels in the dictionaries, became a historical iconoclastic prototype against which other types of image-breaking – for example, the Islamic – have since been compared.

In this way, the study of Calvinism and statehood draws on a set of historicized terms that emerged in response to events in a particular time and place but have since become the lexicon of iconoclasm and modernity. Skinner argues that 'the clearest sign that a society has entered into the self-conscious possession of a new concept is, I take it, that a new vocabulary comes to be generated, in terms of which the concept is then articulated and discussed'.[47] This is historiographically akin to what Danto calls 'past-referring predicates': 'I would recommend that one think of objects in the present world as comparable to words, and the historical use and understanding of them as comparable to reading ... the Sicilian peasant who does not see a certain stone pile as a Norman tower is historically illiterate: he does not know what the stones *say*'.[48] This book attempts such a 'reading' of what the stones of 'iconoclasm' 'say'. That is: from the sixteenth-century reforms and rebellions of a certain type of Protestantism, ideas of both image-breaking and modern political organization were constructed around a common vocabulary. Embedded within this vocabulary, a consensus of 'iconoclasm' as a historical subject took shape: it was considered to represent an urban, bourgeois, and rationalist destruction of the rural, feudal, and superstitious world. This is the prototypical basis of iconoclasm against which other types, for example the Islamic, can be compared.

Specifically, the Calvinist-Christian prototype has been compared to the Islamic movement known as 'Wahhabism'.[49] In 1744, the preacher Muhammad ibn Abd al-Wahhab made an alliance with the Saudi rulers of al-Diriyyah in Najd – now the central territory in modern-day Saudi Arabia – uniting the political factions of the region and coordinating a move on Mecca and Medina. Accounts in both English and Arabic have claimed that ibn Abd al-Wahhab's theological position on images encouraged the Najdi forces to destroy the shrines of both cities during the Saudi occupation. Although Calvin (1509–1564) and ibn Abd al-Wahhab (1703–1792)[50] had no historical connection with each other, they have been compared through the historicized labels of Calvin*ism* and Wahhab*ism*: namely, in terms of the geographical conditions of the Swiss Alps and the Najdi desert; the role of individual charismatic leadership in the interpretation of certain scriptures; the subsequent development or routinization of the charismatic message by its followers; the impact and identity of exile, immigration, and expansionism to these followers in relation to questions of orthodoxy and heterodoxy; their founding of new capital cities in Riyadh and Geneva as bases of 'Puritan' government; and the attacks on images to precipitate and drive such change. The comparison of these features has allowed the ideas of John Calvin and Muhammad ibn Abd al-Wahhab to be presented as a chronologically coherent account of iconoclasm that goes beyond its internal differences, creating a model that extends from the early-modern period to present-day questions of fundamentalism and modernity.

In his text on monotheism, *Kitab al-Tawhid*, ibn Abd al-Wahhab stated that to worship an object as God is to worship a false god, or idol; it signifies an associationism that confuses the unity of God through pluralism and, in its most extreme case, polytheism. This act of faithlessness in loving the created rather than the Creator is related to the question of salvation. Throughout *Kitab al-Tawhid* and his discussion of the relevant *hadith*, ibn Abd al-Wahhab stressed 'that he who meets Him, without associating anything with Him, enters paradise; and he who meets Him, while having associated something with Him enters the fire, even though he may have been the person most prone to worship'.[51] Like Calvinism, then, the 'Wahhabi' theology of iconoclasm inverted the premises of orthodoxy where the image is considered to embody the unity of God on earth. To the iconoclast, this ontology was inverted absolutely: while the world is many, God is

One, and to associate him with the many – through the depiction or veneration of the earthly matter he created – constitutes blasphemy against his unity. Calvin described this blasphemy as 'idolatry' against the 'One' or 'True' God; to ibn Abd al-Wahhab, echoing the Qur'an, the statues and shrines that surrounded the Kaaba encouraged *shirk* (associationism) against the *tawhid* (unity) of the 'One God' (*Allah*).

Like Calvin, ibn Abd al-Wahhab's interpretation of scripture denounced not only those places which harbour idolatrous objects but also the worshippers themselves, making the connection between image-breaking and holy war: 'armed with this concept of *tawhid*,' claims Dallal, 'ibn Abd al-Wahhab was able to change his discourse *on* practice to a discourse *in* practice',[52] reflected in the early nineteenth-century European traveller Jean Louis Burckhardt's observation of an incident during the first Saudi-Wahhabi attack on Mecca:

> Muhammadan saints are venerated as highly as those of the Catholic church … wherever the Wahabys carried their arms, they destroyed all the domes and ornamented tombs; a circumstance which served to inflame the fanaticism of their disciples … At Mekka, not a single cupola was suffered to remain over the tomb of any renowned Arab: those even covering the birthplace of Muhammad … while in the act of destroying them, the Wahabys were heard to exclaim, 'God have mercy upon those who destroyed, and none upon those who built them'.[53]

For the type of iconoclasm that emerged in the Arabian peninsula during the eighteenth century, the violence against the statues and shrines of Mecca was part of a wider military campaign against the orthodox rule (orthodox in that the Hashimite Sharifs claimed a lineage going back to Muhammad) of Hijaz. Historians claim that Wahhabism united much of the peninsula through the 1744 contract with the al-Sauds, the occupation of Hijaz, and the alliance achieved between the nomadic desert communities and the settled citizens of a new capital, Riyadh.[54] Thus Wahhabi Riyadh, like Calvinist Geneva, emerged as a new capital for an iconoclastic society. The construction of such a capital occurred alongside the destruction of Islamic Hijazi and pagan Najdi sacred objects; in this way, the modern city centralized the different communities, traditions, and rituals of the territory. One of the first questions for a comparative study of a Calvinist and Wahhabi politics of iconoclasm is how the scriptural refutation of idolatry was developed in the city and state identity of Geneva and Najd.

THE DEBATE TODAY

The sociologist of religion will note that my use of a normative religious phenomenon like 'Calvinism' as a prototype for further political comparison is not original. It is influenced by Max Weber's analysis of Islam in relation to Western forms of 'rationalized' government and capitalism in *Economy and Society*, where some features of Protestantism are compared to the 'relatively late product of Near Eastern monotheism'.[55] According to Turner, 'we notice the urgency of the question of Islam in relation to Weber's *Protestant Ethic* thesis, since, if the central tradition of Islam is focused on monotheism, predestination and submission, we would expect an Islamic counterpart to the Calvinist calling';[56] likewise for Schluchter, 'in order to conceive of Islam as precisely as possible ... it is reasonable to start with Christianity and with its most important representative in terms of Weber's central question, Calvinism'.[57] Methodologically, the Weberian scholar will also note that my use of a Calvinist prototype (the 'Protestant Ethic') to be tested against an Islamic alternative draws on what Weber called 'abstract dogmas' of 'practical religious interests' to be assessed 'in the artificial simplicity of ideal types'[58] – that is, a way by which different religious and social forces might be conceptualized for the sake of historical understanding.[59] Consequently, my terms of 'Calvinism' and their relationship to the 'rationalized' or 'trained official, the pillar of both the modern State and of the economic life of the West'[60] follow a Weberian approach to the way in which ideas can have material consequences.

However, while this book has been methodologically influenced by a certain type of post-Marxian political thinking in Religious Studies, it is not designed to serve as a response to these questions of Weberian methodology. Rather, it represents part of a wider debate taking place today over the role of iconoclasm in the 'modern' world since the 2001 attacks on the World Trade Center, informed in great part by Latour's 2002 project on the 'Image Wars' affecting science, religion and art: *Iconoclash*. Latour's use of the term 'iconoclash' rather than 'iconoclasm' to structure this debate reflects a perceived ambivalence of symbolism and significance in the destroyed object. It also focuses on a tension within the terms at stake – the *clash* in 'iconoclash' –

which reflects the same semantic struggle described by Skinner in the etymological development of the newly articulated State, as well as Clay's understanding of iconoclasm's 'semiotic turn'. This debate recognizes that the 'contested term' of iconoclasm poses a question that goes beyond the world of Religious Studies, and includes the History of Art, Critical Theory, International Relations, and Philosophy. As such, new possibilities of comparison and contrast are being investigated within an interdisciplinary context. For example, a palaeoecological description of Roman clearances of sacred woodland in Anglesey can be seen to share similar terms of symbolic destruction and political construction as the razing of a Hijazi graveyard by Najdi forces, in that such a considerable alteration to the landscape reflects themes of control, power, domination, and social organization – political features which are also visible in the phenomenological environment.[61] Both the cleared woodland and graveyard also share practical concerns. Rackham explains that slashing and burning a woodland does not prevent it from regrowing again; to destroy it totally, the trees must be uprooted, cut up into pieces, the soil turned over, the ground poisoned.[62] Likewise, incidents such as the Wahhabi destruction of the Janat al-Baqi graveyard in Medina, the French Revolutionary dismantling of the Benedictine Abbey at Cluny, or the Nazi razing of the Warsaw Ghetto represent not singular moments of explosive violence but a lengthy, difficult, organized procedure. Yet while these examples of the uprooting of sacred woodland in Anglesey and the dismantling of an abbey clearly demonstrate similarities of object-obliteration, they differ from Clay's description of the partial breaking and remaking of an object like a statue. Clay notes that 'when Parisians overturned Bouchardon's sculpture they did not simply break it, they remade it'; because of this, 'instead of using terminology that focuses attention on isolated moments' 'in what one might call "the life of the object"', he argues that we should use 'terms that emphasize processes', and 'instead of thinking in terms of their "breaking" or "destruction" ... we think in terms of their transformation'.[63] This focus on the transformation of signs instead of a single moment of an object's final destruction mirrors Latour's notion of semantic ambivalence in the term 'iconoclash'. The fact that it describes the partial breaking of a statue rather than the total obliteration of a city demonstrates how the present-day debate is moving beyond a monoglot use of the term 'iconoclasm' to examine the limits of the attacked, ambivalent object. In this context, Rambelli and Reinders propose a typology of iconoclasm that looks to accommodate the different categories of total and partial destruction. Their typology covers a spectrum, from the irreversible loss of physical integrity of the object to a more reversible damage, where the physical object is left intact, not dissimilar to Morgan's description of 'soft' iconoclasm.[64] This spectrum ranges from 'obliteration without residue' to 'destruction with residue', 'disfiguring: partial destruction, damage', 'humiliation: abuse, insult, demotion', 'theft', 'hiding: burial, disguise, imprisonment', and, finally, 'negative cultural redefinition'.[65]

My emphasis on these issues of typological complexity rather than chronological continuity in the study of Christian and Islamic image-breaking is designed to reassure the reader that this book does not seek to provide a overweening narrative of iconoclasm from Calvin and ibn Abd al-Wahhab to the present day. Rather, the iconoclastic episodes that I have chosen to test the two historical prototypes of Calvinism and Wahhabism are designed to examine the limits of an emerging vocabulary of religious and political modernity. These episodes in Part II, from the French Revolution to the Futurist Manifesto, the razing of Warsaw, the rebuilding of Bosnian mosques, and the changing face of Mecca today – each representing degrees and processes of partial and total destruction – are informed by the religious and political terms laid out in the Christian and Islamic prototypes of Part I.

By attempting a comparative account of Christian and Islamic iconoclasm, then, this book explores the terms with which religious and political history is articulated. When presented with the question, 'how does an abstract metaphysical concept about the structure of reality first articulated by learned humanists, and later applied to scriptural exegesis by theologians, ever come to have any relation with a young Swiss artisan who spat in a holy water font?',[66] the politics of iconoclasm responds: 'some of those who worked as young men on the masonry of these edifices may well have earned good wages for pulling them down'.[67] For both the putting up and the pulling down, money changed hands – as such, each of my case studies will focus on the connection between the destruction of sacred objects and the construction of an organized, wage-paying State. By identifying these terms of the politics of iconoclasm, I hope to contribute usefully to the present-day debate.

Part I

THE PROTOTYPES

CHAPTER 1
Calvinism and Iconoclasm

> Seeing that this brutish stupidity has overspread the globe, men longing after visible forms of God, and so forming deities of wood and stone, silver and gold, or of any other dead and corruptible matter, we must hold it as a first principle, that as often as any form is assigned to God, his glory is corrupted by an impious lie.
>
> John Calvin, *Institutes of the Christian Religion*[1]

On the north wall of Geneva's St. Pierre Cathedral stands a plaque with the following inscription in Latin:

> When in the year 1535 the tyranny of the Roman AntiChrist had been overthrown, and his superstitions had been denounced, the most sacred religion of Christ was restored here to its own purity, and the church was restored to a better order, by the unique goodwill of the Lord: and at the same time when all its enemies had been driven and chased out, the city itself was re-established in its own liberty, not without a miraculous sign: the senate and the people of Geneva took care that this monument be created for the sake of eternal memory, and that it be set up in this place, so that it might serve as witness for their descendants of their gratitude towards the Lord.[2]

Such a monument is not unusual in Geneva. Others exist in the city's churches and municipal buildings, typically featuring the words *Post Tenebras Lux* ('After Darkness, Light'), and are not dissimilar to many statues, tablets, and war memorials in cities throughout the world. Nor is it unusual that the plaque is in Latin rather than the vernacular. The visitor to Geneva today can find other inscriptions written in the language of Rome throughout the French Protestant old town, just as he can find images of the city's image-breakers from the statues of the Monument de la Réformation to the murals of the Hôtel de Ville. These are not paradoxes of particular significance to the Calvinist case. Instead they illustrate how even a people advertising their own iconoclasm use, through necessity, both the visual props and the language of orthodoxy.

What is significant is that the reader of this plaque has no additional sources against which to judge the story that it describes. The words written on memorials dedicated to individuals killed, for example, during events like the storming of the Bastille or the Battle of Passchendaele can be considered alongside a polyphony of other words, images, satires, and critical voices. The reader judges the message of the monument accordingly. But what are the critical voices describing Geneva in 1535 – the year when certain significant acts of image-breaking took place which were subsequently translated into an commonly understood and articulated idea of 'iconoclasm', my historical prototype for this book? To reconstruct the plaque would be to understand something of this prototype's origins.

It is almost certain that the plaque refers to events in St. Pierre on 8 August 1535, after the French reformer Guillaume Farel had preached in the cathedral. Farel himself is believed to have been the author of the Latin text, written a year later when the city's Council adopted a formal 'Reformation' in 1536. However, no records remain of the contents of his sermon. Instead, the response of the congregation was described by his contemporary Antoine Fromment, whose account is the source from which historians describe the events of 1535. But who was Antoine Fromment? Already a well-known individual, he had collaborated with Farel in the early 1530s in Neuchâtel[3] before moving to Geneva. The present-day reader is therefore left with the report of this collaboration to understand what happened in 1535; not only is his reading of Geneva's iconoclasm determined by its inscription on a plaque, it is also unmitigated by any other critical voices. The plaque in St. Pierre was written by Farel, describing an event instigated by Farel, and narrated by his accomplice Fromment. It is a classic example of what Greenblatt has called 'self-fashioning', where beyond mere *apologia* for one's actions 'in the sixteenth century there appears to be an increased self-consciousness about the fashioning of human identity as a manipulable, artful process'.[4] That present-day historical accounts of this event also rely on Fromment as their only source ensures that we are no better off with the history books than we are with the plaque's propaganda.[5] We have not had answered our two critical questions: first, what is specific to *Genevan religious society* (that is, 'Calvinism') at the time of this attack; and second, what makes the events of 1535 specifically *iconoclastic* within the range of possible types of violence against an object – the partial violence, for example, of individuals who seek a target for their boredom, amusement, or rage, and the total violence of a crowd following the orders and the organization of a leader? The lack of an answer to these questions reflects the critical homophony that underlies the historical prototype of Calvinist iconoclasm – the 'self-fashioned' myth of a new Puritanism. My task in this chapter is therefore to outline some of the ways in which this process of myth-making developed – from Fromment's account of the events in 1535, filtered through both Calvin's theological work and a series of political claims, to an established Puritan prototype from which the modern reading of iconoclasm takes its lead.

The following is Fromment's account: Farel stood to preach, surrounded by the images and objects that adorned the walls, columns, and reliquaries of the no-doubt brightly coloured cathedral nave. After giving his sermon, the words of which are lost, the canons sung Vespers. As they did this, some of the boys in the choir began to mimic their chants. To Fromment, these 'little children' were innocents acting 'against all understanding of Man' and their surroundings: 'at the time when the priests were chanting their Vespers and saying Psalm 114 "In extitu Israel de Egypto" etc, these little children, without anybody thinking of it, began to cry, bray, and shout, like the priests'.[6] The Psalm that Fromment claimed was mimicked in this way is relevant. It describes a 'heathen' worship where 'their idols are silver and gold, the works of men's hands. / They have mouths, but they speak not: eyes have they, but they see not'. Thus Fromment adopted the Psalm's distinction between the Jews, whose 'God is in the heavens', and the heathens who resemble their own idols ('they that make them are like them; so is everyone that trusts in them'[7]) and applied it to the Reformers and the Catholics of his day.

Accepting Fromment's account as other historians have done, we read that the ensuing events unfolded quickly. As the Psalm was sung, 'someone said "you are singing that you hate those who make images and trust in them, and yet you leave them here?" These little children continued to make a great noise'[8], described by Eire (following Fromment) as 'staging a counterceremony of their own: hooting and howling, they mocked the Latin chant of the service. Suddenly, the youths charged the sanctuary, overturned the chair on which the canons usually sat, and cursed them for making images and having confidence in them'.[9] With the commotion others ran into the cathedral from the street outside, joining both children and congregation in the nave. Farel had stepped aside, but in his place some of the most prominent reformers in Geneva at the time, including Perrin, entered the fray. By now, a large crowd of people had assembled within the church walls. According to Fromment, they watched for a while the children making their noise and mocking the priests and altar boys[10] until, as a crowd, they 'entered the heart of the temple and in the presence of the priests suddenly threw to the ground their idols and smashed them':

> And my little children ran and jumped after these false gods and cried in a high joyful voice to the people who were outside the church, 'we have the gods of the priests, would you like some?' And they threw them at the crowd. The priests, thinking they were lost, went running out of the church after their gods and to tell the members of the Syndic, and the silly women of the town wept and moaned, hating those who had destroyed their little saints. Some people from the Syndic arrived, Chican and Bandiere, who shouted and harassed those who were there. But in the end they could do nothing but say 'if these are real gods they can defend themselves if they want; we do not know what else we can do'. Then about fifty hosts that had been consecrated by the priests according to their tradition were found, which the magnificent Mesgret gave to his dog to eat, saying 'if these are true gods they wouldn't let themselves be eaten by a dog'. But the dog devoured them in one go, and in this way all the false gods and the idols of the priests were smashed up or eaten by a dog in Geneva.[11]

Having overrun St. Pierre in this way, the crowd moved on to the other churches of the city. Afterwards, according to Eire, 'when questioned about their behaviour, Perrin, Vandel, and Baudichon defended themselves by appealing to divine authority: "concerning the destruction of the images they answered that it was true they had done it, but that they did not think they had erred, because such things [the idols] were against the Word of God". Through iconoclasm the Protestants had circumvented and usurped the power of the magistracy'.[12]

This story is problematic: much has been written about the emergence of 'Calvinist' iconoclasm in the sixteenth century, but the attack on St. Pierre demonstrates that image-breaking existed in Geneva at least a year before Calvin's arrival in the city. To make sense of the Calvinist prototype, then, it is vital that the sequence of these events is properly understood. However, with only Fromment's account and the St. Pierre plaque to guide the present-day reader, how might they be critically assessed, beyond the self-fashioning? It is here that the social and political context must also inform our understanding of the iconoclasm. Certain aspects of the political environment of Geneva were recorded at the time and can be found in material that contextualizes Fromment's account of the events of 1535 and Calvin's theology. It has already been noted that the Genevan Reformation was as much a claim of independence from Savoy as it was a rejection of Roman Catholicism. However, Rome was not so politically preoccupied with Geneva. Many of the Papacy's struggles with France had been settled in 1526 with the League of Cognac; far more immediate a concern for Clement VII in the years immediately preceding Farel's sermon was the danger of Milan and Parma falling to the Turks, and the attacks on Rome itself by the Spanish and Lutheran *Landsknechte*.[13] Chambers argues that in 1535 the Pope's attentions were focussed on a Turkish threat of invasion via Brindisi rather than events north of the Alps. Not until 1546, when a genuinely Protestant militancy had become consolidated, did Rome consider the Swiss Reformation as serious a challenge to its security as the Muslims.[14] This claim can be verified by the literature of Rome at the time, the council reports, and the Vatican records; the material written about the Papacy in 1535 is more prolific than that for Geneva. Indeed, the combination of this *lack* of source material recording Farel's iconoclastic moment, the partisan opposition between Fromment and the Catholic account, the fact that Calvin had not yet arrived in the city, and the general condition of Geneva at the time,[15] indicates that not only was the situation more complex than the proclamation of the plaque of St. Pierre would have us believe, but it is more realistic to talk of events in 1535 as a localized issue pushed by a charismatic individual rather than a more generalized foundation upon which an iconoclastic prototype might be built.

On this level, McGrath accepts that 'the success of the Reformation within a city was dependent upon a number of historical contingencies. To adopt the Reformation was to risk a disastrous change in alignment, in that existing treaties or relationships – military, political and commercial – with territories or cities which chose to remain Catholic were usually deemed to be broken as a result'.[16] In the case of St. Gallen, for example, this 'contingency' was the city's linen industry; 'in the case of Geneva, a paramount historical contingency was the presence of the Catholic duchy of Savoy and its allies on the very doorstep of the city'.[17] Since 1526, the city had allied itself with Bern and Fribourg against Savoy. When Bern – the most powerful of the three – became Protestant, the dynamics of this relationship changed to the extent that 'the history of the Reformation in Geneva', according to Eire, 'is also the history of the growth of Bernese influence at the expense of Fribourg ... in fact, it is difficult to tell whether Geneva would have become Protestant in 1536, or even recognised a Reformed congregation at all, without the constant mixture of threats and encouragements from Bern'.[18]

Taking these details into account, the significance of a peculiarly *Genevan* explanation to the events of 1535 is debatable, as similar social and political tensions were evident elsewhere. For example, one historian states that the region was thriving just before the Reformation, with a university established at Basel,[19] and the same has been written about the military, where 'the problem facing the Swiss states in the sixteenth century was not how to get men into the army but how to keep them out of it'.[20] In contrast, McNeill argues that the region was 'culturally retarded' until the integration of Basel in 1501, and that the crises affecting the Church were precipitated by tensions between the dioceses and the cantons – Geneva under the bishopric of Vienne, Como under Milan, Basel under Besançon[21] – rather than the reformers alone: a claim that might go some way to explaining the gap of authority detected by Bern when it applied its 'tremendous pressure' on the French-speaking cities of Western Switzerland.[22]

For the purpose of understanding the iconoclastic events of 1535, it is not necessary to judge whether these differing accounts are true or not. It is, however, important to understand that the story of Farel's plaque is more complex than the self-fashioning presented to its present-day reader. Critical voices – lacking in coherence by their very nature – realign the limits of how the years leading up to Calvin's 'iconoclasm' can be read. Thus the historian can understand that individuals like Farel and Fromment oscillated between religious and social pressures local to Geneva, without the need to universalize these pressures as 'iconoclastic'. As Bern increased its influence over Geneva, these oscillations became labelled as allegiances either for or against Rome; when these allegiances were tested, they began to break out in occasional iconoclastic riots. The authorities on both sides provided tangible targets with which to harness continually changing patterns of violence in the years leading up to Farel's sermon. By 1532, open displays of disobedience to papal indulgences in the form of placards developed into challenges to a Genevan magistracy that was increasingly trapped between the restlessness of its people, the demands of Bern, and the threat of military action by Savoy. These placards were followed by the destruction of a large cross in front of the Convent de St. Clare.[23] With each act of individual destruction, the pressures became *identified* with a particular type of religious violence increasingly associated with communal image-breaking. At the same time, Farel arrived in Geneva from Neuchâtel.[24]

Despite being temporarily expelled from the city, Farel's presence in Geneva gave weight to a disparate momentum that was gathering pace, translating latent hostilities into increasingly bold attacks on churches, statues of saints, and the stone angels that lined the city's cemeteries. By 1534, The syndic attempted to instil calm by issuing a series of concessionary laws that forbade the abuse of sacraments and preaching without a license while, under pressure from Bern, allowing certain acts of image-breaking so long as they were carried out by the magistracy itself.[25] Any individual act without council ratification would be deemed a riot and punished.[26] If this move on the part of the Genevan authorities was an attempt to preserve its independence in the face of Bern's interference,[27] the outcome was a *de facto* recognition of Bernese rather than Savoyard power. It ensured a degree of calm between 1534 and 1535, despite some unrest when the reformer Viret was poisoned, further riots broke out, the Mass was suspended, and several canons of St. Pierre fled the city.[28] It was during this time of crystallizing concessions and tensions between different authorities, interferences, and rebellions, therefore, that Farel mounted the pulpit in August 1535 to deliver his sermon. The consequences that followed his intervention were absolute: nine months later, on 25 May 1536, 'a General Council of the Genevan people voted unanimously to "live henceforth according to the Law of the Gospel and the Word of God, and to abolish all papal abuses, images, and idols"'.[29] Geneva had ceased to oscillate. Three months later, John Calvin arrived in the city.

CALVIN'S *INSTITUTES*: ON ICONOCLASM

The iconoclastic events of 1535 were individual acts subject to local political oscillations that were subsequently formalized as a religious standard by the charismatic leadership of Guillaume Farel. Calvin's arrival in Geneva took this process a stage further. In order to understand why these individuals are distinguishable from other (to use Ginzburg's words) prophets, visionaries, and preachers who proclaimed revelations in the public squares of European cities in the early sixteenth century,[30] it is therefore necessary to examine the processes by which a charismatic leader governs a religious society and the extent to which that society is fashioned in the leader's own image. Calvin told his own story of coming to Geneva in the 'Preface' to his *Commentary on the Book of Psalms*. In this passage he described how in 1536 he was, as a prominent reformist figure, forced to leave his home town of Noyon in France for the relative safety of Strasbourg:

> As the most direct road to Strasbourg, to which I was then intended to retire, was shut up by the wars, I had resolved to pass quickly by Geneva, without staying longer than a single night in that city. A little before this, Popery had been driven from it by the exertions of the excellent man [Guillaume Farel] and Pierre Viret; but matters were not yet brought to a settled state, and the city was divided into ungodly and dangerous factions. Then an individual, who has now basely apostatised and returned to the Papists, discovered me and made me known to the others. Upon this, Farel, who burned with an extraordinary zeal to advance the gospel, immediately strained every nerve to detain me. And after learning that my heart was set upon devoting myself to private studies, for which I wished to keep myself free from other pursuits, and finding that he gained nothing by entreaties, he proceeded to utter an imprecation that God would curse my retirement, and the tranquillity of the studies which I sought, if I should withdraw and refuse to give assistance, when the necessity was so urgent. By this imprecation I was so stricken with terror, that I desisted from the journey which I had undertaken.[31]

To some biographers of Calvin, this passage 'suggests that he wanted to represent his encounter with Farel as a case – a humanist stereotype – of the scholar drawn against his will into an active life for which he was temperamentally unsuited'.[32] If so, it would be at odds with his contemporary Théodore Beza's claim that Calvin deliberately paid a visit to Farel as he passed through Geneva.[33] As with Fromment's version of Farel's homily, the present-day reader is left with history as it has been written by a few individuals. What can be more critically determined, however, is that after arriving in the city Calvin publicly collaborated with Farel to produce the twenty-one articles of 'The Geneva Confession' on the one God, on the Word, on faith, the law, and on grace. At the same time, he also published the first edition of his *Institutes of the Christian Religion*. This text had been drafted while he stayed in Basel the year before. While it has no *local* connection to Farel's sermon in St. Pierre, it nevertheless coincides chronologically: both discuss iconoclasm independently but concurrently, indicating that the subject of images and image-breaking was of importance to both men and that their coming together a year later in 1536 consolidated an already established, albeit disparate, iconoclastic tradition. In order to gain a clearer idea of Calvinist 'iconoclasm', then, the task must be to assess the points at which the self-fashioning of the individual and his account of the iconoclastic act corresponds with the terms – namely, those of the 'true God', 'the Word', and 'the Church' – that emerged from the writing and the reception of the theological texts.[34]

It is important from the outset to note that Calvin referred to idols and idolatry rather than icons and iconoclasm in his written work. As has already been stated, this is not of particular semantic importance because the term 'iconoclasm' had not yet entered the dictionaries when the *Institutes* were written. The references to idols rather than icons, then, should not present an undue distraction. It is clear that when Calvin refers to the 'idol' he is indicating a sacred image or object that is worshipped in the place of the God it purports to represent. In that respect, his position can be described as iconoclastic. In the 'Prefatory Address' to the *Institutes*, he followed a similar theological premise to other reformists like Farel and Karlstadt (and, indeed, some eighth-century Byzantine theologians), associating images with the miracles, magic, and enchantments that constitute the 'tricks' of Satan, false prophets, and the AntiChrist.[35] Whether his target was labelled an icon or an idol has no more significance – theologically, socially, or semantically – than to demonstrate that before the formalizing of the term 'iconoclasm' in the late sixteenth century, different words were used to describe the same thing.

In this way, Calvin's position against idolatry represented a characteristic example of Reformation iconoclastic theology. In my introduction, I suggested that the orthodox practices targeted by this theology – namely the pilgrimages, miracles, and images codifying ecclesiastical authority – justified themselves by tracing a line of tradition back to the early Church. As with other iconoclasts, Calvin used the same method of inverting that claim: 'It was a father who said, "It is a horrid abomination to see in Christian temples a painted image of either Christ or of any saint". ... an Ecclesiastical Council also decreed, "Let nought that is worshipped be depicted on walls". Very far are they from keeping within the boundaries when they leave not a corner without images'.[36] By citing both the prophets and the Church fathers, Calvin looked to an authority that preceded the Papacy in order to counter its claim to 'orthodoxy'. In the same way, he rejected the notion that images were used by the earliest Christian communities, stating that 'if we attach any authority to the ancient Church, let us remember, that for five hundred years, during which religion was in a more prosperous condition, and a purer doctrine flourished, Christian churches were completely free from visible representations'.[37] To make use of an image in Christian worship, Calvin argued, is as much a deviation from the Church as it is from the true God. He presented these two terms – the *true Church* and the *true God* – as the twin poles of the *Institutes* around which his work on morality, faith, and governance revolved. As such, the question of the image-idol-icon was of central importance to Calvin's theology. He dedicated a lengthy chapter to the subject, introducing the question of the image immediately after the nature of God, man, and creation, and before ecclesiastical history, Christian government, and 'all the churches on which the tyranny of the Roman idol has seized'.[38] For Calvin, then, the question of the image connected the Christian's knowledge of God with Church authority – a theological position which inverted that of orthodoxy.

Calvin's significant work on images is found in Volume 1, Chapter 11 of the *Institutes*: 'The setting up of idols a defection from the True God'. Within this chapter, he constructed his attack on idolatry in four ways. First, he described how God's nature is made known, providing a set of scriptural sources to support this knowledge. Second, he refuted certain orthodox arguments that religious images exist for the 'education of the illiterate'. Third, he denounced the use of images in worship by examining the difference between the Greek words *latria* (as in 'idolatry') and *dulia* (as in 'iconodulia'). Finally, he suggested that humans are naturally prone to acts of idolatry because they seek to understand God according to their own, visual capacity. With this, Calvin established a division between the 'false gaze' of human understanding and the nature of the 'True God'. I shall now expand upon his four arguments.

First, Calvin stated that God's willingness to make himself known to us, 'which we uniformly meet with in Scripture, annihilates every deity which men frame for themselves of their own accord – God himself being the only fit witness to himself'.[39] His scriptural basis for this claim was drawn from the Old Testament, combining the Mosaic Commandments, the Abrahamic Covenant, and the idea of an elect people, and presenting a God who makes himself known in signs of smoke, wind, and fire – none of which are readily made plastic in the human eye. Quoting Deuteronomy 4:15 ('you saw no manner of similitude on the day that the Lord spoke to you in Horeb, out of the midst of the fire, lest you corrupt yourselves, and make you a graven image),[40] Calvin argued that God exists in ways that are too awful for humans to contain in their imagination, let alone capture as images. In order to become knowable, therefore, God limits human understanding as 'the cloud, and smoke, and flame, though they were symbols of heavenly glory (Deut. 4:11), curbed men's minds as with a bridle, that they may not attempt to penetrate further'.[41] This reflects the claim in *Exodus* that the Israelites (with the exception of Moses) were prohibited from looking into the face of God, and that their attempt to circumscribe this prohibition – eventually leading them to worship the golden calf – was to doubt both the promise of Abraham's Covenant and to render God's majesty 'defiled by an absurd and indecorous fiction, when he who is incorporeal is assimilated into corporeal matter'.[42]

From these scriptural verses, Calvin developed an idea of human nature. He argued that throughout the Old Testament could be found examples of societies reducing 'he who fills all space to a bit of paltry wood, or stone, or gold',[43] demonstrating that the human mind needs to compensate for the limits of its knowledge with a visual aid. This limit, he believed, meant that knowledge was replaced by imagination – a moral error that gave license to lascivious depictions of Christ, the saints, and Mary, and ensured that 'brothels exhibit their inmates more chastely and modestly dressed than churches do images intended to represent virgins'.[44] By making this connection between license and lasciviousness from the golden calf to the Catholic Mary, Calvin's message was uncompromising: the attempt to capture God in an image is an ontological error that is contrary to His true nature and which seeks, in Eire's words, to 'domesticate' the divine.

Having considered the relationship between the material world and the nature of God, Calvin dismissed the key orthodox arguments for religious imagery, focusing in particular on the question of educating the illiterate. While conceding that he was 'not ignorant, indeed, of the assertion, which is now more than threadbare, "that images are the books of the unlearned"',[45] he stressed that this was an argument proposed by a Pope, Gregory the Great, whereas in scripture 'the prophets utterly condemn what the papists hold to be an undoubted axiom – viz, that images are substitutes for books'. To strengthen his claim, Calvin quoted Jeremiah 10:8 on the 'doctrine of vanities' that justified using images and, more explicitly, Habakkuk's statement that 'the molten image' is 'a *teacher* of lies'.[46] Concluding that 'the general to be inferred certainly is, that everything respecting God which is learned from images is futile and false', he then broadened his attack to state that 'all modes of worship devised by man are detestable',[47] reiterating the authority of Prophet over Pope.

Next, Calvin dismissed the orthodox belief, originating from the Greek Church, that religious images do not transgress the Israelite prohibition because they depict God's creation rather than God Himself, and that rather than being worshipped as objects in themselves – that is, rather than being idols – they are aids to contemplation of God's glory. For Calvin, this is a 'more subtle distinction' between kinds of worship that has no basis in scripture: 'the worship which they pay to their images and cloak with the name of *idolodulia*, and deny to be *idolatria*. So they speak, holding that the worship which they call *dulia* may, without insult to God, be paid to statues and pictures' – that is, '*dulia*' denotes *service to* rather than *worship of* an image.[48] Calvin denied that it is 'a lighter matter' to serve rather than to worship, and stated that the Greek words themselves are tautological: 'what they say is just the same as if they were to confess that they worship their images without worshipping them', just as 'a murderer or an adulterer will not escape conviction by giving some adventitious name to his crime'.[49] Again he challenged the authority of the Church fathers, asking why 'John the Eastern Legate' – most certainly John of Damascus – stated that he would sooner have brothels in his city than lose religious imagery and asked Christians to 'rejoice and exult, ye who, having the image of Christ, offer sacrifice to it'. In response to this, Calvin demanded 'where is now the distinction of *latria* and *dulia* with which they would throw dust in all eyes, human and divine?'[50] for 'when Christ repels Satan's insulting proposal with the words "it is written, Thou shalt worship the Lord they God, and only him shalt thou serve" (Matth. 8:10), there was no question of *latria*'.[51]

The last of Calvin's main claims concerning images and idolatry in the *Institutes* extended his idea of the 'True God' and the limits of humanity's visual imagination. He argued that humans are naturally prone to idolatry because of their need to understand God according to their own capacities. In this way, he made use of idolatry as a motif to connect his chapter on the nature of God with another on the actions of man. Writing about God and the creation of the world, he stated that God is visible enough in the beauty of nature: 'his essence, indeed, is incomprehensible, utterly transcending all human thought; but on each of his works his glory is engraven in characters so bright, so distinct, and so illustrious, that none, however dull and illiterate, can plead ignorance as their excuse ... the elegant structure of the world serving us as a kind of mirror, in which we may behold God, though otherwise invisible'.[52] At the centre of this beautiful world is the symmetry, function, and form of the human body as made in the image of God.[53] Such a focus on the human body followed biblical teaching on the hierarchy of creation, not the overt humanism that was being developed by some of his contemporaries.[54] Calvin did not propose an anthropocentric version of the universe; his focus on the human 'mirroring' of God's creating grace instead attempted to emphasize the biblical ordering of God, the human body, and the Church while omitting the need for images. His concern was not with making the divine more accessible to human understanding, but the opposite – reinstating the proper 'limit' on the human imagination that he considered to have been lost in the 'false gaze' of imagery. For Calvin, the created and visual world reflects the True God, offering 'a more vivid actual impression than empty visual speculation':[55] an *impression*, like smoke, wind, and fire, being the proper reflection of the ineffable God. Rather than being satisfied with the reflection and impression of God found in the structure and beauty of the world, Calvin argued that humanity renders it plastic, imaginary, and, in this way, creates 'petis dieux' of its own.

Calvin defined idolatry as an intrinsic part of human nature recurring throughout scripture: 'in the fact that the people every now and then rushed forth with boiling haste in pursuit of idols, just like water gushing forth with violence from a copious spring, let us learn how prone our nature is to idolatry'.[56] He suggested that the very existence of a second commandment means 'we may infer, that the human mind is, so to speak, a perpetual forge of idols' that 'stuffed as it is with presumptuous rashness, dares to imagine a god suited to its own capacity'.[57] In short, Calvin believed that idolatry is a particularly human folly, a perversion of the image of God where 'the flesh is always restless until it has obtained some figment like itself, with which it may vainly solace itself as a representation of God'.[58] Faced with the True God, he argued, 'it is not him they worship but, instead of him, the dream and figment of their own heart', a fault repeated throughout human history until 'idolatry has as it were raised its banner'[59] in the traditions of the Church.

In this way, Calvin presented the question of images as the fundamental test by which God's people might approach their Creator in opposition to the orthodox Church. In the *Institutes*, his theory of image-breaking provided a way of combining certain issues concerning God's nature, human imagination, and Church tradition. Before examining the ways in which he applied these principles to a theory of government, it is necessary first to expand on an idea that will become relevant to Chapter 2. Within the study of Wahhabism, the concept of *tawhid* arises – that is, the Islamic understanding of the 'true' God's ineffable unity as opposed to its human versions (*shirk*). *Tawhid* provides the justification for much Islamic iconoclasm. It is therefore important to introduce Calvin's similar notion of an ultimately unknowable 'True God' whose unity with the world precludes any need for visual interpretation.

THE TRUE GOD

In the *Institutes*, Calvin placed the question of images at the forefront of his theological priorities. To summarize his argument: the nature of God is unknowable, and human beings are bound to approach Him according to the limits of their own capacity. As they visualize, imagine, and illustrate God they mistake that which is intended for the glory of God to be God Himself, and make the error of worshipping the creation instead of the Creator. Over time, this error has been repeated to the point where it has become enshrined within the traditions of the Church. Orthodoxy, in its desire to preserve tradition (that is, its own survival in the face of dissent), further complicated the matter by associating the image with the Incarnation. This association, confusing the image of Christ with the objects of tradition, was promoted throughout the Middle Ages artistically and architecturally until it reached its apogee in the sixteenth-century papacy and its allied princes (most immediately, for Calvin, those of France and Savoy, as well as the theologians of the Sorbonne). In order to return properly to approaching knowledge of the true God – and, by extension, supporting the true Church – the destruction of images was therefore of central importance to Calvin's theology. I have examined something of what he meant by that destruction. Now, it is necessary to expand upon what he meant by the 'true God': specifically, the terms he used to describe God's unity, the Word of God, and the difference between the true and the false Church.

Calvin claimed that the attributes of the true God 'are these three: Loving-kindness, on which alone our entire safety depends; Judgement, which is daily exercised on the wicked, and awaits them in a severer form, even for eternal destruction; Righteousness, by which the faithful are preserved, and most benignly cherished. The Prophets declare, that when you understand these, you are amply furnished with the means of glorying in God'.[60] For Calvin, understanding these attributes does not necessarily bring humanity closer to understanding the true God Himself. Rather, it enables a proper way of glorifying Him in the worship and regulation of daily life. In the first passages of the *Institutes*, Calvin claimed that the limits of the human capacity to comprehend God could be transcended through worship rather than imagination, writing that 'our mind cannot conceive of God, without rendering some worship to Him'.[61] As God is ineffable, 'the pious mind does not devise for itself any kind of God, but looks alone to the one true God',[62] exemplifying the kind of seeking worship that constitutes true or 'pure' religion.[63]

For Calvin, then, the 'true' God and 'one' God are synonymous. This is not a question of semantics but instead of theological importance to a study of the question of images in worship. The concepts of unity and ineffability are associated in the description of the true God. For ibn Abd al-Wahhab, the connection between unity and *Al-lah* is encapsulated in *tawhid*. For Calvin, the unity of God is contained within the Trinity, where 'in each hypostasis the whole nature is understood, the difference being that each has its own subsistence'.[64] Crucially for the question of images, the Trinitarian unity incorporates 'the flesh as Mediator' – that is, God 'clothed in our flesh',[65] His nature reflected in us through the mediation of Christ. However, Calvin is clear that the mediation points to the glory of the true and unknowable God, rather than to the limits of our humanity. Thus the use of an image in Christian worship or education makes a fundamental mistake in how it intends to reflect the incarnation and the nature of the true God. Quoting 1 Corinthians, Calvin emphasized that the unity in which humanity is involved through the mediation of the flesh is made possible only by the grace of God; in this way the spirit inhabits the human body as a temple of God:

> Paul infers that we are the temple of God, from the fact that 'the Spirit of God dwelleth in us' (1 Cor. 3:16, 4:19; and 2 Cor. 6:16). Now, it ought not to be slightly overlooked, that all the promises which God makes of choosing us to Himself as a temple, receive their only fulfilment by his Spirit dwelling in us. Surely, as it is admirably expressed by Augustine (*Ad Maximinum*, Ep. 66), 'were we ordered to make a temple of wood and stone to the Spirit, inasmuch as such worship is due to God alone, it would be a clear proof of the Spirit's divinity; how much clearer a proof in that we are not to make a temple to him, but to be ourselves that temple'.[66]

This passage combines Calvin's ideas both of the true God (in unity) and physical representation (in mediation and worship), and connects them with a passage from scripture. From this premise, it is reasonable to agree with Parker's claim that 'it cannot be emphasised too strongly that the concept of unity dominates his thinking ... since Christ's unity with mankind depends upon the unity of God with man in Christ'.[67] However, the nature of that unity extends beyond orthodox Trinitarian thinking. The God described in the *Institutes*, supreme and ultimately unknowable, involves us in 'mediation' by the gift of grace alone, making the otherwise 'filthy' human body a temple while denying the body itself any cause for glory; the idea that a portion of humanity is admitted to this unity (and elected to eternal salvation) through grace underpins Calvin's soteriology and ultimately his view of predestination. Once again, the language used by Calvin and by orthodoxy inhabits similar theological territory – taking the incarnation as the foundation for the worship of God – but the conclusions then reached at these pressure points diverge. Indeed, the very use of the word 'unity' by Calvin would be deemed preposterous by some proponents of orthodoxy who consider its proper use to be in describing the relationship between Christ and the universal (that is, the 'Catholic') Church.[68] In terms of images, the conclusions drawn from the Trinity differ in the emphasis they place on human worship: orthodoxy reflects the incarnation through visual representation; for Calvin, the image of God is another way of describing 'the Word'.

Calvin's *Institutes* urged the worshipper of the true God to focus his attentions on the Word of God as found in scripture and (following John's Gospel) in Christ. 'The Word of God', he wrote, 'was the supreme angel, who then began, as it were by anticipation, to perform the office of mediator'.[69] In the *Commentary on John*, he developed this principle that within the unity of the true God both mediator and Word are one and the same:

> The Evangelist assures us that we do not withdraw from the only and eternal God, when we believe in Christ. ... As to the Evangelist calling the Son of God *the Speech*, the simple reason appears to me to be first, because he is the eternal Wisdom and Will of God; and, secondly, because he is the lively image of his purpose; for, as *speech* is said to be among men the image of the mind, so it is not inappropriate to apply this to God, and to say that He reveals himself to us by his speech.[70]

It will be noted that in this passage Calvin used 'the Speech' rather than 'the Word' for the Latin *verbum*. Indeed, in the *Commentary on John*, he explicitly differentiated between the two, stating 'I wonder what induced the Latins to render ὁ λόγος by *Verbum* (the Word); for that would rather have been the translation of τὸ ῥῆμα. But granting that they had some plausible reason, still it cannot be denied that *Sermo* (the Speech) would have been far more appropriate'.[71] This debate over *Verbum* had already occupied the theologians of his time, leading to a dispute between Erasmus and the Sorbonne, with Calvin dismissing the latter for teasing Erasmus because 'he had changed a single word for the better'.[72] Following his own logic, then, the present-day reader should also consider it a futile exercise to become trapped in a semantic quagmire over 'a single word'. *Verbum* is one word or phrase; *sermo* is speech in general, a speech, or a manner of speech.[73] Different translations of Calvin use either term. The Latin word in John's Gospel is *verbum*; any uncertainty over whether this should be translated into 'the Word' or 'the Speech' is not only due to semantics but also because theologically the idea being conveyed contains two senses: first, as a description of the Incarnation, the mediator of the true God's unity; and secondly, as human speech (that is, as the limit in the human articulation of God). Christ belongs to the first meaning; scripture belongs to the second. This is the ambiguity contained within 'the Word' which led Calvin to concern himself with how it could best be translated. The present-day historian of iconoclasm should not feel the same anxieties; it is more significant that Calvin wished to convey the dual sense of John's *verbum* in that the *Word* (Christ) is 'the lively image' of God but that as '*speech* is said to be among men the image of the mind' the bond between visual image and incarnation is broken. To this purpose, translating *verbum* as 'the Word' is acceptable, although it is useful to make the minor distinction of a capitalized 'Word' to denote the incarnate Christ and 'word' to denote human speech.

The Word, according to Calvin, combines the nature of the true God with the limits of human understanding as an active part of the true God's unity. Christ (the Word) is the *image* of God, whereas the human body is described as God's temple; the word (speech) is the image of the mind and as such is the appropriate way for humanity to approach the knowledge of God. In this scheme there is no need for the poor substitute of the plastic image. The image falls short, Calvin argued, on every level, failing to reflect either the Incarnation, the human body, the capacity of knowledge, or the unity of the true God. Instead, scripture is the means by which man might come to know the true God, for 'whenever Scripture asserts the unity of God, it does not contend for a mere name, but also enjoins that nothing which belongs to Divinity be applied to any other'.[74] Like worship, scripture transcends the limits of human capacity through the grace of God. In short: the Word of the true God is expressed only by the true word.

Calvin's position against images in Christian life is put into context when it is understood as a question of how Christians might practically implement the Word over human 'elaboration'. From this premise he developed his argument by including those Church traditions that appeared to invert this order of the true God's unity. In claiming that 'the only things, therefore, which ought to be painted or sculptured, are things which can be presented to the eye; the majesty of God, which is far beyond the reach of any eye, must not be dishonoured by unbecoming representations',[75] he was making a critical leap within his ontological thinking. These theological principles, however, needed a practical framework, leading him to consider his work on imagebreaking within the terms of the true Church – the Church representing the point of transition between the theology of iconoclasm and its politics.

The rejection of images contained in the *Institutes* was presented as a fundamental part of how humanity might approach knowledge of the true God. In practical terms, it indicated how Christians should structure themselves as a Church. Parker summarizes the thinking by arguing that 'the Church is Church if and because she proclaims nothing but the Word of Christ. Thus, as the mouthpiece of Christ, the Church has a supreme authority in the *regnum spirituale*. The two aspects have to be held together. It is only as the mouthpiece of Christ, the minister of the Word of God, that the Church has supreme authority'.[76] In other words, the Church is bound, through the Word (both as Christ and Scripture) to the one and true God, so that each part of the whole corresponds with the other according to the unity of God. In the *Commentary on the Book of Micah 4:2*, Calvin wrote:

> Here in a few words the prophet defines true worship of God. For it would not be enough for the nation to come together to one place to confess that they are worshippers of one God if they did not also show real obedience. True obedience depends on faith, as faith depends on the Word ... Hence we conclude that the church of God can be established only where the Word of God rules, where God shows by his voice the way of salvation ... Clearly, then where the teaching is corrupt or is despised, there is no religion approved by God.[77]

The true Church is therefore that which follows the Word of the true God in obedience. Calvin's use of the word 'nation' adds a soteriological dimension to his ontological thinking, so that the Church is also considered a particular 'people' of God to be judged separately from the traditional or orthodox church. The adherence to scripture rather than tradition provides the premise for the structure that the true Church should take in its quest for election. Calvin wrote that 'three evangelists give a narrative in a mean and humble style. The proud often eye this simplicity with disdain, because they attend not to the principle heads of doctrine'.[78] In contrast, he argued, Church tradition confuses how 'it is necessary to apply to Scripture, in order to learn the sure marks which distinguish God, as the Creator of the world, from the whole herd of fictitious gods',[79] meaning that 'a most pernicious error has generally prevailed – viz. that Scripture is of importance only in so far as conceded to it by the suffrage of the Church'.[80] However, these statements should not be read as an outright rejection of the organized church. Calvin also maintained that 'with the Church we wage no war, since ... we worship and adore one God'.[81] Instead he took for his target 'their contending that the form of the Church is always visible and apparent;

and, secondly, in placing this form in the see of the Church of Rome and its hierarchy. We, on the contrary, maintain, both that the Church may exist without any apparent form, and, moreover, that the form is not ascertained by that external splendour which they foolishly admire'.[82]

In this way, the question of images combined Calvin's ontological and institutional (that is, ecclesiastical) thinking. Parker states that he contested the orthodox position that 'the Church must have a visible form and that that visible form consists in the hierarchy in communion with the Pope. Against this Calvin, arguing from actuality to possibility, insisted that the Church could lack a visible form. It lacked a form in the days of Elijah who, seeing none like-minded in Israel, believed that he alone was left, whereas the Lord knew the invisible seven thousand who had not bowed the knee to Baal'.[83] Likewise, Höpfl writes that 'what is crucial for salvation is not membership of *a* church, but membership of the true church, the communion of saints, which, since it is composed of the dead as well as the living, and, furthermore, contains none but true Christians (a state of soul discernible only by God), can give scant guidance about the ordering of a "particular" church'.[84] On this level, it could be argued that for Calvin the true Church is expressed by faith rather than form – an opposition to what he called (in the same terms as Zwingli)[85] the false church of Rome and the false gods (Fromment's *'petis dieux'*, both as images and hosts) of idolatry.

According to Calvin, the true God is reflected in the true Church, where the faithful look to the one Word. While the Papacy has been corrupted by Satan, the faithful are the nation of a new Jerusalem.[86] Their creed states not 'I believe *in* the Church' but 'I believe the Church', for they 'believe in God'.[87] He wrote that 'if the true Church is "the pillar and ground of the truth" (1 Timothy 3:15), it is certain that there is no Church where lying and falsehood have usurped the ascendancy' – with the exception of the false church of Rome where 'instead of the ministry of the word, prevails a perverted government … a government which partly extinguishes, partly suppresses, the true light', breeding a 'school of idolatry and impiety'.[88] These statements on the Church consolidated the various lines of thought, from scripture to education, that have been presented in this chapter. Crucially, they made the connection between image and ontology that proved central to Calvin's iconoclastic thinking: the true Church's approach towards the one God is considered absolutely different from the 'false and vain' gaze, to which all humans are prone and which constitutes the 'shadow of religion'[89] in Rome. This is the theological link between image-breaking and the nature of God as outlined in the *Institutes*. In the words of Eire, 'when one considers that Calvin regarded knowledge of God and of oneself to be the proper end of all human beings, it is easy to see why the idolatrous impulse seemed so heinous: it produced a complete reversal of the true, natural order, and perverted the *cogito* that alone could make life good'.[90] For Calvin, 'the communion of the Church was not instituted to be a chain to bind us in idolatry, impiety, ignorance of God, and other kinds of evil, but rather to retain us in *the fear of God and obedience of the truth*'.[91]

In summary: Calvin argued that truth (the true Church reflecting the true God) stands over orthodoxy (the false church) as the word (scripture, the worship of the true Church) and the temple of God (the human body) stand over the image (the object of the false church). We may conclude from this brief examination of Calvin's theology, developing an understanding of the nature of God to the organization of Christian life, that the logic of the *Institutes* revolved around the question of images and image-breaking. The question that remains is how this theology was interpreted in the streets of the 'new Jerusalem': Geneva in the 1540s and 1550s.

THE *INSTITUTES* AND SOCIAL GOVERNANCE

How did the theology contained within the *Institutes* relate to Calvin's thinking on political society? Specifically, how was a 'Calvinist' theology of the true God and the true Church organized at a local and governmental level in the Geneva of his day, and to what extent was this related to iconoclasm? I have argued that 1536 was a critical year in iconoclastic history, as it saw both Farel's preaching throughout Vaud and Calvin's work on the *Institutes* in Basel brought together within the walls of one city. Furthermore, I have suggested how the historical understanding of this event is problematic in the extent it relies on accounts that Farel, Calvin, and Fromment themselves gave of the 'new Jerusalem' or *Hieropolis*,[92] the 'Holy City'. However, from 1536 a series of institutional changes can be noted alongside these accounts, providing the historian with moments of 'singular clarity' (to use a phrase of Foucault) against which the society of Calvin's Geneva can be assessed. The issuing of the Geneva Catechism was one such moment. So too were other legal and social decisions made at the time. Under Calvin, new records of births, marriages, and punishments were written down. Each exist as a series of indications of the direction Geneva was taking, enabling the historian to trace the process of what would eventually become 'Calvinism'. As such, the theological study of Calvin's iconoclastic thinking remains incomplete unless it is reflected in the institutions of Calvin's society.

The reader will note that this approach differs from an anthropological concern with how belief relates to practice in religious communities. I am concerned with moments of change both institutionally (that is, explicitly civic) and linguistically (that is, what was added to the dictionaries). This modifies the belief/practice axis. Instead of comparing 'what was believed to be the case' with 'what was evidentially the case', the institution / language axis asks 'what was declared to have been the case', or, more precisely, 'what might as well have been the case' for the purpose of reading a written history. Fact, fiction, and fashioning remain equal parts of the historical whole, to the extent that the fact might even be predominantly fictional – that is, mythological – and everything that we understand to have been the case in 1530s Geneva was nothing of the sort. The myth was built upon a record of some sort, and as such must be read with as much 'historical literacy' (as I have used Danto's phrase) as the 'evidence' of practice. I offer these thoughts for a specific reason. Although Calvin wrote about images in the *Institutes*, the chroniclers of image-breaking and the image-breakers themselves were Calvin*ists*. By examining, then, how the theology of 1535 related to the political life of the 1540s and beyond, the momentum of the pendulum that swings between the myths and the myth-makers of iconoclasm can be observed without stopping it dead with the conclusion of belief through practice. The question left to be asked of the theology within the *Institutes* is this: how did the oscillation of iconoclastic thinking during those years become *codified* into the prototype that we recognize today? What were the institutions of image-breakers?

To answer this question requires an understanding of political Calvinism. As such, I shall conclude this chapter by outlining Calvin's theory of government in the *Institutes*. From this, I shall consider how his theory of government related to Geneva, both economically and demographically. The use of economic and demographic material in this context represents more than a short-hand for describing political society. Both are intimately connected with the development of Calvinist self-fashioning. *Demographically*, Geneva in the 1530s and 1540s saw a substantial influx of French immigrants fleeing Catholic persecution. Both Farel and Calvin were such immigrants – Farel originating from Gap in Savoy, and Calvin from Noyon in Picardy. To an extent, the implementation of their theology in the political life of Geneva was also a case of introduction and, at times, imposition. When this is considered in the light of the 'international Calvinism'[93] propagated through the Low Countries, England, and eventually America, the question can be asked whether immigration and exile should be deemed important factors in a study of Calvinist iconoclasm. *Economically*, it is important to understand how the financial culture developed in sixteenth-century Geneva in order properly to approach those parts of Calvinist society which have been compared, notably by Weber, to aspects of Islam and, by extension, 'Wahhabi' society.

Calvin's work on government in the *Institutes* contains four key parts. First, he developed the ideas that had informed earlier chapters on scriptural authority and the example of the prophets, to argue that the reformed Church was not something new but instead part of a true religion pre-dating the 'perverted government' of Rome. This located the question of ecclesiastical organization in the context of an enquiry into political government. As such, Calvin argued that acknowledgement of the true God's supremacy must be reflected in Christian obedience to the political rule imposed by God. Third, he posited a division between the spiritual and the earthly or political kingdoms, in part to counter the accusation that he was an Anabaptist. Calvin claimed that a human action on earth (for example, that of obedience) can 'begin' the heavenly kingdom in Christian life – a soteriological premise that formed the basis for Weber's description of Calvinists making money on earth in order to reflect God's grace and ultimately secure election to heaven. Fourth, Calvin ended the *Institutes* with a practical question pertinent to his followers throughout Europe at the time: under these terms, should a Christian obey an evil or tyrannical ruler? This final question, as well as his wider political theory, informed his efforts to establish a reformed church in Geneva.

For Calvin, political life is an extension of the organization of the true Church. As something founded on the authority of scripture, he stressed that this organization was not something new to the Church. In the *Institutes*, he wrote that 'first, in calling it new, [the papists] are exceedingly injurious to God, whose sacred *word* deserved not to be charged with novelty ... those who are acquainted with the old saying of Paul that Christ Jesus "died for our sins, and rose again for our justification" (Romans 4:25) will not detect any novelty in us'.[94] Likewise, 'Moses does not introduce a new Deity. He only sets forth that doctrine concerning the eternal God which the Israelites had received by tradition from their fathers'[95] – a tradition pre-dating the papacy as 'the seed of Abraham, and the fruit of the loins of David'.[96] In this way, Calvin declared the so-called new Church to be as old as the prophets, and emphasized Christ's lineage with Abraham and David over Peter. In terms of Church organization, he took the prophets as an example:

> In the present day, therefore, the pretence of the Romanists is just the same as that which appears to have been formally used by the Jews, when the Prophets of the Lord charged them with blindness, impiety, and idolatry. For as the Jews proudly vaunted of their temple, ceremonies, and priesthood, by which, with strong reason, as they supposed, they measured the Church, we are presented by the Romanists with certain external masks, which often are far from being connected with the Church, and without which the Church can perfectly exist.[97]

Calvin made his argument against 'novelty' for two reasons. First, he wished to counter the accusation of theological innovations typically associated with heresy. Second, his claim to legitimate reform with reference to parallels in the Bible provided a bridge between scripture and the case for political change. He considered iconoclasm to be the first step on this bridge because it enabled the Christian to revert to the Word. From the empty space created by iconoclasm, Calvin believed, the political question that followed was how the building of civil institutions could also relate to scripture and the true Church, adding that '[the papists] forgot this landmark when they enacted so many constitutions, so many canons, so many dogmatic decisions, without authority from the Word of God'.[98] His concern, under these terms, was not with institutions *per se* – within the context of the true Church, they could provide the foundation for political reform – but rather with the traditions developed by the false church. Thus the legitimacy of iconoclasm in Calvin's mind: it destroys false traditions in order to give space for Godly institutions to be built and, in this sense, is presented as an act of *constructive* ordering of a religion as old as the prophets.

The emphasis on 'order' in Calvin's work contained a complex political stance that was, contrary to partisan accounts, often in line with orthodoxy. Steinmetz states that 'large portions of Calvin's teaching, even when judged by the strictest standards of mediaeval Catholic theology, remained traditionally orthodox ... Calvin was committed to reforming the old faith, not to minting an altogether new one'.[99] This is not to insinuate a Catholic reading of Calvin; on the contrary, it highlights an important detail that is otherwise hidden by the blanket of the Calvinist myth. The same can be said for his political theory. In the *Institutes* Calvin presented a line that supported the integrity of royalty as a matter of order. His address to the King of France denounced 'what lying calumnies it is daily traduced in your presence, as aiming at nothing else than to wrest the sceptres of kings out of their hands, to overturn all tribunals and seats of justice, to subvert all order and government, to disturb the peace and quiet of society, to abolish all laws, destroy the distinctions of rank and property, and, in short, turn all things upside down'.[100] Predicting the accusation that (as an exile) he sought to appease the king in order to be allowed to return to Noyon, Calvin added 'let it not be imagined that I am here framing my own private defence, with a view of obtaining a safe return to my native land', stressing that though he loved France he could 'be absent from it without regret'.[101] Instead, he presented his defence of the king as an extension of his theology: 'the characteristic of a true sovereign is, to acknowledge that, in the administration of his kingdom, he is a minister of God'.[102] Aligning the question of political order in terms of obedience – Christian obedience to the monarch, and the obedience of that monarch in turn to God – Calvin's thinking was concomitant with much sixteenth-century orthodox teaching on the divine right of kings, emphasizing that Christians ought not to rebel against a figurehead placed on his throne by divine will, 'nothing being less accordant with the nature of God',[103] within the context of individual liberty determining the form of ecclesiastical organization.[104]

These twin principles of obedience and order shaped the concluding chapter on government in the *Institutes*. Calvin wrote that just as men should curb any natural inclination towards idolatry in their attempt to know God, so too they should curb any propensity towards disobedience of being governed. The limits of human imagination connect the theology of images and the politics of government; in both cases, obedience to the true God represented the goal for Christian life. He stated that the 'law of God' (that is, the will of the true God on earth) is a 'bridle to curb men', and while men cannot fully comprehend this law,[105] it exists nevertheless as 'restraint' or 'order' on so-called 'liberty'.[106] This, in turn, reflects a difference or division between the realms of the 'spiritual' (the heavenly) and the 'worldly' (the governmental or legal; 'the law of God'):

> He who knows to distinguish between the body and the soul, between the fleeting life and that which is future and eternal, will have no difficulty in understanding that the spiritual kingdom of Christ and civil government are things very widely separated. Seeing, therefore, it is a Jewish vanity to seek and include the kingdom of Christ under the elements of this world, let us, considering, as Scripture clearly teaches, that the blessings which we derive from Christ are spiritual, remember to confine the liberty which is promised and offered to us in him within its proper limits.[107]

While civil government extends from ecclesiastical organization according to the Word, Calvin argued, the civil and the religious 'kingdoms' which Christians inhabit are separate. This is the 'two-fold regime' proposed in the *Institutes*,[108] invoking the debate over ecclesiastical and secular authority that had, since *Dictatus Papae* in 1075, defined orthodox polity. As those who denied the papal assertion could be accused of heresy, Calvin was adamant that his distinction between civil and spiritual obedience was different from radical Manichaeism. He contended that Christians should not neglect civil or worldly obedience in their quest for spiritual salvation. Answering the Anabaptist contention that 'after we are dead by Christ to the elements of this world, and being transformed by the kingdom of God sit among the celestials, it is unworthy of us, and far beneath our dignity, to be occupied with those profane and impure cares', he maintained that 'as we lately taught that that kind of government is distinct from the spiritual and internal kingdom of Christ, so we ought to know that they are not adverse to each other. The former, in some measure, begins the heavenly kingdom in us, even now upon earth, and in this mortal and evanescent life commences immortal and incorruptible blessedness'.[109] Obedience is one such 'incorruptible blessedness'. It is an attribute of political life on earth that, while 'distinguished' from the kingdom of heaven, remains one of its most immediate reflections. To be governed is thus to begin and bridge the two kingdoms.

It is evident that Calvin's political theory was designed to draw together the theology that threads throughout his *Institutes*: from his first remarks on creation, to the following chapters on the nature of the true God, the nature of mankind, the question of images, the true Church's governance, doctrine, and finally, political government. Steinmetz writes that the structure of the book 'is an orderly compilation of extended discussions of central themes and problems in the Christian faith'; as God 'was reclaiming his fallen creation, not only through the church but also to some extent through the restoration of order by the state'[110] ('sin makes government necessary'),[111] it is logical that Calvin positioned the work on government after the theology. Throughout the *Institutes*, and specifically on the subject of images, he made a moral case for human self-limitation. According to Steinmetz, 'the practical implication' (that is, the political application) 'of God's establishment of specific limitations on human action should now be clear. God exercises his power for a *purpose*: he seeks through the rule of Christ and the work of his Spirit to reclaim, restore, renew, and revitalise all that his own'.[112] However, Calvin was not explicit as to how this 'practical implication' should be resolved, preferring to expound a theory of obedience and order without providing a detailed economic or legal framework. This lack of a practical political guide for his followers had two exceptions: first, in those demands that developed alongside his functioning role as a pastor; and second, in a specific question concerning the code of obedience presented in the *Institutes*: namely, should a Christian obey an 'unchristian' (in other words, an immoral or tyrannical) ruler?[113] Before examining the role of the Reformist pastor in Genevan society, I shall turn briefly to this latter question.

The question of obedience to a tyrant occupies the last pages of the *Institutes*. In order to provide an answer, Calvin took his portrayal of the true God's utter supremacy to its final conclusion. He wrote that various kinds of government exist – monarchical, aristocratic, and democratic[114] – with each kind ruling over different countries as God sees fit. Thus tyranny will exist in some places at some times. Within this context, Calvin argued that the duty shown by Christians to kings[115] should be extended also to despots, because the obedience yielded 'is rendered to God himself, inasmuch as [the ruler's] power is from God'.[116] To quote at length:

> As we have hitherto described the magistrate who truly is what he is called – viz. the father of his country, and (as the Poet speaks) the pastor of the people, the guardian of peace, the president of justice ... in almost all ages we see that some princes, careless about all their duties on which they ought to have been intent, live, without solicitude, in luxurious sloth ... others pillage poor people of their money, and afterwards squander it in insane largesses; others act as mere robbers, pillaging houses, violating matrons, and slaying the innocent; many cannot be persuaded to recognise such persons for princes, whose command, as far as lawful, they are bound to obey. For while in this

unworthy conduct, and among atrocities so alien, not only from the duty of the magistrate, but also of the man, they behold no appearance of *the image of God* ...

But if we have respect to *the word of God*, it will lead us farther, and make us subject not only to the authority of those princes who honestly and faithfully perform their duty toward us, but all princes, by whatever means they have so become, although there is nothing they less perform than the duty of princes ...

We need not labour to prove that an impious king is a mark of the Lord's anger ...[117]

This passage contains each element of Calvin's theology hitherto introduced and applies it to a question of practical and political significance. The king rules not necessarily according to the will of God but always under the will of God,[118] and obedience to the Word guides Christians even when the image of God is obscured. Indeed, Calvin suggests that Christians living under a tyrant are possibly being punished by God ('if ... we are persecuted for righteousness' sake by an impious and sacrilegious prince, let us first call up the remembrance of our own faults, which doubtless the Lord is chastising by such scourges')[119] and that tyranny might be contained within an overall order of good.[120]

In the case of obeying a tyrant, the will of God remains supreme. However, the final page of the *Institutes* contains a piece of mitigating advice: 'in that obedience which we hold to be due to the commands of rulers, we must always make the exception, nay, must be particularly careful that it is not incompatible with obedience to Him to whose will the wishes of all kings should be subject'. Calvin stated that 'we are subject to the men who rule over us, but subject only in the Lord. If they command anything against Him let us not pay the least regard to it, nor be moved by all the dignity which they possess as magistrates – a dignity to which no injury is done when it is subordinated to the special and truly supreme power of God'.[121] This complicated practical matters. For example, when the French-speaking church at Wesel in Cleves was pressed to follow Lutheran Eucharistic rites, the congregation wrote to the Genevan ministers to ask what should be done in terms of obedience. The reply from Geneva was to conform 'in all those ceremonies, which do not have a decisive influence on our faith so that the unity of the church is not disturbed either by our excessive severity or timidity'.[122] However, 'a decisive influence' remained open to debate. If a secular ruler was to enforce a liturgical tradition of the 'false church' (for example, a Catholic Mass or the use of images), this would be grounds for political disobedience.

The reader of these last pages of *Institutes* is not given a clear idea of how these measures might be implemented. Höpfl's introduction to the separate edition of the chapter (published as *Luther and Calvin on Secular Authority*) states that 'he virtually abandoned the attempt to distinguish an area of secular matters, over which secular rulers were to have jurisdiction, replacing it with a much more defensible distinction between the *means* employed by secular and spiritual governors respectively'.[123] The reader is left with little more than an overall theory of the political osmosis between Church and government. However, within this theory remained some indications of a practical guide – first, to comfort those reformers who were being persecuted and to remind them that their actions were not a novelty but older than Rome; and second, to stress that the true Church was not opposed to secular rule. In this way, the *Institutes* represented something of an instruction or handbook (*Institutio*) specific to the needs of the day as much as it proposed a general soteriology. Calvin was writing for fellow exiles, and many of his later ideas on the election of Christians find their origin in his rough guide to the early French reformers. The political conclusion to the *Institutes* heralded the radical predeterminist position (inasmuch as it called for complete obedience according to the supreme will of God and the restoration of order) that would shape the later treatise on predestination (1552) and the *Commentary on the Psalms* (1557). Thus Calvin concluded his work on ontology, images, and civil government. It now remains to be examined how this was developed around the specific dilemmas facing pastors in his Geneva.

THE POLITICS OF CALVINIST ICONOCLASM

By outlining the political dimension to Calvin's theological ideas in the light of Farel's sermon in St. Pierre, I have sought to present something of both material and methodological importance to a study of iconoclasm: that is, most image-breaking that occurred in Geneva took place under the instigation of French immigrants *before* Calvin arrived in 1536, and as such Calvin's connection with image-breaking remained theoretical, expressed as ideas in the pages of the *Institutes*. Calvin the individual is clearly of importance to this discourse, even though he himself did not engage in image-breaking. However, in terms of *iconoclasm*, it is more precise to talk of 'Calvin*ism*' – an idea applied as an explanatory label to the actions of individuals associated with Calvin's theories. To make sense of these labels and events, a lexicon was established to describe – sometimes by the protagonists, sometimes pejoratively by their opponents – the 'iconoclasts', 'Calvinists', and 'Puritans' influencing the religious and political landscape. Once groups of these Genevan individuals had turned outwards in a diaspora the lexicon was propagated, particularly throughout England, Scotland, and the Low Countries, through further acts of image-breaking. As described in my introduction, the dictionaries of the time used new words to define the iconoclast and his political or 'state' territories – words or terms that were taken to their final conclusion by Weber when he connected the clergy (whom Calvin called 'pastors'), commerce,[124] and tyranny[125] in the same 'Protestant Ethic'. This represented the development of 'Calvinist' image-breaking that became intellectualized and historicized into a prototype or myth of 'iconoclasm'. In other words, through a process of linguistic and institutional change, the iconoclast was developed into 'iconoclasm' as Calvin was developed into 'Calvinism'.

As Calvin's theory of government stemmed from the principle of ecclesiastical organization, his notion of the role of a pastor was politically significant. This was something new to Geneva. When he arrived in the city in 1536, the political system was based around four categories of inhabitant: *citoyen* (someone native-born), *bourgeois* (someone naturalized, often on payment), *habitant* (a legally resident alien), and *natif* (a local with no civic status). Both *citoyens* and *bourgeoisie* could vote in the annual meeting of the *Conseil Général*, ratifying different council decisions and electing magistrates.[126] It was the *Conseil*, for example, that decided to accept the tenets of the Reformation during the struggles between Bern and Savoy. The same body, still undecided in its direction, was also responsible for the temporary expulsion of both Farel and Calvin soon after 1536. This fact alone highlights the differences between Calvin's political thinking and the practical demands that he faced. The idea that Calvin dominated Genevan political life in an absolutist manner is part of the Calvinist mythology. When he introduced the twenty-one articles of the 'Confession of Faith' (the prototype for the 'Geneva Catechism') he restricted his demand for subscription to *habitants*.[127] As a French immigrant, he was bound to address his fellow resident aliens rather than the *citoyens* who approached him with some reservations; after being expelled for some time by the latter, he was only granted *bourgeois* status later in his life.

Considering these factors, it is reasonable to state that while Geneva was religiously open to change (following the dismissal of its Savoyard Catholic bishop), it remained politically fixed. The immigrant French pastor must be understood in this context. During his expulsion, Calvin's letters described the process of reform and the state of government in Geneva. In a letter to Henry Bullinger written in 1538 (soon after returning to the city), he wrote 'we have not yet been able to obtain ... that the city, which in proportion to its extent is very populous, may be distributed into parishes, as is rendered necessary by the complicated administration of the Church. The generality of men are more ready to acknowledge us as preachers rather than as pastors'.[128] Calvin's early experiences indicate that he sought to ensure that the role of pastor was deemed administratively relevant, whereas the *Conseil* considered it to be primarily religious (that is, not of mechanical importance to the political system). As Calvin believed that much of the religious work of dismantling the false church had already been achieved through iconoclasm, his intention was to consolidate it within Geneva's administrative system by institutionalizing the reforms. The role of pastor was therefore of central importance. In one letter of 1536 he wrote to Francis Daniel that while 'already in many places, the idols and altars of Popery have begun to disappear, and I hope it will not be long before all the remaining superstition shall be effectively cleared away ... you can hardly believe the small number of ministers compared with the very many churches which need pastors. How I wish, seeing the extreme necessity of the Church, that, however few they may be in number, there were at least some right-hearted men among you who may be induced to lend a helping hand'.[129]

Such practical concerns affected the application of Calvin's political theory. Höpfl contends that 'in 1535, when he wrote all or most of the *Institution* [sic], Calvin was entirely innocent of any pastoral experience, and *a fortiori* of any experience in matters of ecclesiastical polity or the councils of princes and magistrates'.[130] This changed with his growing experience as a pastor in Geneva, governing a local church.[131] Initially, he operated outside the political system, catering to *habitants* rather than *citoyens*. However, following his expulsion and subsequent return to Geneva, Calvin worked to build both a 'Company of Pastors' and a group of councillors to work with the Company in the 'Consistory'. This had political as much as religious ramifications. According to Naphy, 'by 1546, Calvin had gathered round himself a group of extremely gifted, well-educated, socially prominent and financially secure French religious refugee ministers',[132] indicating that by the middle of the 1540s he was politically more established. Naphy states that 'by 1546, Calvin's theories of ecclesiology were nearly complete in practice. The Company of Pastors met every week for discussion, improvement, admonition, and support as a Genevan national synod. The Consistory was an ecclesiastical court which, on its own, could become the local governing body of the church'.[133] In short, church and government (we cannot yet talk of Church and 'State') were combined to consolidate the reformers' position in Geneva, the pastor becoming a prominent figure in Genevan political and legal society.

Naphy describes Geneva at the time as a city 'overcrowded and stuffed with refugees'.[134] The question to be asked in terms of iconoclasm is: how reliable is such a description, and to what extent did the issue of immigration effect the development of 'Calvinism'? The most complete study dedicated to the demographic situation in Geneva was written by Monter in 1979; prior to that, almost no such work had been undertaken. Monter states that 'there has been too little cross-fertilization between demographers and specialists in traditional fields', while stressing that 'this neglect is not due to any lack of records. On the contrary, raw demographic data from Calvin's Geneva are remarkably complete'.[135] Like Eire, Monter notes the wealth of records in Geneva during Calvin's pastoral rule. Historiographically, this is a significant point. Compared to the lack of material other than Antoine Fromment to describe Farel's iconoclastic sermon in St. Pierre in 1535, one effect of Calvin's role as a pastor was not only the reorganization of the city's parishes but also an increase in its documentation of baptisms, marriages, and deaths. For Monter, 'the problem for historians is to know exactly what questions to ask of this information ... First, how do Geneva's demographic data affect our knowledge of the French Reformation? Second, how do they affect our knowledge of Calvinist morality in action?'[136] These questions can be recast according to the terms I have put forward. To what extent did the political and demographic expression of morality help institutionalize Calvin's followers into becoming 'Calvinists'? And how do these individuals of the 1540s and 1550s relate to the image-breakers of St. Pierre in 1535?

Monter explains that the prominent demographic feature of Genevan society during Calvin's 'tenure' was its influx of Huguenot refugees. This was already the case during Farel's time in the city, when St. Pierre was attacked. Eire writes that the kind of riots involving Farel and acts of image-breaking were precipitated by local Catholics attacking Protestants over perceived privileges, and that friction between *citoyens* and *habitants* was as significant a reason for the attacks as the wider struggle between Bern, Savoy, and the oscillating *Conseil*.[137] This demographic friction intensified once Calvin had settled in the city. According to Grell, 'Geneva, a city of around ten thousand, more than doubled its size because of the arrival of religious refugees of mainly French and Italian origin, from Calvin's recall in 1541 to his death in 1564'.[138] Valeri's economic study of Geneva at the time claims that 'a nearly seventy-five per cent rise in population during Calvin's tenure, from twelve thousand to twenty-one thousand, put immense pressure on economic resources, especially welfare institutions and food supplies'.[139] Valeri is referring here to the 1550s, meaning that the seventy-five per cent rise in population took place in the fifteen years following Calvin's arrival. In terms of the documentary evidence, Monter notes that 'Geneva's official immigration records only exist from 1549 until January 1560, again from 1572 to 1574 (the aftermath of the St. Bartholomew's Massacre), and again from 1585 to 1587 (during a blockade of the city by the Duke of Savoy)'.[140] Thus a correlation is found between these records, the surges of immigration, and key moments of crisis affecting the reformist movement. Monter uses this evidence to explain that the French stayed only a short time in Geneva as a place of refuge,[141] claiming that 'the Huguenots were an extremely mobile group which left Geneva as massively as it had entered'.[142] Referring to baptism and marriage certificates, he notes how 'transitory this Huguenot colony was ... between 1560 and 1590, the city lost close to half of its population'.[143] If we accept the claims of McGrath[144] and Höpfl – that Geneva 'was not on the great trade routes, it no longer had its own fair, it had neither imposing civic buildings nor a university. It had neither great wealth, nor great manufactures, nor guilds of artisans; Genevan watch-making and printing are the consequences of French immigration ... politically, too, Geneva was a city of no great consequence'[145] – the evidence would seem to strengthen the claim that Huguenot immigrants were responsible for the city's wealth. As Geneva was not an economic centre, it is apparent that the surges in migration occurred for reasons of religious refuge rather than economic gain, even though the effect was a change in both the market and the political structure along religious lines (that is, pastors now negotiated, traded, and voted with *citoyens*).

Having described the flux of people in and around Calvin's Geneva, Monter examines its effects on the system of government. He writes that the *citoyens* had prevented the French migrants from acquiring the status of *bourgeoisie*; in 1555, however, 350 reformers were granted the status, including Calvin himself.[146] This detail reveals something of critical importance to my study on iconoclasm in Geneva:

> Most of the refugees who became citizens after 1555 had arrived in Geneva long before then. Among the 390 men whose names appear in both the *Livre des Habitants* and the *Livre des Bourgeois*, well over half (215) had signed the former before 1555. Measured another way, we can say that about 22 per cent of the refugees recorded before 1555 eventually became full Genevan citizens, but fewer than 5 per cent of those who arrived afterwards ever did so. *Thus, the permanent settlers among Geneva's enormous Huguenot colony of the 1550s were for the most part the earliest arrivals – a group which also included the richest and most famous refugees.* Apparently Geneva assimilated her masses of refugees with increasing difficulty; only the earliest arrivals (particularly the wealthiest and famous among them) found enough opportunity to establish themselves permanently.[147]

This passage contains a subtext that provides a critical context to Farel's monument and Fromment's self-fashioning, and explains something of the development of the Calvinist prototype. The documentary evidence it uses shows that most of the records describing the lives of the reformers in Geneva were written during and after Calvin's time (from 1536 onwards). However, the majority of Genevan image-breaking took place before this date under Farel, as described by Fromment. To use recorded evidence from the 1550s to make a social statement about events of the 1530s would be disproportionately speculative, even anachronistic, were it not that the records then show that many of the individuals who instigated the attacks in the early 1530s were *also* those who remained in the city during the years that followed, despite the temporary expulsion of Calvin, the departure of Farel to Neuchâtel, the wavering of the Genevan *citoyens*, and the massive shifts in population affecting their fellow religious exiles. These early reformers became more established within the otherwise fixed structure of Genevan political society. Despite the early instability, they were eventually granted official status in the city. The detailed records attributed to Calvin's tenure begin at the same time as this later assimilation. However, the people mentioned in the records are predominantly the same in 1555 as in 1536.

The 'Monument International de la Réformation' in Geneva, featuring Farel, Calvin, de Bèze, and Knox (1909)

Rather than being an anachronistic leap of imagination, then, it is safe to say that the documentary evidence of the old Huguenots refers to the young image-breakers at the moment that they became *institutionalized* in the political system. This is the moment of institutional 'iconoclasm', even though little image-breaking was taking place. It reflects the axis of institution and language; by writing themselves into history in such a way, the 'Calvinists' began to shape their own identity. This represents a turning-point in the politics of iconoclasm.

The self-fashioning, or myth-making, of this new Calvinist, iconoclastic class, is also of vital importance if we are to make sense of the connection between image-breaking and political society. When considered in terms of the institutionalization of Calvin's ideas into a collective that would later be called 'Calvinism', defined around certain labels – namely, those of the religious *émigré* becoming, through a series of civil stages, the urban *citoyen* – it is apparent that the historian is also dealing in the transaction between institutions and language that constitutes a myth. The veracity of this myth has been fought over by partisans since its origin, but I am more interested in its usefulness, reduced to two points: the 'Calvinist' as recorded in 1550s Geneva enables me to reach at one point the otherwise unknowable individual who attacked St. Pierre in 1535, and at another point the popular image of Calvinism today – an image which provides one of the prototypes of this book.

To conclude: Calvin established a theory of government in the *Institutes* around the twin principles of order and obedience shown to the ruler by the ruled. Men should obey the rule of kings, he argued, because those kings in turn are ruled by God. This followed a theological premise outlined in earlier chapters on the absolute supremacy of the true God and took it to a political conclusion which, he indicated, might instruct his fellow religious exiles. Despite the provision of some practical pointers in the final pages, however, his instruction remained in the main theoretical. Once he was established in Geneva, Calvin developed the theory through his practical experiences. His primary concern at this time was to establish the religious role of pastor within the political framework of *citoyens*. In 1546, the Company of Pastors was initiated. In 1555, several hundred French reformers, including Calvin himself, were accepted as official *bourgeoisie*. Once politically established in Geneva, Calvin's letters show that his early ideas of political obedience articulated in the *Institutes* were then sent to instruct other reformist groups in the Low Countries and England.

The significant acts of image-breaking in Geneva, notably the attack on St. Pierre in 1535, took place before Calvin settled in the city, and while he was writing the *Institutes* in Basel. Thus the 'Calvinist' image-breaking which is taken by present-day historians as a prototype for Reformation iconoclasm occurred in the main *before* Calvin's arrival in 1536. In order to understand the events of 1535, the historian relies on the singular account of Antoine Fromment. The records of civil life in Geneva, detailing baptisms, marriages, and laws, increased in volume *after* Calvin had established the Company of Pastors. In other words, the later records of social and political life in Geneva do not describe the earlier acts of iconoclasm. It is possible to identify, through the records, certain attributes of the immigrant Frenchman in Geneva during the 1550s, but the same cannot be done for the image-breakers of twenty years beforehand. However, the available demographic material indicates that those French reformers who remained in Geneva during the later years were in the main the same individuals who had first arrived with Farel and Calvin during the 1530s. Thus a historical leap is able to be made, and some of the attributes of the later 'Calvinists' can be applied to those who attacked

St. Pierre in 1535. The records and the labels refer to the same individuals. It is therefore appropriate to refer to 'iconoclasm' in terms of 'Calvinism' rather than Calvin. Under these terms, it is not necessary to attempt the identification of an act but rather its translation into an idea, a myth, a prototype. Calvin*ism* took hold in Geneva, organized around a new political class, and was subsequently promoted through various reformist groups throughout Europe and eventually to America.[148] As such, acts of iconoclasm took place in these countries that were labelled Calvinist but had limited historical connection with Geneva in 1535.[149] This process of dislocation and translation is the origin of a Calvinist, iconoclastic mythology that serves as a prototype in the dictionaries today – a historical standard that is comparable, as shall be examined in the next chapter, to certain traditions in Islam.

CHAPTER 2
Wahhabism and Iconoclasm

There can be little doubt that the Wahhabite assault on popular practices and other manifestations of devotional and doctrinal difference was directed not only against dogmatic and devotional aberrations, but was also the counterpart of the fact that these were not only aberrant, but also and decidedly local. This acted to fragment religious authority in this world as well as in others, and militated against the emergence of a political authority which, busily devouring and incorporating social and geographical territory into a unifying vortex, was sustained by the Saudi-Wahhabite alliance.

Aziz Al-Azmeh, *Islam and Modernities*[1]

The historical identity of Saudi Arabia, presented through the narratives of local partisans and the memoirs of European visitors, has had its origins traced to a movement that emerged in the Arabian peninsula during the eighteenth century and is labelled as 'Wahhabism' after the preacher Muhammad ibn Abd al-Wahhab. The nature of this movement has been the subject of controversy and debate due to a lack of source material: ibn Abd al-Wahhab's followers typically came from outside the line of Ottoman control and the main coastal trading routes, and as such there is a scarcity of contemporary literature, either in Arabic, Turkish, English, or French, to provide a critical voice to the standard account of Wahhabi history.[2] In this respect, the first acts of 'Wahhabism' (and therefore the first events of Wahhabi iconoclasm) represent something historiographically similar to the first acts of 'Calvinism' under Guillaume Farel in Geneva's St. Pierre, in that the historian is presented with a limited discourse consisting of the claims of the iconoclasts, partisans for or against their iconoclasm, and the empty spaces that once contained sacred objects. Like those who attacked St. Pierre in 1535, the individuals who destroyed images in eighteenth-century Arabia left little with which the modern historian might understand them. Their acts have been translated into a label or type, comparable to the development of the 'Calvinism' that I have described in Chapter 1 – a label of 'Wahhabism' which aids the historical legibility of what might or might not have taken place. The following chapter will examine the development of this label.

Contrary to Delong-Bas' argument that ibn Abd al-Wahhab 'had no political motives [and h]is efforts were limited exclusively to religious *dawa*' (a call to Islam),[3] the historical label 'Wahhabism' denotes both a religious and a political agenda. Religiously, it has promoted a reformist version of Islam based on an adherence to the absolute unity of God (*tawhid*) and the refutation of associationism (*shirk*). In the opening statement of his *Kitab al-Tawhid*, ibn Abd al-Wahhab emphasized these twin principles by quoting the Qur'an 4:36 – 'worship (*abudu*) Allah and do not associate (*tushriku*) anything with him' – where the verb *tushriku* relates to *shirk*, and *abudu* to *al-ibadah*, 'the worship' that ibn Abd al-Wahhab stated refers specifically to *tawhid* (*an al-ibadah hiya al-tawhid*).[4] This emphasized those verses in the Qur'an which declare that the worship of the one God (*Al-lah*) precludes his association with anything else, and where the worship of Allah is literally synonymous with the destruction of idols as the words used to describe both idolatry and unbelief (in this case, that of the Christians) are the same.[5] The importance of this theological stance illustrates why the 'Wahhabis' called themselves 'proponents of *tawhid* ' – *muwahhidun* – a term that is often translated into English as 'Unitarian' in order to avoid the pejorative connotations of the label 'Wahhabism'.[6]

Politically, in the desire to create a society that followed absolutely the teachings of the Qur'an (that is, in the desire to recreate an idealized first Islamic community), the Wahhabi destruction of idols attempted to eliminate certain local traditions throughout the Arabian peninsula that were deemed to deviate from *tawhid*. These ranged from incidents of Najdi tribal worship of non-Islamic deities, dead ancestors, and natural objects, such as the male palm tree at Bulaydat al-Fidda,[7] to the veneration of Islamic shrines in the Hijazi cities of Mecca and Medina under the cosmopolitan auspices of the Hashimite Sharifs. The rejection of such diverse local traditions reflected a desire for unity not only in the theological approach to God but also in the political approach to land; from the beginning, the Wahhabis attempted to unite both under the rule of Najd following the 1744 contract between ibn Abd al-Wahhab and the Najdi al-Saud family. Thus iconoclasm represented, for Wahhab*ism*, a means of bridging the principles of theological and political unity.

The following chapter will attempt to outline these elements of Wahhabi iconoclasm: first, in the account of its historical origins; second, in the theological analysis of ibn Abd al-Wahhab's ideas of *tawhid* and image-breaking; third, in the description of certain acts of image-breaking that accompanied the first Wahhabi attack on Hijaz; and finally, in the way that these ideas were applied institutionally, in the emergence of Saudi Arabia as a modern nation state retaining a 'Wahhabi' identity. Throughout the chapter, I shall have in mind the question as to whether a comparison can be made between 'Calvinism' and 'Wahhabism' in the light of their image-breaking and social organization and, by extension, whether it is possible to identify the terms that can provide the framework for a wider definition of iconoclasm shared by different historical, religious, and cultural traditions – that is, the case studies in Part II of this book.

THE SOCIAL CONTEXT TO WAHHABISM

In the early eighteenth century, the Arabian peninsula was populated by communities of nomadic tribes, family clans, and oasis cities from which settled urban (*hadar*) amirs reigned. Towards the south of the peninsula, today described as the *Rub al-Khali* – the 'Empty Quarter' – was desert, separating present-day Saudi Arabia from Yemen and Oman. The mountainous West included the Hijaz region and the holy cities of Medina and Mecca, ruled by the Sharifs and dominated both culturally and economically by the *Hajj* pilgrimage. This area of international influence and trade extended northwards towards present-day Sinai, Syria, and Jordan, a territory that was later connected in 1908 by the construction of an Ottoman railway from Damascus to Medina. Between the *Rub al-Khali* and Hijaz was situated Najd, a semi-desert region with a settled capital, al-Diriyyah, under the control of the al-Saud family. The degree to which Najd at this time was influenced by either cosmopolitan Hijazi or nomadic desert culture has been the subject of recent academic debate, as it would indicate the extent to which Wahhabism was either isolated from or part of a wider Islamic context.

The eighteenth-century Arabian context should not be considered in purely religious terms. Many of the changes experienced by its different communities at the time reflected the demands of social organization in desert conditions. A vivid example of these conditions was provided by Daniel Saunders, an American mariner who was shipwrecked on the east Arabian coast en route to Bombay in 1792, and who described his group of castaways trying to find Muscat and discovering villages that had been deserted because the date trees were barren,[8] leading him to declare that the Bedouin 'even make no difficulty in saying, that the religion of Mahomet was not made for them – "For (add they) how shall we make ablutions, who have no water?"'.[9] This kind of foreign depiction of geographical and social hardship was instrumental in the eighteenth and nineteenth-century construction of an 'Arabian' myth. While Western portrayals of the Ottoman Muslim, including the Levantine Arab, typically promoted an image of wealth and luxury (an image criticized by Said as 'Orientalism'), the portrayal of the 'Arabian' Arab, particularly the Bedouin and the rural Najdi, was one of hardship and poverty. It located Wahhabi history within a context of 'isolation due to its huge geographical area and the unique features of its society',[10] where international trade had a limited influence on inland Najd.[11] Indeed, this account has been developed into an official Saudi claim today that Arabia was never either conquered or colonized because external forces were unable to settle in so harsh a climate,[12] a claim that seems to be supported by al-Rasheed's statement that when foreign intervention did take place (for example, by the British in the early twentieth century), it had as significant an effect on the building of a unified Arabian state as religious Unitarianism.[13] Under these terms, a historical identity of 'Arabia' was promoted that remained both isolated from international relations and the effects of European industrialization, and was defined by the severities of its landscape. This myth extends from early nineteenth-century European depictions of how 'the wild freedom of the neighbouring Bedouin tribes, their endless wars and predatory expeditions, rendered Najd and the surrounding country a scene of perpetual disorder and bloodshed'[14] to the present-day official Saudi position that Wahhabism was a necessary reform of nomadic desert life, an urban movement that emerged as a 'natural event' under the charismatic leadership of ibn Abd al-Wahhab.[15]

This social context was defined by the issue of coexistence between nomads and settled communities. Writing about agricultural organization from the Arabian peninsula to Syria, Hourani states that 'the symbiosis between cultivators and pastoralists was a fragile one ... the mobility and hardiness of the nomadic pastoralists tended to give them a dominant position ... On the fringes of the desert too the pastoralists might be strong enough to levy a kind of tribute, *khwuwwa*, on the settled villages ... they regarded themselves as having a freedom, nobility and honour which were lacking to peasants, merchants and craftsmen'.[16] In turn, Hourani notes, the influence of the nomads was curbed once they came into the realm of the larger settlements. For the leading families of settled agricultural communities, 'the ties of tribal solidarity linking them with the local population might have grown weak, but in their stead they might possess some degree of coercive power, based on the control of strong places and possession of armed forces'.[17] As such, the social life of the inhabitants of villages, towns, and cities on the Arabian peninsula was shaped by different challenges and claims to the identity of clan ties (*asabiyyah*) and nomadic 'independence'. In eighteenth-century Najd, the majority of the population (and therefore the majority of those who were subsequently called 'Wahhabis') were nomads, but it is important from the outset to stress that the Saudi family with whom ibn Abd al-Wahhab forged his pact were urban *hadar*. Al-Rasheed writes that 'both the Saudi leadership and the *mutawwaa* [the enforcers of 'Wahhabi' law] represented the interest of the Najdi *hadar* communities at the expense of those of the Bedouin tribal population'. Indeed, she adds, 'most probably the al-Saud were a sedentary group ... the [1744] settlement recognised the authority of the Saudi amir as a result of ... his residence in the oasis and his ownership of cultivated land and wells around the settlement'.[18] Thus the Arabian context introduces some important features to a study of 'Wahhabi' iconoclasm – first, that the origins of Wahhabism reflected overtly social conditions as much as religious complaints; second, that Wahhabism emerged within a settled community, but depended on nomads to further its influence through clan ties and conquest; and third, that the urban base of the settled Saudi family, al-Diriyyah, became the central influence in Najd, pulling the nomadic communities and the lands they occupied towards its own orbit and creating, in the process, a new region under Saudi rule. With the tribes united around a central settlement in al-Diriyyah, both *hadar* and Bedouin interests in and around Najd were satisfied, dispelling the notion that the large uninhabited desert areas of the peninsula could not be both conquered *and* controlled. A new balance of power took shape in the region around al-Diriyyah. The question that remained was how this would function when the newly powerful Najd turned towards its cosmopolitan neighbour, Hijaz.

Eighteenth-century Hijazi culture was dominated by two international factors: first, the Ottoman rule over the indigenous Arab population; and second, the economics of having thousands of people from across the Islamic world performing the *Hajj* pilgrimage. Prior to the emergence of Wahhabism, Faroqhi explains of the Ottomans that 'large sums of money were spent upon the pilgrimage every year, and most of these expenditures yielded no economic return. This fact alone indicates that the Sultan's title "Servant of the Holy Places" was more than a matter of rhetoric, and formed an important aspect of the Ottoman state's legitimation *vis à vis* the society it governed'.[19] The sums spent on the maintenance of the mosques, shrines, and hospices of Mecca, for example in Sultan Ahmad's addition of a golden water spout to adorn the Kaaba, were intended to strengthen the position of an absent patron.[20] Such signals of legitimation reflected the complex levels of authority over Hijaz, where the governor of Egypt acted as a liaison in Jedda between Mecca and Istanbul,[21] but where the Hashimite Sharifs enjoyed significant degrees of autonomy, having ruled in the city since the tenth century and claiming a royal lineage tracing back to Muhammad. In legislative terms, according to Teitelbaum, 'the structure of the Ottoman state in the Hijaz was unlike that in other Ottoman vilayets, or provinces; it was, rather, more like a "state within a state", where the Ottoman Vali and the Sharif each had their own administration, armed forces, courts, prisons, and representatives in the major towns. This state of affairs caused perpetual tension between the two authorities',[22] reflecting a wider antagonism between Arabs and Turks. To complicate these tensions further, towards the beginning of the eighteenth century, British and French forces began to explore trading routes along the Hijazi coast. Reacting to such increasingly cosmopolitan influences, Hourani argues, a growing number of Arabs voiced their concerns that an erosion of their cultural identity was taking place.[23] Accordingly, the period saw a series of revivalist movements emerge, not unique to Hijaz, which fused claims to 'true' Islam, localism, and anti-Ottoman sentiments.[24] In response, the Ottomans continued to strengthen their ties with Mecca, from an annual delivery of gifts and garrisons to the holy city to the encouragement of Turkish settlers.[25] This contest over legitimacy and revivalism, orthodoxy and localism, on the part of both Ottoman and Arab interest groups, was a defining feature of Hijazi culture in the years preceding the emergence of Wahhabism in Najd, and provided part of ibn Abd al-Wahhab's justification for reforming what he saw as corruption surrounding Mecca and the *Hajj*. In other words, the status of the pilgrimage was a contested symbol of political as well as theological authority. For the Wahhabis in Najd, concerned with the unification of a growing orbit of political alliances, the issue of a culturally unpredictable *Hajj* grew in importance. To control it, however, along with its economic profitability, necessarily involved a military move on Mecca. Thus the attentions of Wahhabism were directed from its origins towards the conquest of Hijaz.

MUHAMMAD IBN ABD AL-WAHHAB

I have thus far focussed on the overtly social context to the origins of Wahhabism. This is because the social questions surrounding the control of Hijaz and the *Hajj*, the unification of the nomadic and settled groups throughout the Arabian peninsula, and the pull of Saudi authority towards Najd, were each as central to the identity of Wahhabism as the theology of *tawhid*. These social questions were also reflected in controversies over the details of Muhammad ibn Abd al-Wahhab's own life.

Who was Muhammad ibn Abd al-Wahhab? While his religious thinking was recorded in books, correspondence, and refutations by other Arabian scholars, the only contemporary local biographical account of his social context was Hussain ibn Ghannam's (d. 1811) *Tarikh Najd*,[26] an apology which influenced a later Najdi account, Uthman ibn Bishr's *Unwan al-Majd fi Tarikh Najd*. While not an exact contemporary, Uthman ibn Bishr was a Najdi student who met groups of people who had known ibn Abd al-Wahhab in order to develop ibn Ghannam's work. Drawing on these sources, he described ibn Abd al-Wahhab as being born in 1703 or 1704 into relatively impoverished circumstances in al-Uyainah, from which as a child he showed 'prodigious' talent, while adding that his father was a judge and, as a result, that he grew up with a degree of education.[27] This claim of education was reiterated by another nineteenth-century source on Hanbalism which stated that ibn Abd al-Wahhab's father was trained in *fiqh* and wrote legal epistles[28] – an argument for the intellectual origins of Wahhabism that has been emphasized by its present-day apologists, from theological commentators[29] to historians.[30]

The lack of reliable biographical source material enabled a mythology to develop around ibn Abd al-Wahhab during the nineteenth century, fuelled by the disputes between Najdi followers, Arab scholars, and European visitors. Ibn Bishr's chronicle likened the so-called persecution of the early Wahhabis to that of the first Muslims, seeking, in the words of Delong-Bas, 'to demonstrate continuity in the Muslim experience'.[31] Such 'continuity', however, was not considered to diminish the belief that Wahhabism emerged from isolated desert conditions, without social parallel; on the contrary, ibn Abd al-Wahhab's association with the first Islamic community, dismissing both that which had come between them and before the Prophet, supported his argument that he was responding to godlessness (*jahiliyyah*) in Arabia. Thus his followers equated 'continuity' with 'revivalism'. From this context, legends about the life of ibn Abd al-Wahhab emerged. For example, certain local rumours were recorded by the French consul to Aleppo in Syria, Alexandre de Corancez, of Sulaiman, the grandfather of ibn Abd al-Wahhab, who was said to have dreamt that he saw a flame leave his body and trail into the desert, consuming in its wake tents and city dwellings. The Najdi shaikhs are reported to have informed Sulaiman that this dream signified he would have a son who would initiate a revival of religion; instead it was his grandson that became the famous Imam.[32] However, Muhammad ibn Abdallah ibn Humayd al-Najdi (d. 1878) claimed that ibn Abd al-Wahhab's father 'was angry with his son Muhammad because he would not study *fiqh* as his predecessors and peers had done. His premonition concerning him was that he would bring about a calamity, saying to the people, "One day you will see Muhammad cause evil"'.[33]

The absence of contemporary source material makes judging these claims critically problematic, and has ensured that biographical accounts of ibn Abd al-Wahhab's life have been shaped by the labels of a mythology which occupies the historical gaps between Najdi, Arab, and Muslim identity, and ranges from the partisan descriptions of 'reformer', 'revivalist', 'puritan', and charismatic 'prophet', to even – according to reports sent back to Napoleon Bonaparte – a renegade French Jesuit.[34] As such, it is a futile task to attempt an explanation of Wahhabi political and religious teaching through stories of a young ibn Abd al-Wahhab. However, there is a consensus among scholars that at some point before 1744 he studied outside Najd, probably in Medina, that he travelled towards Basra around the 1730s,[35] was expelled from that city, and returned to his native al-Uyainah to preach.

According to al-Rasheed, this moment of return to Najd marks the point when his teaching began to take a form that would be recognizable today as 'Wahhabism', and is particularly associated with the story that he commanded the stoning of a woman accused of fornication, citing the *Shariah* as his authority. He is also described at this time of persuading the amir of al-Uyainah, Uthman ibn Muammar, to destroy the tomb of the companion Zayd al-Khattab and to cut down certain trees that were being venerated by the townspeople.[36] Despite the lack of contemporary sources, these stories nevertheless introduce the first features of a recognizable 'Wahhabi' identity: the association with absolutism, the first acts of iconoclasm, and the suggestion that ibn Abd al-Wahhab's reputation was known outside Najd during his lifetime. They also provide an explanatory context for the question over why, having antagonized the amir and clerics of al-Uyainah, he left for al-Diriyyah and gained asylum under the ruling al-Saud family.[37] With this in mind, then, the critical question for the historian must be to what extent the wider Islamic thinking to which ibn Abd al-Wahhab was exposed in Hijaz and Basra before 1744 influenced his ideas and acts once he had returned to Najd and forged a pact, eventually, with the al-Sauds.

The debate over whether ibn Abd al-Wahhab's theology was the product of a socially isolated Najd or a wider Islamic tradition has been summarized in two articles by Voll and Dallal. Voll states that ibn Abd al-Wahhab was influenced by Muhammad Hayya al-Sindi, a 'quiet scholar who attracted a variety of students and who participated in a vigorous community of *Hadith* scholarship in Medina' and who encouraged the Najdi preacher to 'denounce rigid imitation of mediaeval commentaries and to utilize informed individual analysis (*ijtihad*)'.[38] Al-Sindi was part of a broader network of Persian, Arabian, and Indian *Hadith* scholars working in Medina at the time, who in turn were influenced by two older teachers, Ahmad al-Qashashi in Arabia and Muhammad al-Babili in Egypt. 'If one constructs an "intellectual family tree"', writes Voll, 'Muhammad Hayya had at least eight lines of connexion with al-Babili ... the picture that emerges from this pattern of student-teacher relationships is one of a closely intertwined intellectual community'[39] involving Sufis, Shiite and Sunnis, and stretching from India and Persia to Algiers and Morocco. Voll's point is this: the community at Medina was a cosmopolitan centre of Islamic thought, and it is from this nexus that ibn Abd al-Wahhab emerged. In other words, the pluralism of eighteenth-century Hijaz that has been described by historians as provoking the

Najdi-Unitarian reforms instead provided, according to Voll, the intellectual environment from which Wahhabism emerged.

Dallal rejects Voll's depiction of an 'intellectual family tree', writing that 'this theory is attractive in many ways, primarily because it allows the student of modern Islam to analyse and understand a complex set of variables in the context of one coherent whole', but 'the connections made to achieve this coherence are at best fragile'.[40] Stressing that the parts of a sum do not necessarily constitute its whole, Dallal points to the fact that ibn Abd al-Wahhab studied under Muhammed Hayya with the Sufi Shah Wali Allah *after* being expelled from Basra (where he wrote the *Kitab al-Tawhid*) for extremism, indicating 'that his ideas were articulated before establishing connections with the Haramayn network'.[41] However, in an article examining contemporary refutations of ibn Abd al-Wahhab, Traboulsi suggests that while an international context to the theological origins of Wahhabism should not be over-stated, the movement was already known outside Arabia before the Saudi pact of 1744. Traboulsi writes that ibn Abd al-Wahhab's early sermons in al-Uyainah were refuted by clerics in towns around Najd, but that these disputes were also recorded at the time by the Egyptian scholar al-Tandatawi, who was in turn recorded by al-Shafi al-Basri, a prolific refuter of ibn Abd al-Wahhab who cited now lost works such as *Kashf al-Hijab an Wadjh Dalalat ibn Abd al-Wahhab*, used as a source by ibn Ghannam. Noting this succession of influences on the origins of Wahhabism, Traboulsi concludes that 'Tandatawi's refutation also shows that the Shaikh was still a local Najdi figure at this early period. However his actions were not. By stoning the tombs of the saints and stoning the adulteress, ibn Abd al-Wahhab was undermining the authority of both *ulama* and the Sufis, to exist. However minor a figure he was at that time, the Shaikh had crossed a red line and action was necessary to prevent such an "aggressor" from moving forward in his destruction of the established system'.[42]

These details of ibn Abd al-Wahhab's life, combined with the overall social picture of Najd and Hijaz, help the historian make sense of certain features of the social climate from which 'Wahhabi' iconoclasts emerged – first, in an Arabian context defined by continual exchanges of power between nomads and settled communities, where belief in Islam combined with the conditions of desert life; second, in the differences between ibn Abd al-Wahhab's native Najd region and the cosmopolitan influences on Hijaz and Mecca, the site of the *Hajj* pilgrimage; and third, in the degree to which ibn Abd al-Wahhab was informed by a wider Islamic heritage through his experiences in Hijaz and Basra. These issues contextualize the particular combination of a political ambition to unify local clans and a theological ambition to uphold the monotheistic principle of *tawhid*. Their social expression, dependent on a collaboration of nomads to spread Wahhabi-Saudi power through military conquest, was instrumental to the development of a 'Wahhabism' that operates in the historical mind as a prototype of religious and political absolutism. It is under these terms, and with the potential for comparison with Calvin's *Institutes* in mind, that the theology of ibn Abd al-Wahhab can be understood, notably in his *Kitab al-Tawhid*.

SHIRK AND *TAWHID*

Muhammad ibn Abd al-Wahhab's *Kitab al-Tawhid* consists of quotations from the Qur'an and different *hadith* to support some brief lines of commentary on the absolute unity of Allah. As such, an examination of his book constitutes little more than an acknowledgement of the different scriptural sources that underpin the theology of *tawhid*. However, it is possible to identify an emphasis on the ideas of covenant, worship, and unity that is particular to ibn Abd al-Wahhab: namely, that the *la ilaha illa Allah* of the *Shahada* ('there is no god but the God') is the declaration of *tawhid*; that the *face* of God can be found only in this declaration; and, concerning the unbelievers and associators – the *mushrikun* – that both Jesus and Muhammad were 'worshippers of Allah' (where 'worship', as already noted, denotes *tawhid*) and Isa or Jesus was the 'word' of God.[43] In a chapter entitled 'Explaining *tawhid* and the testimony *la ilaha illa Allah*', ibn Abd al-Wahhab referred to the Abrahamic Covenant as an example of the 'greatest and most important of issues – that is the explanation of *tawhid* and the explanation of the *Shahada*',[44] as the true worship contained within the *Shahada* is connected with the salvation of the Muslim who utters it.[45]

Before elaborating on ibn Abd al-Wahhab's development of these ideas, it is important to note that *tawhid* is differentiated by three types in Islamic teaching: the oneness of the lordship of Allah (*tawhid al-Rububiyyah*), the oneness of the worship of Allah (*tawhid al-Uluhiyyah*), and the oneness of the names and qualities of Allah (*tawhid al-Asma wa Sifat*). The first, professing the 'lordly unity', asserts that there is only one (*ahad*, from which the word *tawhid* is derived) God (*Allah*)[46] who created and sustains the universe, and from whose creation come both goodness and salvation. Dallal claims that belief in *tawhid al-Rububiyyah* 'is held by most people, and was even held by the Arabs before the advent of Islam' as the *jahiliyyah* also believed in an all-creating God, followed the Abrahamic example, and performed a pilgrimage to Mecca, but still committed *shirk* by seeking the intercession of prophets and saints and associating partners with God.[47] Specific to Islam, and constituting the focus of *Kitab al-Tawhid*, is the question over the *worship* of Allah's unity (*tawhid al-Uluhiyyah*), and its relationship to salvation,[48] where a recognition of *shirk* in religious life is required in addition to acknowledging the lordship of Allah. For ibn Abd al-Wahhab, *tawhid* is 'the first obligation' to prayer,[49] as the *Shahada* distinguishes the Muslim from the *mushrikun*; this represented, according to Dallal, 'an act of repudiation, which functions as a rite of intellectual initiation into Wahhabism [as] the non-initiated remains guilty of *shirk*'.[50] As such, the following pages shall have in mind, when considering *tawhid* and *shirk*, the question of worship contained in *tawhid al-Uluhiyyah*.

Drawing on the Qur'an 4:48 ('Allah does not forgive if partners are set up [*yushraka*, from *shirk*] with Him, but he forgives [everything] except that ... Whoever sets up partners with Allah in worship, he has indeed invented a tremendous sin'), and echoing the Qur'an 2:22 ('Do not set up rivals against Allah'), ibn Abd al-Wahhab argued in *Kitab Kashf al-Shubuhat* that the greatest threat to *tawhid* is *shirk*, the act of worshipping something other than or associated with Allah, and the only sin that remains beyond redemption.[51] Indeed, much of his commentary on *tawhid* in both the works *Kitab Kashf al-Shubuhat* and *Kitab al-Tawhid* centred on an explanation of *shirk*, noting that 'it is the most dangerous thing for the righteous' as it brings closer the possibility of both 'Paradise and the Fire' through worldly acts. Associationism by itself, he concluded, can determine whether or not a Muslim is saved, regardless of other virtues or circumstances.[52] This soteriological statement followed the same reasoning as that of *tawhid*: namely, a linear understanding of God's unity contained in the creation of the world and the breaking of the Abrahamic Covenant by the *mushrikun*. Under these terms, the premise of absolute monotheism is that *tawhid al-Rububiyyah* or the unity of Allah preceded *shirk* or its human misrepresentation, and that *shirk* is therefore a corruption of the natural state of humanity, which originally testified to the unity of Allah's lordship. It follows the Qur'an 7:172, which states '[remember] when your Lord brought forth from the Children of Adam, from their loins, and made them testify as to themselves: "Am I not your Lord?" They said "Yes! We testify", lest you should say on the Day of Resurrection: "We have been unaware of this"'. According to *Hadith al-Bukhari*, Muhammad is reported to have said that 'every child is born upon the *fitrah* [an innate nature or virtue of humanity, tied to the unity of God]. Then, his parents make him a Jew or Christian'[53] – a claim that Islam is the natural state of social human beings, and as every child is 'born upon the *fitrah*' he or she are also 'born upon' *tawhid* inasmuch as *tawhid* reflects the truth of the *Shahada*. While Jews and Christians remain *al-Kitab*, of the same scripture as Islam, they have corrupted both Allah's Covenant and their own *fitrah* through their rejection of *tawhid*. For this reason, ibn Abd al-Wahhab concluded that 'Allah therefore sent Prophet Muhammad, to revive their old religion – the religion of their father Ibrahim'.[54]

Shirk is defined most readily as idolatry; accordingly, the argument against *shirk* in *Kitab al-Tawhid* and *Kitab Kashf al-Shubuhat* can be considered to represent ibn Abd al-Wahhab's argument against images, presented as a commentary of the Qur'an and *hadith*. In this format, he claimed that pre-Islamic society was characterized by *shirk*, describing how Nuh (Noah) offered the first warning against associationism but was ignored, with a 'woeful scourge' then engulfing his community,[55] and that Muhammad cleared the Kaaba of its idols, returning the 'house' of Ibrahim to the proper worship of 'The One God'. However, the Qur'an also states that the *shirk* of the *jahiliyyah* was mitigated to an extent because pre-Islamic society created intermediaries in both saints and sacred objects as an attempt to maintain a purity of worship through *distance* from Allah.[56] On this level, ibn Abd al-Wahhab judged the pre-Islamic Arabs to be less sinful in their *shirk* than his contemporaries, whom he denounced as polytheists, necromancers, and distracted by the devil.[57] This distinction corresponds with Islamic teaching that, as with different types of *tawhid*, there are two types of *shirk*: a 'minor' or accidental type, involving boastfulness, pride, and celebration of man's creation above Allah,[58] and a 'major type' involving the corruption of *tawhid al-Rububiyyah*. The latter of these two can make a Muslim a *kafir*, something against which ibn Abd al-Wahhab argued (following a *Hadith*) the believer should fight:

> Fight in the name of Allah, killing whoever disbelieves [*kufr*] in Allah. Fight, do not be excessive, nor take the spoils of war, nor mutilate. Do not kill a child. When you meet your enemy

among the *mushrikun* ... invite them to Islam ... If they accept this then accept it from them and leave them. If they refuse, then seek Allah's help and fight them.[59]

This edict takes shape within the social context that I have outlined, namely the Wahhabi perception of the *Hajj* under Ottoman rule, and adds a religious motivation to the Wahhabi attacks on Mecca. The followers of ibn Abd al-Wahhab's teaching on *tawhid* considered the Hashimite rule of Mecca to be a case of 'major' *shirk* in the location of the Abrahamic Covenant, the Kaaba. His call to fight *al-Mushrikun* echoed the Quranic call to fight those disbelievers who corrupted worship in the Kaaba.[60] Under these terms, the subsequent move against Sharif Ghalib in Mecca fifty years later represented a statement of worship (*al-ibadah*) as much as Arab communality (*al-asabiyyah*), driven by the belief that to revive the teachings of the Qur'an and to uphold *tawhid* involves not only an attack on the objects of *shirk* – idols or images – but also on those who worship them, the *mushrikun*.[61] As I have stated, this made a connection between image-breaking and holy war that fuelled an association of 'Wahhabism' with expansionism, absolutism, and violence in the historical mind.

I have taken the argument against *shirk* contained in both the Qur'an and certain texts by ibn Abd al-Wahhab to provide the theoretical premise for the prohibition of images that emerged in Najd during the eighteenth century and which led to acts of image-breaking, notably in the 1803 attack on Mecca under ibn Saud. However, this prohibition was not symptomatic of all Arabian or Islamic traditions – the very community and type of worship that ibn Abd al-Wahhab sought to reform or revive. It is important to acknowledge this caveat to the definition of 'Wahhabi' iconoclasm as the expression of the theology of *tawhid*.

Iconoclasm was not symptomatic of Arabian culture in general, as can be understood from the complaints of ibn Abd al-Wahhab in his work on *shirk*. The veneration of tombs and saints in the region preceded Islam, reflecting 'a religious factor in the inner life of pagan Arabs', as well as a cultural practice common to different communities across the peninsula.[62] For example, the Nabathean tombs at Madain Salih in northern Hijaz (designated an UNESCO World Heritage Site in 2008) were the subject of a Quranic denouncement,[63] and a series of wall-paintings have been excavated at al-Faw in south-west Saudi Arabia.[64] Fahd has suggested that pre-Islamic Arabia was influenced by a Hellenistic tradition of representing deities in paintings and sculpture,[65] while similar influences were evident from sizable Christian and Jewish communities living in, among other places, Mecca. The tradition of building domes over the tombs of saints was also characteristic of the region south of Hijaz, in present-day Yemen. For example, the concept of a 'sacred territory' (*hijrah*) to which a holy man or saint would emigrate (*hijrah*), designating it inviolable, has been associated with Hadramawti society. According to a sociological study by Knysh, many settlements valued the reputation that such a claim brought them, and expressed this by painting brightly coloured domes over the tombs of their local saint. In turn, the tomb could become a centre of religious and social activity, with classrooms and ibex hunting being held in its vicinity.[66] When the debate over the tradition of such tombs spread to Yemen, fuelled by the northern influence of Wahhabism, Knysh argues that it centred around an opposition between image-breaking as an expression of universal Islamic law on the one hand, and the building of domes over tombs as an expression of clan solidarity on the other – an opposition between claims of universalism and localism that has partly defined the issue of iconoclasm in general.

Despite the Quranic prohibitions, iconoclasm was not indicative of all Muslim denominations. On this question, King's article on 'Islam, Iconoclasm, and the Declaration of Doctrine' examines examples of Muslim image-breaking across different centuries. He claims that while early examples such as the destruction of crosses in the Egyptian delta in the seventh century and the fixing of Quranic verses above church doors reading 'Muhammad is the great apostle of God, and Jesus is also the apostle of God. But verily God is not begotten and does not beget'[67] affected events in Byzantium, this did not necessarily influence other Islamic traditions, as 'outside Arabia itself, the only evidence of iconoclasm until the fall of the Umayyad Caliphate in 132/750 is confined to the well-known attack on images and statues carried out on the orders of Yazid II b. Abd al-Malik (101–105/720–724)'.[68] King argues that the early Muslims believed 'the matter of representations of God had already been settled in Islam in the lifetime of the prophet: the inconceivable was beyond encompassing by any artistic repertoire; and meanwhile idolatry was suppressed and the pre-Islamic religious images were overthrown inside Arabia itself. The pagan idols of Mecca were destroyed by the Muslims in 8/630, and although the Prophet may have spared a picture of Mary and Jesus in the Kaaba, he nevertheless destroyed the rest of the numerous images which it had housed before his entry to Mecca,' adding that 'for the early Muslims, the underlying religious meaning attached to what was represented was of greater importance than the fact of representation as such. The *jahiliyyah* idols in Arabia had been destroyed first and foremost because they were idols and thereafter, beyond Arabia, objections to Christian pictures were made because of what they portrayed, not because of the fact of portrayal in itself'.[69] The connection between this early Islamic example and the situation in eighteenth-century Najd was made through ibn Abd al-Wahhab's own notion of scriptural revivalism and the *hijrah*, or emigration, of the first Islamic community. 'Wahhabi' puritanism invoked an Islamic norm that raised the question, like Calvinism, of an orthodoxy that depended on this first community for its authority.[70] However, the claim of orthodoxy was made by both iconoclasts and iconophiles alike – a conflict which explains why those Ottomans whom ibn Abd al-Wahhab opposed themselves produced images of Muhammad, albeit without hands or face, standing beside the Kaaba.

On both the Arabian-cultural and the Islamic level, then, iconoclasm was not symptomatic. On the contrary; Muhammad ibn Abd al-Wahhab's focus on the issue of *tawhid* represented an attempt to denounce what he saw as a corruption of worship, community, and ontology through the sin of *shirk*, or associationism, that he believed was endemic in his society. Under these terms, his theological reasoning was comparable to that of John Calvin outlined in Chapter 1, inasmuch as both individuals used the same scriptural examples of the Abrahamic Covenant and Mosaic law to support the breaking of images. Likewise, ibn Abd al-Wahhab considered this theological position to be revivalist because it held both the Qur'an and the first Islamic community above the traditions of his community – a claim that is also comparable to that of Calvin in the *Institutes*. Like John Calvin, who wrote his *Institutes* in Basel before moving towards political life in Geneva, and who despite writing a theological justification for iconoclasm was not himself engaged in the major acts of 'Calvinist' image-breaking in that city, ibn Abd al-Wahhab wrote *Kitab al-Tawhid* as a younger preacher moving between al-Uyainah and Basra, before his 1744 pact with the al-Saud family of al-Diriyyah and significantly before the 'Wahhabi' attack on Mecca in 1803.

Thus a comparison can be made between the two preachers, through the interpretation of their theology by their followers, without forcing the narrative: that is, both John Calvin and Muhammad ibn Abd al-Wahhab were *theoretical* iconoclasts, concerned with similar themes of the unity of God, the limits of human imagination, and the relationship between scripture and 'true' worship; these ideas were then applied to political issues of community, obedience, and the law; iconoclasm was the bridge between the religious and political concern over unity; once located within a particular city (Geneva or al-Diriyyah, later Riyadh), the theology of the two preachers was translated, routinized, and politicized by 'Calvinist' or 'Wahhabi' followers; and finally, crucially, the majority of acts of image-breaking that took place were at the hands of these followers, committed in the name of two men who by that time were no longer alive. In this way, like 'Calvinism', the notion of 'Wahhabism' took shape as a myth, both in the Islamic world and beyond – a myth acknowledged by Ibn Saud's declaration in Mecca in 1929 that 'they call us "Wahhabis" and they call our creed a "Wahhabi" one as if it were a special one … this is an extremely erroneous allegation … we are not proclaiming a new creed or a new dogma. Muhammad ibn Abd al-Wahhab did not come with anything new … it is a creed built on the oneness of the Almighty God'.[71] This creed, comparable to the Calvinist notion of the 'True God', provides the terms from which a prototype of Wahhabi iconoclasm is historically understood. It now remains to describe the consequences of that creed following ibn Abd al-Wahhab's death, in the iconoclastic acts of his followers.

THE ATTACK ON HIJAZ

I have claimed that the theological justifications for image-breaking made by ibn Abd al-Wahhab can be compared to those of John Calvin: namely, that the theology of unity was not something new but rather represented a scriptural and communal revival, providing a guide for the proper worship of the 'true' or 'one' God according to his nature and as expressed in his creation, and that the associationism of 'idolatry' or *shirk* denoted an error of human imagination which had, with time and tradition, become part of the culture of orthodoxy and which needed to be reformed by exiles (whether as Huguenot or through *Hijrah*), if necessary by violent means. This claim for such strong similarities between two theologians who lacked any connection of either time or place should not surprise the reader. Both men took as their premise the same scriptural narratives of the Torah, in particular those describing the creation of the world, the Abrahamic Covenant, and the Israelite worship of the golden calf. Furthermore, when this is considered alongside the social context, another similarity between Calvin and ibn Abd al-

Wahhab emerges: that is, both men agitated for iconoclasm on the theoretical level of their writings, but neither were involved in the acts of image-breaking that have since been attributed to them – the 'Calvinist' attacks of Guillaume Farel and the 'Wahhabi' attacks of Saud on Geneva and Mecca respectively. From these points of comparison, then, certain terms can be ascertained with which a wider study of Christian and Islamic iconoclasm might proceed. They are the questions of: the nature of the 'One' God; the worship of this God; the charismatic agitation of an individual preacher against images; his scriptural revivalism, invoking an ideal community; the exile of his followers as proof of their part in that community; the translation of his charismatic message into acts of image-breaking; the gap between the individual preacher and the historical labels used to describe his followers; the translation, routinization, or self-fashioning involved to bridge this gap; the absolutism of this routinization – that is, the absolutism of *iconoclasm* as the '-ism' of the iconoclasts; the political formalization of this routinization in the control of a city, its institutions, and its surrounding land; and finally, the expansion or propagation of this process over other societies, typically in acts of war. These are the terms that have thus far been generated in order to define the 'iconoclasm' of both Calvinism and Wahhabism. With them in mind, I shall look to combine the social context and the theology through the description of an act used to translate the theology of *tawhid* – namely, the Wahhabi-Saudi attack on Mecca and the *Hajj* in 1803.

With the Wahhabi-Saudi pact of 1744, the pull towards a unified Najdi orbit was inevitable. As I have described, this orbit had from its origins the conquest of Hijaz and the control of the *Hajj* as its primary objective, in order to unify the Arabian peninsula both religiously and politically as a revived model of the first Islamic community. Consequently, the emergence of 'Wahhabism' as a social and political implementation of ibn Abd al-Wahhab's theory of *tawhid* can be considered as synonymous with its territorial expansion. This involved a particular combination of settled Saudi leaders and an army of nomadic fighters, the dynamics of which influenced the later formation of a 'Saudi Arabian' state. At the time of the first attack on Mecca in 1803, however, the organization of the Saudi-Wahhabi forces remained informal. As such, the control of the pilgrimage in Mecca represented an available and achievable symbol for a variety of 'unifying' factions. The destruction of images was a part of that availability.

The justification for the control of Mecca focussed on perceived abuses of the Kaaba with the idols and rituals that had become associated with the *Hajj* through a combination of local Hijazi tradition and the influence of thousands of foreign visitors. As early as Burckhardt's description of his visit to the city following the death of ibn Abd al-Wahhab, 'the scandalous conduct of many hadjys who polluted the sacred cities with their infamous lusts; the open license which the chiefs of the caravans gave to debauchery ... the numerous acts of treachery and fraud perpetrated by the Turks, were all held up by the Wahabys as specimens of the general character of unreformed Muselmáns'.[72] While this is a European account, it is, as I have suggested, no more removed from the actual events of 'Wahhabism' than the Arabic reportage of ibn Ghannam or ibn Bishr and, on that level, should not be considered as less accurate. Burckhardt's description of Mecca, referring to the *towaf* with the Kaaba now stripped of its icons, and unpaved streets which 'plagued the lungs' with sand during the summer but which turned to mud on the roads in the winter, making them impassable when 'destructive rains' raged on the city and destroyed its ancient buildings, provides the historian with a vivid portrait of the city at the time. Importantly, he also stated that while the *muwahhidun* (that is, the 'proponents of *tawhid*', the Wahhabis) were instrumental in the decline of the *Hajj*, there had been a reduction in the number of pilgrims *prior* to the Wahhabi attacks due to problems of infrastructure: 'since the pilgrimage which has begun to decline (this happened before the Wahaby conquest), many of the Mekkawys, no longer deriving profit from the letting of their lodgings, found themselves unable to afford the expense of repairs; and thus numerous buildings in the outskirts have fallen completely into ruin'.[73] When considered alongside the significant Ottoman investments that had been made in Hijaz during the sixteenth and seventeenth centuries, it appears that the *Hajj* (and therefore the city of Mecca) in the years preceding the attack of 1803 was in a state of decline.

When describing the first Wahhabi attack on Mecca in 1803, two caveats must be made from the outset. First, as has already been stated, ibn Abd al-Wahhab died before the event. The attack on the city and the breaking of its shrines and images was therefore a Saudi act facilitated by 'Wahhabi' forces. Second, according to ibn Ghannam, rather than being a case of unmitigated Najdi aggression, both the Wahhabi-Saudis and the Sharifs had engaged in dialogue concerning the question of worship and the *Hajj* before 1803. As a precaution against the changes taking place in Najd, Sharif Masud had banned the *muwahhidun* from taking part in the *Hajj*; following this ban, a Najdi delegation visited Mecca and discussed the matter of the pilgrimage with the Sharif over a number of years. When these talks faltered, they attacked other pilgrims in order to push a lifting of their own ban – a strategy which led the new Sharif, Ahmad, to invite another delegation to Mecca to debate the differences between the two groups, including the veneration or destruction of tombs, and the rejection of saints as intercessors with God. By this account, according to Bari, Sharif Ahmad was impressed with the 'Wahhabis', and as a result was forced from office by the Ottomans, placing Hijaz once again in opposition to Najd.[74] By the time that Sharif Ghalib assumed power in Hijaz, in the early 1790s, relations between Saudi al-Diriyyah, Hashimite Mecca, and Ottoman Istanbul were at a low. With Ghalib failing to meet the Saudi-Wahhabi demands, and with most of the Najdi clans now unified into a single military unit, the once-disparate reformist movement turned into a powerful and aggressive force.[75] In the face of this, Ghalib allowed the Saudi amir to perform the *Hajj*. By now, however, the Wahhabis had already encircled Mecca and Medina, and demanded the Sharif's abdication. When he refused, appealing in vain to the pilgrims of the wider Muslim world, including the rulers of Cairo, Damascus, and Jedda, the Najdis moved on Mecca. Ghalib fled, setting fire to his palace, and allowing Saud to enter the city in 1803.

As with other aspects of early Wahhabi history, there are conflicting versions over Saud's entry into Mecca. Contemporary European accounts were sympathetic and described this event as one of pilgrimage and peaceful. For example, Burckhardt referred to the 'catechism' that Saud distributed to the Meccans as proof of his 'integrity':

> When Saoud took possession of Mekka, he distributed copies of this catechism among the inhabitants, and ordered that the pupils in public schools should learn it by heart. Its contents are nothing more than what the most orthodox Turk must admit to be true ... Nothing, however, was contained in this catechism which the Mekkans had not already learned; and when Saoud found that they were better informed than his own people, he desisted from further disseminating it among them.[76]

Likewise, the Spanish traveller Domingo Badia y Leblich / Ali Bey al-Abbasi, 'an eye witness to Saud's second entry into the city in 1221 AH [1806 CE]', claimed that 'the Wahhabis were thoroughly well-behaved and requited every service rendered to them by whatever means they could and "thus this political revolution terminated without one single drop of blood being shed"'.[77] This was echoed by another European at the time, the British envoy to Basra Sir Harford Brydges, who claimed that 'the tenets professed by Saoud, contained much that was captivating to the minds of those who panted for civil as well as religious freedom; who had long considered the voluptuousness, and corruption of their Turkish masters as ill according with the simplicity recommended and enjoined by the Arabian prophet and legislator'.[78] While Brydges noted that once Mecca had been taken its Syrian pilgrims were banned from performing the *Hajj*[79] and that this issue, along with the destruction of tombs and domes, led to reports circulating among both Hajjis and European observers that the Najdis were committing atrocities, he shared Burckhardt's opinion that such stories were exaggerated by the Turks who, he claimed, worked through the Sharif to 'artfully and unremittingly spread reports of the Wahábys being really infidels'.[80] In other words, both the contemporary Arabic Najdi and European accounts of the entry into Mecca were supportive of the new 'Wahhabis': as ibn Ghannam and ibn Bishr were open to ibn Abd al-Wahhab's theology,[81] Burckhardt and Brydges approved of Saud inasmuch as he was fighting a proxy war against a common Ottoman enemy. Consequently, reports of Wahhabi violence against pilgrims and shrines in Mecca in 1803 were considered to be dubious. Even when he received reports of British frigate ships being attacked in the Gulf, Brydges was prepared to justify such accusations against the Wahhabis as a 'popular clamour' propagated by the Turks.[82]

The claims of Arab over Ottoman identity were relevant also to the question of image-breaking in 1803. Al-Azmeh argues that the attack on Mecca (and later Medina) used the destruction of images and shrines in order to clear – literally – religious and political territory for the building of a revivalist community, and that the events in Hijaz against the Hashimites were an extension of previous events against local Najdi traditions. As such, he claims, Wahhabism conflated different cultural Arab traditions in order to present a target – in his words, an 'otherness' – for a single religious Islamic movement. Thus the earlier 'concrete manifestation of otherness to be suppressed was the particular Najdi forms of *shirk* ... such matters as the idol Dhal-Khilsa, destroyed very early in the history of Wahhabism, against which apparently infertile women rubbed their buttocks in the hope of fertility ... the felling of sacred trees and the destruction of shrines', these 'very first acts of ibn Abd al-Wahhab, who was particularly vehement in his condemnation of devotional acts directed towards any objects of sanctity other than God' were later transferred to Hijaz, where 'some of the first acts of the Wahhabite forces of Saud b. Abd al-Aziz upon the invasions of Mecca in 1803 and Medina in 1805 were the destruction of sacred domes designating shrines',[83] including that of Muhammad's daughter Fatimah. Observers noted that the Wahhabis spared Muhammad's tomb, although Burckhardt suggested that this might have been due to the difficulties involved in demolishing large structures rather than theological reluctance:

> Even the large dome over the tomb of Muhammad, at Medinah, was destined to share a similar fate. Saoud had given orders that it should be demolished; but its solid structure defied the rude efforts of his soldiers; and after several of them had been killed by falling from the dome, the attempt was given up. This the inhabitants of Medinah declared to have been done through the interposition of Heaven.[84]

As with the biographical details for ibn Abd al-Wahhab's life, a lack of contemporary source material prevents the historian critically from accounting for the image-breaking carried out in his name in 1803 and 1805. However, it is evident from the range of reports at the time – common both to Arab accounts such as ibn Ghannam and ibn Bishr and European accounts such as Jean Louis Burckhardt and Harford Brydges – that an association between the *muwahhidun* attack on the *Hajj* and the destruction of domes, mosques, and tombs was taking shape in the historical mind. The levels of this association were complex and dependent on cultural circumstance: while those Europeans who were at odds with the Ottomans were supportive of the Najdi actions in Mecca, for the Ottomans themselves (including the Hijazi and Levantine-Syrian Arabs) the attacks on both the religious sites of the early Islamic community and the expensive developments and adornments in which they had invested a century beforehand were deemed serious enough to warrant the sending of Egyptian troops to repel the Saudi forces. Furthermore, the fact that these attacks on the images of a cosmopolitan Hijaz operated as an extension of earlier assaults on local Najdi traditions involving the worship of natural objects and holy men meant that the relationship between the 'Wahhabi' implementation of a theology of *tawhid* bridged complex divides between the blocs of Najdi-Hijazi, Wahhabi-Najdi, Hijazi-Ottoman, and Arab-Turk interests. This was the 'conflation', as al-Azmeh calls it, of targets against which a single Islamic movement could identify itself and be identified. In other words, the cultural overlaps involved in acts of image-breaking during the Najdi attack on Mecca provided the context for a 'Wahhabi' myth to develop and be reinforced by comparable later events, from nineteenth-century assaults on Shiite sites in Karbala to Ibn Saud's final move on Mecca in 1925. Thus in 1954, Muhammad Asad, an Austrian Jewish convert to Islam, friend of Ibn Saud, and representative to the United Nations for the new state of Pakistan, noted how this mythology maintained a reputation for the Wahhabis during the *Hajj*, as 'to the men of Najd, men of the Central Arabian highlands, war and pilgrimage spring from the same source ... and the numberless pilgrims from other lands – from Egypt and India and North Africa and Java – unaccustomed to such wild abandon, scattered in panic before our approach'.[85]

THE POLITICS OF WAHHABI ICONOCLASM

The organization of the Saudi sphere of influence after the attack on Hijaz provides the historian with a way of understanding the development of a 'Wahhabi' society towards its final, formal expression as 'Saudi Arabia' in the twentieth century. In the previous sections of this chapter, I have endeavoured to describe how a code of 'unity' not only connected similar interpretations of scripture, law, and worship under the theological rubric of *tawhid*, but also territorially served both nomadic and settled groups across Najd and Hijaz, and that this code was communicated, on many levels, by acts of image-breaking. I shall now examine some of the institutional mechanisms of this process as a way of assessing the social life of 'Wahhabi' image-breakers and the potential for their comparison with Calvinism.[86] The idea of an institutionalization of a charismatic message of *tawhid* during the nineteenth century provides a useful way of considering the increase of Saudi cultural and territorial hegemony. It also relates to the building of a new capital, Riyadh, after the repulsion of the Saudi-Wahhabi forces by the Ottomans following the first attack on Mecca in 1803 and the razing of al-Diriyyah in 1818.

The development of early Saudi-Wahhabi society was structured around the conditions of organizing nomadic desert communities around a central urban powerbase. These conditions became pronounced during times of territorial expansion. When needed, a call would be made from al-Diriyyah to the Najdi tribes for soldiers; the reward for their participation would be the spoils of war. Once the 'Wahhabi' army was assembled, it proved adept at rapid offensive action, long sieges, and the negotiation of difficult terrain. However, these advantages could in themselves produce problems. Zdanowski notes that as war-spoils were not a guaranteed revenue and participation in a military campaign could be costly for an individual clan, the call from al-Diriyyah would often be ignored. In these cases, he states, as well as in those where soldiers engaged in battle without adequate equipment, the Saudis were known to penalize the entire community.[87] Zdanowski adds that the nomads were considered to be both cheaper and better-suited to desert conditions than a standing army, reportedly eating only milk and dates and using camels rather than horses both as transport and as living shields. However, such unstable conditions meant that these fighters could also, should the spoils diminish, switch allegiances, as they did in 1818 when they joined the Egyptian army and turned to defeat their old Saudi patron.[88] Furthermore, the rapidity and mobility of the nomadic fighters ensured that while large amounts of land could be covered quickly, it was not then held with settled garrisons – a problem that partly explains why the Wahhabis invaded and were pushed out of Mecca twice over a century before Ibn Saud finally retained the city in 1925.[89]

The nomadic allegiance to the Saudi rulers elided a religious call with territorial expansionism under a single cultural (and eventually historical) identity. Central to this arrangement was a belief in the ideal authority of early Muslim patriarchs where, in the words of al-Azmeh, 'kings were likened to herdsmen and helmsmen. A king, according to a saying attributed to the Prophet, is God's shadow on earth ... moreover, like divinity, kingship is indivisible',[90] and where the king, or later the Caliph, 'came increasingly to be formally conceived as the successor of the Prophet'.[91] This mediating role between Allah and the people depended on the guardianship of the Kaaba, increasing the importance of controlling Mecca. As such, the Saudi-Wahhabi expansionism of 1803 represented, as well as an implementation of the theology of *tawhid*, an attempt to revive the ideal early Islamic model around these social dynamics of guardianship. This developed the particular Najdi relationship between settled *hadar* leadership and nomadic fighters into a new 'desert polity'. The process, according to al-Azmeh, was 'based on the *patrimonial* ascendancy of a particular clan – here the Sauds – which holds in tow an alliance of other clans which are by definition tributary and excluded from power'[92] – an exclusion, he continues, which is 'the means by which the tribal society is stratified', leading to 'the subjugation of nomadic tribes to the centre'.[93] In other words, Saudi-Wahhabi social identity became defined after the attack of 1803 by the division or 'stratification' of a 'patrimonial' powerbase, which had developed as a routinization of the relationship between settled and nomadic communities in proximity to a sacred place, the Kaaba. This connected the theology of *tawhid* with the social settlement of nomads into a new class of urban dwellers. Thus the emergence of a central powerbase in Riyadh served three interconnected functions: first, it consolidated Saudi patrimonial rule over Najd; second, it expressed institutionally the theology of *tawhid*; and third, it settled the fighters and nomadic *muwahhidun*.

This does not imply that al-Diriyyah was merely a primitive desert settlement that was eventually replaced by a more advanced urban system in Riyadh. Al-Diriyyah was an influential city even before the Saudi-Wahhabi pact of 1744. Dresch writes that as the Saudis expanded from Najd through al-Ahsa, 'they drew clothes, food and even cooks from there; the great historian of Wahhabi Najd, ibn Ghannam, was brought from al-Ahsa to al-Diriyyah. The second Saudi state (c. 1824–91), based in Riyadh, repeated the process'.[94] Likewise, Delong-Bas notes that 'those who responded positively to ibn Abd al-Wahhab's invitations sometimes made a migration (*hijrah*) to al-Diriyyah to study with ibn Abd al-Wahhab and his followers',[95] supporting the argument that his theology had international influences beyond Najd. The emergence of Riyadh was a consequence of the 1803 attack on Mecca, when Egyptian forces led by Muhammad Ali's son Ibrahim Pasha responded by expelling the Saudi-Wahhabis from Hijaz and, with around nine thousand soldiers, cavalrymen and artillery, moved on al-Diriyyah in 1818. Having razed the city, these troops took the Saudi ruler Abdullah to Cairo and eventually Istanbul, where he was beheaded. As such, according to al-Rasheed, 'the sacking of Diriyyah marked the end of the first Saudi-Wahhabi emirate'; two years later, Abdullah's son 'Turki (1824-34) benefited from the partial retreat of the Egyptian troops from Najd under pressure from its local inhabitants',[96] but instead of attempting the rebuilding of al-Diriyyah, he chose to establish his authority in the smaller settlement of nearby al-Riyadh. This time, with its influence extending again over neighbouring regions, including Arid, Kharj, Sudayr and Aflaj, Saudi rule experienced internal conflicts rather than external threats. Turki was assassinated on the order of his cousin Mishari, and only when his son Faisal reclaimed Riyadh with the help of the Rashidi amir of Hail did the 'second' Saudi rule of Najd (and with that, the growth and the institutional fabric of the city) experience some degree of stability. As such, the Saudi authorities today mark the centenary of their Kingdom not from the 1932 declaration of independence but rather the third and final capture of Riyadh from the Rashidis by Ibn Saud in 1902.[97] This emphasizes the importance of Riyadh for the identity of Saudi-Wahhabi 'polity': if Wahhabi theology depended on the control of Mecca and the *Hajj*, Saudi society depended on the regularization of its urban centre.

On this level, the sociopolitical strengthening of Riyadh as a regional capital represented the regularization or routinization of Saudi-Wahhabism – a historical feature of homogenization that echoes Ernest Gellner's distinction between a 'high' Islam inhabiting an urban environment of scriptural and legal formalism (what he terms Islamic 'Puritanism') and the differentiation and superstition of 'folk' Islam.[98] However, the Wahhabi desire to recreate an idealized early Islamic society did not necessarily correlate with an early Islamic version of the city. Lapidus argues that 'although newly founded cities were sometimes the sole Muslim places in their region, so that migration to them constituted a *hijrah* (a conversion to Islam) the evidence does not show such cities to be necessary to the Arab-Muslim concept of a full Muslim life. Cities were important to early Islam, but any exclusive association of Islam and urbanism would be misleading'.[99] Lapidus is referring here to early Islamic examples of urban systems and Abbasid Baghdad, both of which contained (as did the Rashidi capital Hail in the nineteenth century) quarters for Christians, Jews, and foreign craftsmen.[100] For Riyadh, a city constructed for the purpose of consolidating a particular local settlement between Saudi king and nomadic *muwahhidun*, the question must be whether the range of its institutional variety (that is, the range of variety between its religion, law, and market) was *limited* to serving this arrangement between *hadar* and nomadic communities under the same patrimony. If so, this would provide the limits within which a social life specific to Wahhabism can be defined, and would indicate that the development of the nineteenth-century Wahhabi city represented exactly the kind of elementary 'fusion of fortress and market' that Weber described in *Economy and Society* as lacking the kind of *gemeinde* instrumental to a civil society[101] – a political economy that has been described, in its present-day context, as 'hyper-tribalism'.[102]

Keddie claims that in the early nineteenth century, 'there was no state structure in Najd, and there were increasing problems and divisions that could best be met by a unified state and legal system. The decline of Ottoman power in Arabia opened the way for the rise of an independent and powerful state, at least until the Ottomans could suppress it via Muhammad Ali in the early nineteenth century'.[103] I have suggested that these conditions created a space that was occupied by a particular 'Wahhabi' combination of military, religious, and legal interactions structured around a theological and territorial idea of unity. Socially, this combination was reflected in Riyadh through the stratification of two groups: the *mutawwaa* (a Najdi word referring to typically settled *hadar* religious specialists) and the *ikhwan* (an Arabic word meaning 'brother', but in this sense referring to typically nomadic fighters). Writing about the development of later nineteenth-century Wahhabi society, al-Rasheed describes the *mutawwaa* as follows:

> A mutawwa was a member of the *hadar* who had acquired a religious education after a period of study with a distinguished member of the *ulama*, based in the main towns of southern Najd (mainly Riyadh) and Qasim (Unayzah) after which he became a specialist in jurisprudence ... The term mutawwa embodies both obedience and compulsion. A mutawwa was a volunteer who enforced obedience to Islam and performance of its rituals. The *mutawwaa* were a Najdi phenomenon. They differed from religious scholars in other parts of the Islamic world, commonly referred to as *ulama*.[104]

The *mutawwaa*, she adds, 'were active agents in state *building*; they were also a pre-existing force ready to be mobilised in the service of the state. In contrast, the *ikhwan* were a crucial military force created as a result of the *mutawwaa*'s efforts for the purpose of Saudi expansion',[105] a process she describes as 'domesticating' the Najdi population into accepting the political authority of the al-Sauds. The emergence of these two classes reconfigured the different levels of unification shaping Najdi society – that is, the levels of religious, legal, and political unification on the one hand, and the levels of *hadar* and nomadic unification on the other – into a polity that could be described as peculiarly 'Wahhabi'. The *mutawwaa* and *ikhwan* of nineteenth-century Riyadh and Najd reinforced the 1744 pact made between ibn Abd al-Wahhab and the al-Sauds, developing it from the context of *dawa* and war booty into that of an increasingly urban society, and incorporating the institutional matters of justice and taxation. As such, al-Azmeh notes that 'in the religious terms of Wahhabite divines and of the principles of government they imparted to the House of Saud, this reduction of nomads, agriculturalists and townspeople equally into subjects of the Saudi polity, this compact of protection and allegiance, was expressed in terms of the canonical alms tax, the *zakat*,[106] where both a religious pillar of Islam and a requirement of civil regulation was combined for the first time in a unified Najd. Indeed, the loyalty of the *mutawwaa* depended on the question of the *zakat* tax and the development of a professionalized political economy.[107] According to al-Rasheed, religious specialists had traditionally existed as either merchants, farmers, or mendicants through charitable income. By the end of the nineteenth century, ibn Saud had 'enlisted them in the service of his domain as he employed them and paid their salaries in cash and kind. He thus transformed them into full-time religious ritual specialists, loyal to him and dependent on his resources'. In turn, the *mutawwaa* collected the *zakat* tax for the central government. This arrangement between 'both the regime of moral discipline and the collection of *zakat* were important mechanisms behind the consolidation of Saudi authority in Arabia';[108] by the time of the third attack on Mecca and the *Hajj*, the question of tax regulation had replaced the claims for war booty with which the Wahhabi fighters were formerly associated. Vassiliev quotes a Soviet consular report from Jedda after the final Wahhabi taking of Mecca, writing that 'possession of Hijaz with its returns from the pilgrimage, customs, etc enables Abd al-Aziz [Ibn Saud] to use all these resources (the pilgrimage alone yields up to £2m annually) to strengthen his power in Najd to great political advantage by aiding new settlers and subsidizing the shaikhs of Bedouin tribes ... the Bedouin are dissatisfied: they pay *zakat* of 2.5%, plunder is prohibited, imports of trucks have deprived them of their income ... the *Hajj* guides are also dissatisfied, being no longer able to fleece pilgrims, since the state regularises the *Hajj* and appropriates the proceeds from it'.[109]

I have argued that the emergence of a Saudi-Wahhabi polity during the nineteenth century was determined by the dynamics between settled and nomadic communities, religious and territorial claims, an unresolved co-dependency between the ruling and fighting classes, and the idealization of a first Islamic community. This distinctive 'Wahhabi' polity shaped the institutional regulation of Riyadh. It amounted to the regulation of local Najdi dynamics between nomadic, *hadar*, and religious communities by consolidating the issues of the settlement of soldiers and the collection of tax as both an Islamic and civil matter. This process of regulation, necessarily focused on life in

Riyadh, saw the emergence of new classes of *ikhwan* and *mutawwaa* and a gradual centralization of Najdi society around a new city – a centralization that included within its orbit Hijaz and culminated in Ibn Saud's final taking of Mecca and Medina (and with that, the guardianship of the Kaaba and the destruction of shrines and tombs, including those of Muhammad's wife and grandfather, as well as the Janat al-Baqi graveyard) in 1925. Thus certain terms can be identified that describe institutional or political Wahhabism, combining 'kin-related political behaviour' with a 'territoriality shared by both nomadic and sedentary populations alike'.[110] The social classes that emerged from this combination operated between the religious call of the *muwahhidun* and the civil needs of regulating *zakat*, reinforcing the Saudi-Wahhabi pact of 1744 within a new, urban context.

Despite this emergence of hegemony within newly defined territorial borders, the term 'State' is a problematic label for describing *mutawwaa* obedience to a Saudi patrimonial authority. This is not unique to the case of Wahhabism, and poses a wider question over the formal (and typically Western) terms used to describe a political Islam. Hourani includes chapters on 'The Age of Nation States' only after 1939 in his *History of the Arab Peoples*, focussing on the examples of Egypt and Algeria; however, the declaration of the independence of the *Kingdom* of Saudi Arabia – *al-Mamlaka al-Arabiya as-Saudiya* – was made almost a decade previously. Thus Asad, examining the relationship between Islam and Arab nationalism, argues that while many Islamic societies have been forced to assimilate or adopt Westernized political models, this has not necessarily been translated into an Islamized version of the Western State. He writes:

> Both Arab nationalism (whether of the 'liberal' or the 'socialist' variety) and Islamism share a concern with the modernizing state that was put in place by Westernizing powers – a state directed at the unceasing material and moral transformation of entire populations only recently organized as 'societies'. In other words, Islamism takes for granted and seeks to work through the nation-state, which is so central to the predicament of all Muslims. It is this *statist* project and not the fusion of religious and political ideas that gives Islamism a 'nationalist' cast.[111]

For Asad, then, the idea of a State represents the means rather than an end to an Islamic polity. When considered alongside Muslim ideas of kingship, al-Azmeh questions the appropriateness of referring to

Islamic states at all, when the types of government at stake often operate around 'the sum total of royal activities, which are described and tabulated but not theorized' (that is, the types of government represent 'a typology of royal motivation, not a theory of the state'),[112] extending a mediaeval notion of sultanship where 'the body politic, whose *locus* is the king, constitutes the body social and maintains it. The relationship is not the other way round'.[113] On this level, it is possible to consider the emergence of a recognizable 'Wahhabi' polity during the nineteenth century as the consolidation within a single territory of a system of patrimonial succession and domination. It does not follow, however, that such a territory should necessarily be defined as a 'Wahhabi State' in the civil – that is, Weberian – sense.

The emergence of a recognizable 'Saudi' Arabia also depended on factors imposed from outside the forces and self-fashioning of a Saudi-Wahhabi polity. These factors involved the drawing of permanent borders for the Middle East following the collapse of the Ottoman Empire. For the nomads of the Arabian peninsula during the nineteenth century, international boundaries were meaningless. Migrating with the grazing patterns of their livestock and the need for water, they moved seasonally into present-day Iraq and vice versa. The British treaties of 1922 separated Najd and Hijaz from Iraq, Trans-Jordan, and Kuwait, creating a political divide between nomadic and settled communities. 'To draw a hard frontier across the desert', Vassiliev writes, 'seemed to the Najdis to threaten the very existence of those tribes'.[114] When the British allocated neutral grazing zones between Najd and Iraq to resolve this problem, increasing numbers of *ikhwan* exploited the gap in power to move across these zones and attack British interests, particularly in Trans-Jordan. In response, a border was formally drawn with the proviso that the integrity of Saudi territory would be respected by the British as long as Ibn Saud restrained the *ikhwan*.

It is important to note that these external factors were as independently influential to the formation of a now-identifiable Saudi Arabian territory as the internal settlement made between the religious *mutawwaa* and their political rulers in Riyadh. The pressure to agree on an internationally recognized border pushed the al-Sauds in two ways. First, the fact that the *ikhwan* were operating militarily independently from Riyadh changed the previously established dynamic between the king and his soldiers. Ibn Saud now turned against the *ikhwan*, and only declared Saudi Arabian independence once he had defeated them in 1932. This also signalled new tensions between the religious demands of Wahhabi iconoclasm and the political concessions needed to be made with the British in the formation of an independent Saudi Arabia; when the image-breaking of the *ikhwan* began to jeopardize Ibn Saud's territorial negotiations, as in their attempted destruction of the Egyptian *Mahmal* in 1926, he restrained them with force.[115] Second, as the borders north of Najd were effectively sealed by British interests in Iraq and Trans-Jordan, Ibn Saud's territorial claims could only move westwards, towards Hijaz. Vassiliev suggests that this factor was as instrumental to the final Saudi-Wahhabi conquest of Hijaz and the control of the *Hajj* as a religious desire to implement *tawhid* in Mecca[116] – a caveat to Ibn Saud's 1924 declaration that 'the sole purpose of the invasion of Hijaz was to "guarantee the liberty of the pilgrimage and to settle the destiny of the Holy Land in a manner satisfactory to the Islamic world"'.[117] Thus a dislocation emerged between these external conditions and the internal idea that 'the rise of the Wahhabi movement in Najd was a "natural event" in an area predestined to play a leading role' in the reform of Hijaz, and where the term '"unification" rather than "conquest" is used to describe the military campaigns in Arabia after the capture of Riyadh by Ibn Saud'.[118] The levels of localism and universalism contained within this dislocation are complex. Politically and externally, Saudi rule was presented to the British as a moderating influence on the nomads; religiously and internally, its 'guardianship' of the Kaaba, previously held by the caliphs, presented to the *ummah* a single authority to unite fragmenting Muslim communities following the decline of the Ottoman Empire, where 'salvation came with the Wahhabi reform movement and its adoption by the Saudi rulers'.[119] In this way, difficult questions over the construction of such a 'state' were answered, often with force, by the increase of Saudi hegemony. For al-Rasheed, this process of historical self-fashioning represented the identity of a Saudi state, reinforced in the present day:

> Although the Saudi state is now highly visible, thanks to the infrastructure it has created, its relations with its people and history remain contentious. For this reason, state-sponsored representations of the past, embedded in official historiography, political rhetoric and festivities create a historical memory that serves to enforce obedience to the ruling group ... While the state dominates the material infrastructure and resources of the country, it has become increasingly important to extend this

domination to the symbolic realm of ideas and visions of the past, present and future.[120]

This account of the formalization of Wahhabi polity indicates that the label of a 'state' is applicable only inasmuch as it reflects the combined forces of religious, cultural, and political homogenization that were fashioned into a single Saudi Arabian identity by its ruling classes. Like the label 'iconoclasm', the Wahhabi 'state' should therefore be read as a historicized rather than a historical subject – a part of the developing lexicon, if we follow Skinner's thinking, with which an emerging society understands itself on a universal level.

As such, Wahhabi political society today is typically described in terms of the State. Writing about this, al-Azmeh concedes that 'the conditions of Western economic and political conquest and hegemony in the modern age have engendered, for good or for ill, correlative conditions of equally real ideological and cultural hegemony. The East – and I only use this term for convenience – has been heavily impregnated with novel categories of thought, methods of education, contents of knowledge, forms of discourse and communication, aesthetic norms and ideological positions. It has become impossible to speak with sole reference to traditional texts without reference to Western notions'.[121] This position, acknowledging the cross-fertilization of labels of explanation without necessarily acknowledging their intrinsic value, is a useful way of considering the development of an idea of the Wahhabi State. I have examined the institutional features of a Saudi-Wahhabi polity emerging in the nineteenth century, but the *formal* expression of those features as a single territory in 1932 was not wholly separate – not least due to the influence of external conditions in drawing the borders of that territory and the final move on Hijaz – from international ideas of state-formation. Thus it is not unreasonable to consider the articulation of Saudi Arabia's final and formal development in terms of 'state-building' and 'iconoclasm' as labels of what Danto would call historical legibility, while recognizing that both these labels 'iconoclasm' and 'state' are Westernized ways of describing, as Asad has noted, an Arab and Islamic polity. The particular Saudi-Wahhabi identity I have endeavoured to describe in this chapter, pulling inwards rather than pushing out, had at its heart a logic of unity – both in religious *tawhid* and in territorial *Lebensraum* – that, once fulfilled in the Najdi domination over Hijaz and the control of the *Hajj*, was translated into the institutional practice and historical labelling of the first charismatic message of ibn

Abd al-Wahhab. It is this process of *translation*, not a fixed stage of polity, that represents the politics of Wahhabi iconoclasm.

SUMMARIZING THE CALVINIST AND WAHHABI PROTOTYPES

A comparative study of Calvinist and Wahhabi iconoclasm generates a set of terms that can now be summarized in their full theological, social, and historical context. Theologically, both John Calvin and ibn Abd al-Wahhab drew on similar scriptural sources, particularly those of the Abrahamic Covenant and the golden calf, to present an ontology that placed the idea of the unity of the one God or the *tawhid* of Allah above all else. They depicted an order of the world where the ineffable nature of God is reflected in the beauty of His creation alone. Within this order, human beings are called to focus their worship on the Creator, not the created, but their inability to comprehend God's nature in His creative elements leads them to supplant knowledge with imagination. This is an error to which they are predisposed by the limits of their minds, according to Calvin; for ibn Abd al-Wahhab, these limits of association or *shirk* separate them from their natural union with God, the *fitrah*.

The absolutism of this theology denies a distinction between the use of images as an aid to worshipping God and the worship of them as God, as such a distinction is judged to be a product of the imagination. Likewise, the traditions that have been shaped around the so-called orthodox use of images – an orthodoxy that for Calvin was based in Catholic Rome, for ibn Abd al-Wahhab in Hashimite Mecca – represent formal corruptions of the union between humanity and God. This absolutism is therefore revivalist inasmuch as it looks to a first community of worshippers who preceded the traditions of orthodoxy. The emphasis on the scripture of the first community over the traditions of orthodoxy has led historians to describe both Calvin and ibn Abd al-Wahhab as 'Puritans', creating a commonality that goes beyond other divisions within and between Christianity and Islam. By reviving the idea of the Abrahamic Covenant, both were preoccupied with fulfilling the role of God's chosen people. Thus their question over images was connected with that of being chosen and saved, and the ontological error of associationism or idolatry cast in terms of sin and communality. In this way, both Calvin's *Institutes* and ibn Abd al-

Wahhab's *Kitab al-Tawhid* can be read as guidebooks to their communities in salvation.

The absolutism and revivalism of this theology claimed a new type of orthodoxy; socially, this created a division between the followers of the true God and the corrupt. That the corrupt were also the formally orthodox through the power of tradition meant that the advocates of this theology were typically the peripheral and the exiled – in the case of Calvin, as a French immigrant living among Genevan *citoyens*; in the case of ibn Abd al-Wahhab, as part of a small Najdi *hadar* community neighbouring a cosmopolitan Hijaz. These ideas of order, orthodoxy, separation, and exile helped shape a political identity for those who chose to follow and implement the teachings of Calvin and ibn Abd al-Wahhab. Consequently, a common theology was reflected in similar social practices. Both 'Calvinists' and 'Wahhabis' sought to implement the theology of unity in a government that mirrored the idealized first community and looked towards the occupation of sacred places. Political contingencies were subject to the religious premise of these goals, and both Calvin and ibn Abd al-Wahhab highlighted the issue of obedience to secular rulers. The Najdi oath of allegiance in 1744 established that 'Wahhabi religious specialists accepted the doctrine that power is legitimate however it may have been seized, and that obedience to whoever wields this power is incumbent upon all his subjects',[122] as the politicalization of *tawhid* holds the authority of the ruler as an extension of the will of God. Likewise, in the last chapter of the *Institutes*, Calvin argued that 'subjects, in submitting to princes and governors, are not to be influenced merely by fear ... because the obedience which they yield is rendered to God himself, inasmuch as their power is from God'.[123] Socially, this was expressed in legal negotiations between a new, religious class and their rulers in urban communities. When the negotiations worked, the community was fortified; when they broke down, the theology of unity became a question of territorial domination.

This translation of a common theological premise into systems of political behaviour between groups who had otherwise no cultural connection to each other is historiographically problematic. How can the study of iconoclasm account for such shared developmental patterns without venturing into a kind of religious-historical Lamarckism? While both Calvin and ibn Abd al-Wahhab wrote against images, it was their followers who engaged in acts of image-breaking; the movements of iconoclasm in their name occurred often years after their death and in cultural circumstances removed from their own.

The dislocation between the preacher, the individual image-breaker, and the '–isms' attributed to them requires a developmental approach to the levels of association between the theology and its political expression. This kind of developmental tracing of an idea in both Christianity and Islam, clearly influenced by Weber's work in *The Protestant Ethic* and *Economy and Society*, goes beyond the material restrictions of that idea, and touches also those stages or levels of historical association that occupy the space between a shared theology and its political organization. This tracing does not demand the question 'who were the image-breakers?', but rather 'how did their actions come to be known as iconoclasm?' – a matter of translating the individual event into a label available for historical scrutiny. It enables a study of iconoclasm to go beyond the comparison of individual acts of image-breaking taking place in Geneva and Mecca and recasts that comparison as an account of how such acts have been translated into the label 'iconoclasm'. Thus the two prototypes of 'Calvinism' and 'Wahhabism' that I have provided are exactly that – historicized labels through which the study of later, diverse, continually developing acts of 'iconoclasm' might be understood.

In this way, I approach the problematic of what Boldrick and Clay have called the 'contested term' of 'iconoclasm' through its proper semantic context. Within this context, the terms that emerge from the 'Calvinist' and 'Wahhabi' prototypes – those of image-destruction, self-fashioning, and city-building – make possible a network of comparison between individual events that would otherwise be unconnected. This network of comparison extends beyond the Calvinist and Wahhabi prototypes to influence and inform subsequent cases of iconoclasm: that is, during the French Revolution; in the decay of nineteenth-century monuments and the artistic response; in the cities razed during World War II; in the mosques destroyed during the Balkan conflicts; and in the changing urban face of 'Wahhabi' Mecca today. It is to these cases that I shall now turn.

Part II

THE CASES

Chapter 3
The French Revolution and Iconoclasm

> A multitude of men are made one person when they are by one man, or one person, represented; so that it be done with the consent of every one of that multitude in particular. For it is the unity of the representer, not the unity of the represented, that maketh the person one. And it is the representer that beareth the person, and but one person: and unity cannot otherwise be understood in multitude.
>
> <div align="right">Thomas Hobbes, <i>Leviathan</i>[1]</div>

The terms of a politics of iconoclasm outlined in Part I of this book were generated from two prototypes within Christianity and Islam – Calvinism and Wahhabism – connecting religion and politics in a discourse of destruction. For the cases to which I shall now turn in Part II, this connection was less direct. For example, while the question of religion was important in the case of the image-breaking of the French Revolution, specialists of the period like Clay and Gamboni are also concerned with the breaking of sculptures and statues within the context of aesthetics or visual space and Art History. This points to a wider challenge for scholars working today on the question of iconoclasm, where each specialist field within Art History, Religious Studies, Anthropology, Critical Theory, and Philosophy is prone to accommodating similar individual accounts of the same subject but with little interaction with each other. On a personal note, to illustrate this potentially frustrating state of affairs: I remember as a graduate student in a faculty of Religious Studies meeting art historians from another university who, while working from a different school of thought and using an entirely different category of sources, had arrived at fascinatingly similar conclusions about the broken object to my own. Part of the challenge for the present-day debate is to explore the potential of this kind of interdisciplinary interaction.

On that level, then, it is appropriate that the first of my short case studies should be that of the French Revolution. If, as suggested by Clay, the word 'iconoclasm' represents a complex transformation of signs that occurs within an ongoing process rather than a fixed or final moment of destruction, then the image-breaking of the French Revolution is rich with religious, artistic, and political overlaps. Targets of image-breaking at the time included religious buildings, relics, and artifacts, but also emblems of royal rule and sculptures associated with political oppression. In churches as well as in the streets, attacks on images of saints occurred alongside attacks on images of the king. This reflected the extent to which the religious and political dimensions of society were interwoven in a Bourbon France which, as the 'eldest daughter' of the Catholic Church, upheld the role of the king as a quasi-divine function and exhibited this function in the visual and urban environment. The kings of France had been buried since Clovis I in the Basilica of St. Denis (situated today in the northern suburbs of Paris); when their tombs were attacked and the contents emptied in 1793, this necessarily involved acts of violence against the surrounding religious imagery. As Burleigh argues, 'the assault on the Church served to undermine one of the essential supports of monarchical authority, namely the supernatural element'[2] – as such, an event like the destruction of the Abbey of Cluny in 1793 involved a complex combination of rebellions, partly against the religious symbolism of the building, partly against the hierarchy of the *ancien régime*, and partly also against the land ownership of the abbots.

This combination of political and religious, royal and divine imagery, not peculiar to Bourbon France but certainly exaggerated by the notion of a 'Sun King', meant that the iconoclasm of the Revolution conflated different symbols and signs in attacks on single objects. This conflation is understood by some historians to represent a linear connection between the Revolutionaries and the Calvinists. Van Kley claims that 'even if it had been possible – as was emphatically not the case – to distinguish cleanly between Catholic and royal relics and remains in France, Calvinist iconoclasts in the 1560s cannot be credited with having tried very hard', adding that 'Calvinist iconoclastic crowds in Capetian France implicitly struck at symbols of the monarchy along with those of Catholicism'.[3] This suggests that a culture of combining attacks on images of the king with attacks on images of the Church existed *before* the Revolution, leading us to ask two questions: first, to what extent were the revolutionaries influenced, directly or indirectly, by the Huguenots or Calvinists; and second, did the Revolution mark a moment when the target and transformation of iconoclasm shifted from an overtly religious basis to one of a more pronounced political nature? If so, what effect did the iconoclasm of the French Revolution have on the concept and terminology of the State? The historical evidence indicates that iconoclasm was codified in new laws and statutes at the time. Idzerda notes that in 1792 a 'definitive law applicable to the whole nation' was passed which 'made its general purpose – iconoclasm – quite clear'. This decree *institutionalized* the conflation of the religious and political target, announcing:

> Whereas, the sacred principles of liberty and equality will not permit the existence of monuments raised to ostentation, prejudice, and tyranny to continue to offend the eyes of the French people; whereas, the bronze in these monuments can be converted into cannon for the defense of *la patrie*, it is decreed; I. All statues, bas-reliefs, inscriptions, and other monuments made of bronze or other metals, which exist in public squares, gardens, parks, public buildings ... will be removed by the communes. [The second article provided for the conversion of this metal into cannon.] III. *All monuments containing traces of feudalism, of whatever nature, that still remain in churches, or other public places*, and even those in private homes, shall, without the slightest delay, be destroyed by the communes.[4]

The reference to churches among 'other public places' within the context of 'feudalism' encapsulates the conflation of targets by the French Revolutionary iconoclast. By relegating the sacred importance of the Christian place of worship and codifying the destruction of its monuments in law, it represents a transformation of religious and political signs that had implications for the construction of a new social identity around the rubric of the State. In this chapter, I shall examine the relationship of those signs and that rubric. First, I shall begin by considering some of the points of connection between the sixteenth-century Calvinists and the eighteenth-century revolutionaries.

THE FRENCH REVOLUTION AND CALVINISM

The idea that a connection can be made between Calvinism and the apparent anti-clericalism of the French Revolutionaries has been promoted by partisans pursuing both a Protestant and Catholic agenda. Two late nineteenth-century examples illustrate this kind of historical partisanship. For a Presbyterian like Nathaniel S. McFetridge, writing about the movement as a moral and political force in Europe and America, Calvinism was the religion of liberty and, as such, the Calvinist migrants in America were working alongside Rousseau in France towards 'the promotion of one great purpose'.[5] For a near-contemporary Catholic like Hilaire Belloc, the opposite was true. Belloc wrote that 'in France there had arisen, during the movement of the Reformation, a wealthy, powerful and numerically large Huguenot body ... the Huguenot had in France a very special and permanent quarrel with the monarchy, and therefore with the Catholic Church'.[6] Ignoring Calvin's call for obedience shown towards the king, and reinforcing the idea that the French monarchy and the Catholic Church were inseparable institutions, Belloc depicted the eighteenth-century French Protestant: 'the peculiar phenomenon remained of a body powerful in numbers and (what was far more important) in wealth and social power, scattered throughout the territory of the kingdom, organized and, by this time, fixedly anti-Catholic, and therefore anti-national', which amounted, in his words, to 'a State within a State'[7] – an accusation which is reflected to some extent in van Kley's description of Calvinism's independence from and potential threat to the 'State'.

Both of these accounts, despite their different agendas, present the French Revolution as a development of Calvinist political ideology. However, the reader should not therefore assume that an uncomplicated line of chronological influence from Calvin to the *sans-culottes* can be interpreted as defining the terms of their iconoclasm. Indeed, the nature of that influence is the subject of historical debate today. Besançon states that 'after Calvin, texts dealing directly with the representation of the divine become increasingly rare'[8] (tellingly, Besançon refers to the French Revolution only twice in his epic treatment of iconoclasm from the Bible and Plato through Calvin and Hegel to Malevich, Kandinsky, and contemporary abstract art). However, Weinshenker describes an increasing preoccupation with the issue of idolatry and sculpture within the practices of Catholicism during the *ancien régime*. She states that 'visual artists during this period also created many works depicting the linkage between idol-worship and sculpture, matching the textual reiteration of this *topos*. They introduced it into scenes drawn from the Bible and the legends of the saints; in the decades around the mid-eighteenth century they also derived subject matter from increasing archaeological knowledge based on such publications as Bernard de Montfaucon's *Antiquité expliquée* (1719)', and adds that, reflecting the Protestant focus on the Torah, many Catholic 'images of idol-worship were selected from episodes in the Old Testament and illustrated or implied the guilty character of the rituals. The individuals or peoples revering the false gods were represented as having turned away from the true faith to this wicked practice'. A 'major milestone' of this 'linkage', she concludes, was Nicolas Poussin's painting of the Israelites worshipping the Golden Calf.[9]

The idea of Poussin, a French painter who spent much of his life in Rome working under papal patronage, painting the golden calf – the emblem of Calvinist iconoclasm – in a manner that would eventually be described as 'classical' and part of a cultural movement that looked towards ideals of logic and 'Enlightenment', is rich with the overlaps and tensions characterizing the French attitude to idols at the time. So too is Weinshenker's reference to Bishop Bossuet of Meaux's work on the connections between sculpture, idolatry, and human vanity,[10] when we note that Bossuet himself was accused of appeasing Protestants. However, such tensions within Catholic rhetoric on the image do not detract from the explicit connections between a Calvinist-Huguenot religiosity and an anti-royalist politics. Weinshenker notes that 'one prominent Huguenot pastor expresses indignation at a Catholic publication that "exaggerates the apotheosis of the King in so impious and scandalous a manner that he is compared to the true God and twelve times all the praises that the Scriptures give to the Divine Majesty are conferred upon him"', describing Protestant converts to Catholicism as leaving '"the religion of Jesus Christ, the King of Kings, in order to enter that of a mortal Prince, where ... they kneel before the idol"', and adding that 'there is "nothing more contrary to the word of Jesus Christ and to the spirit of the Gospel than the worship of images ... which today comprises almost the entire devotion of the Papists"'.[11] Indeed, such rhetoric intensified after the Revocation of the Edict of Nantes in 1685 and the renewed persecution of Huguenot communities in France under the forces of Louis XIV – a turning-point that can be placed chronologically almost exactly between the Calvinist image-breaking of the 1530s and the destruction of the royal tombs of St. Denis in 1793.

In this way, while recognizing the complex relationship that Catholics themselves had with images during the *ancien régime*, it is reasonable to accept the connections that both van Kley and Weinshenker make between the early Huguenots and the anti-clericalism of the later revolutionaries. In political and cultural terms, this connection was often indirect; a combination of diverse religious and anti-royalist voices, including a marginalized Protestantism, the rise of what is now called Enlightenment philosophy, and the influence of an English coffeehouse culture, where for the first time newspapers and satirical journals were being printed outside of the control of the authorities, created what Habermas has described as a new kind of public space in the mid-eighteenth century. As was the case in England, this public space became increasingly an arena for the new urban classes, including both the 'Calvinist' bourgeois communities which I have described in Chapter 1 and the educated opponents of feudalism. Such a 'structural transformation' of society, as Habermas termed it, changed the *representational* power of royalty from monuments of religious association to a public 'sphere' (*Öffentlichkeit*) which, while amorphous, served to unify a range of dissenting voices.[12] Habermas used the term within a Marxist context of commodity exchange and the transition from feudalism to a kind of democracy. However, his idea of the rejection or the decline of 'representational' (visual) power involving the rise of a new public class is also pertinent to the study of iconoclasm in eighteenth-century France, as it accommodates the complex interactions between Catholic rejections of idolatry, the connections between Calvinism, the Enlightenment *philosophes*, and the revolutionaries, and the fact that even in pre-revolutionary Paris, statues of the king were sometimes graffitied with anti-royalist slogans.[13]

It is within this new public sphere, then, that the historian can identify a common voice between the 'Calvinist' and 'Revolutionary' classes, and make the link from their iconoclasm to their forms of political organization. It is within this sphere, too, that these classes can be considered in the philosophical context of the Enlightenment as, according to Burleigh, 'the *philosophes* were the beneficiaries of those Calvinists and Jansenists who had propelled an infinitely good God further away from this corrupt world'.[14] Indeed, the subject of idolatry was discussed by many seventeenth- and eighteenth-century philosophers. Examples such as Voltaire's 1757 submission on 'Idole, Idolâtre, Idolâtrie' for d'Alembert's *Encyclopedie*, which by examining Greek and Roman forms of worship served 'to demonstrate the idolatrous character of contemporary religious observances',[15] had the effect – whether deliberately or not – of contributing to the Huguenot controversy over idols and iconoclasm. According to Morgan, the philosophy of reason became as much of an 'instrument of iconoclasm' as the Calvinist theology of the 'True God'. I shall quote Morgan at length here, for he provides a paragraph which summarizes the key terms of connection (which I shall italicize) between religion, the public sphere, and the Enlightenment which have enabled a semantic-historical line to be drawn from the image-breaking of the Calvinists to the French Revolution and, ultimately, modern notions of 'reason' and the 'secular':

> Idolatry and its extirpation are rooted in the history of religion, but they extend beyond strictly sectarian experience. In the *modern* West, often characterized as a *secular* culture, as the offspring of the Enlightenment quest for *liberation* from oppressive institutions such as the Church, idolatry and *iconoclasm* have remained vital categories of cultural criticism. The view installed during the seventeenth and eighteenth centuries has remained a force in scientific, academic and political discourse: freedom rests in liberation from superstition and authority ungoverned by *reason*. In the *lexicon* of the *Enlightenment*, superstition is another word for idolatry ... *science* and *philosophy* are the instruments of iconoclastic enlightenment. Reason is the tool that will smash their hold on the human mind.[16]

In this way, the label 'iconoclasm' becomes part of the lexicon of Habermas' new public sphere in eighteenth-century France, alongside the terms of science, reason, modernity, and the State. It represents a network of ideas and events which developed the sixteenth-century Calvinist organization of a class of once-exiled, now-urban *citoyens*. It is with this lexicon that the politics of iconoclasm can be understood, and can be considered alongside other semantic-historical investigations, such as Latour's deconstruction of the term 'modern' and Milbank's or Asad's critique of the 'secular'. Within this network, the study of iconoclasm inhabits the realm of a constructed, self-fashioned semantic-history, not entirely reducible to the material world of broken objects.

In terms of this wider connection between iconoclasm and scientific invention, Schaffer notes that Isaac Newton used the same vocabulary of idolatry when describing 'the worst corruption of religion' and 'that an improved natural philosophy of light and matter would destroy the idols' power and restore true faith'.[17] This idea of 'light and matter' referred to a connection made at the time between idols and 'bad optics'. For figures like Bacon, Niceron, and even Hobbes, the unclear, disunified, or broken image was both a cause and a consequence of human error which could be resolved by the clarity and unity of science – an 'optical salvation', according to Schaffer, which encouraged Protestants to accommodate the presence of scientific empiricism and the machine in their lives. The reader will note that these terms of 'truth', 'unity', and 'salvation' are rich in Calvinist significance. Scientists like Niceron sought to solve the question of the false image with advances in optical knowledge. For the political thinker Hobbes, who described the 'idols of the brain, which represent bodies to us, where there are not' – for example, the turning of 'Bread into a Man' – the idea of unifying the many, broken idols of men's minds into a single social body was represented by the 'Leviathan', the image of which had the body of the king made up of the many bodies of the people.[18] Clearly this is not to draw a direct line of influence from Calvin to Hobbes, and from these individuals to the French Revolution; rather, it is to describe the intellectual environment preceding the events of 1789–1793, and to demonstrate the extent to which the terms of religion, science, and politics made use of the same iconoclastic rhetoric against idolatry. Such rhetoric was then manifested by the French Revolution's conflation of attacks against images of both feudalism and superstition.

Burleigh notes that Revolutionary attacks on idols occurred alongside a promotion or construction of imagery celebrating the new political order – in his words, a 'political religion' based around the State's images of liberty, equality, and fraternity. He argues that the emblems of the State replaced the idols of the Church to the extent that 'the Revolution adopted Voltaire and Rousseau as its intellectual parents, translating their earthly remains to the Pantheon, in 1791 and 1794 respectively, with elaborate ceremonies that echoed religious processions'[19] – a moving of body parts which mirrored, as we shall see, the emptying of tombs in St. Denis. According to Burleigh, this inversion of idolatry-iconoclasm rhetoric permeated Revolutionary France. He refers to the example of Wieland, who 'regarded religion as a private matter, and not something that should be compelled by the state. He was especially appalled by what he called "a type of new political religion", which was being "preached by [French generals] at the head of their armies". They worshipped the idols "freedom and equality" with a degree of intolerance that reminded Wieland of "Mohamed and the Theodosians"',[20] an accusation which echoes Burke's statement that 'a theory concerning government may become as much a cause of fanaticism as a dogma in religion'[21] and rejects, ironically, the very idea of a 'civil religion' as espoused by Rousseau in *The Social Contract*. As idols of the State were put up to replace those idols of the Church pulled down (a scenario not dissimilar to the opening quotation of this book, from Amis' account of the Bolshevik attacks on the bodies of Russian saints and their subsequent embalmment of Lenin's corpse), this was expressed by quasi-religious scriptures, liturgies, and sacraments. Burleigh refers to such an example, a kind of revolutionary catechism:

Question: What is Baptism?
Answer: It is the regeneration of the French begun on 14 July 1789, and soon supported by the entire French nation.

Question: What is Communion?
Answer: It is the association proposed to all peoples by the French Republic henceforth to form on earth only one family of brothers who no longer recognize or worship any idol or tyrant.

Question: What is Penitence?
Answer: Today it is the wandering existence of traitors to their Fatherland ...[22]

This was, in effect, the deeper influence of Calvinism on the French Revolution: beyond the debates over the extent to which the revolutionaries were or were not the direct heirs of Calvinism, a more profound change had taken place, articulated by the lexicon of the new public sphere, and from which the same rhetoric against Catholic imagery in sixteenth-century Geneva could be echoed in eighteenth-century Paris.

It was, to borrow Anderson's words on nationalism, part of the 'slow, uneven decline' of the 'interlinked certainty' 'in which cosmology and history were indistinguishable', to be replaced by the new certainties of a self-fashioned consciousness of the State.[23] Thus the link between iconoclasm and the State mirrors the link between Calvinism and the French Revolution. It reflects the tension that can be identified between what is destroyed and what is built, and is the window through which the historian can consider the image-breaking or sign-transformation of the French Revolution – a window through which, in the words of Taussig, the apparent paradox 'defacement is like Enlightenment' is resolved.[24] On that level, then, we can consider the image-breaking that occurred during the French Revolution.

IMAGE-BREAKING DURING THE FRENCH REVOLUTION

As with many acts of organized image-breaking during a time of political conflict, including the events of Geneva in 1535 and Mecca in 1803, the attacks against images of the Church and king that took place in French cities in the early 1790s were performed quickly. This rapidity has often been depicted as due to the frenzies of mob violence, but the speed of destruction was more often than not because of military and administrative demands for decisive action. Idzerda writes that 'many complaints were voiced in the Convention that the destruction of symbols glorifying the past was not being accomplished with sufficient rapidity or thoroughness ... in October, 1793, it was required that all symbols of the *ancien régime* were to be destroyed within eight days, upon pain of confiscation of the property where such symbols still existed'. This sense of urgency explains partly why iconoclasm became enshrined within a law for the destruction of monuments which was enforced by the central government and a 'Committee of Public Safety'. It also reflects practical concerns. The combined act of destruction with the construction of a state identity did not always respond directly to political or philosophical ideals; often, the practical issues of dismantling a church or obliterating stone tombs and monuments required a level of organization that could only be achieved, like much manual work that is dependent on committee deadlines and paying wages, in short, concentrated bursts.

Owing to their symbolic importance, some of the key targets of iconoclasm during the French Revolution were the royal tombs in the Basilica of St. Denis, described as 'monuments of idolatry' which 'still nourished the superstition of some Frenchmen'. Idzerda notes that 'within a month of the directive from the Committee of Public Safety some fifty of the tombs were destroyed',[25] an act depicted by Hubert Robert in his painting 'La violation des caveaux des rois dans la basilique Saint-Denis'. Robert portrays a group of revolutionaries removing, workmanlike, the tombs in the crypt. One leans on his elbows and watches the others work, another looks down from a ladder. Above this crypt, a gap in the floor exposes the window tracery of Abbot Suger's gothic building. This image of carrying, shifting, and resting depicts the manual realities of 'attacking' large blocks of stone. It implies a level of effort and organization which resists Réau's notion of the vandalistic 'mob', or what Taussig calls the 'fury' of defacing 'the lies, or the repressed history, of the regime' while 'awaiting the resurgence of the truth of the past'.[26] Furthermore, the depiction of the image-breaker as a manual worker following the orders of a central committee, rather than an individual engaged in a moment of frenzied violence, reflects 'the painful dilemma of the revolutionaries' at the time: that is, while some revolutionaries emptied the crypt of St. Denis, the new Monuments Commission was seeking ways of protecting some of the tombs for their artistic value. Idzerda notes that the Commission 'had to demonstrate that the fine arts would not suffer under a revolutionary regime, but many of the social, political, and religious values expressed in the art of the pre-1789 era were, in revolutionary terms, "untrue", and had to be destroyed'.[27] A distinction was drawn, as with Calvin's separation of the 'true God' from 'false idols', between the object of 'true' artistic value and the contents or 'untrue' signification of the object. Thus, in the words of van Kley, 'by defacing churches, changing sacral place-names, and forcing priests to marry, the dechristianizers mainly mimed the iconoclastic gestures of sixteenth-century Calvinists'.[28]

These two declared intentions – one to destroy the symbol, the other to preserve the object – created a complex iconoclastic culture within which attacks such as that on the tombs of St. Denis took

Hubert Robert, 'La violation des caveaux des rois dans la basilique Saint-Denis'
(1793)

place. This culture was reflected in the legal pronouncements and new institutions which appeared at the time legitimizing certain acts of destruction and preservation. Idzerda states that the nationalization of Church property in 1789 led to a concern over protecting examples of French art that were within church walls, as 'the sale of many church buildings to private individuals raised fears that the mosaics, stained-glass windows, statues, and paintings in these buildings would be either destroyed or dispersed'. He adds that 'to avoid the danger of such an artistic loss to the nation, the Constituent Assembly in 1790 created a Monuments Commission composed of members of several royal academies. The chief duty of this group was to inventory and collect in various depots those works of art thought worthy of preservation by the State'.[29] In this way, preservation, like destruction, became a matter of state control, achieved through its administration. The creation of a commission to achieve this control marks the moment of *institutionalization* that operates at the heart of a politics of iconoclasm. Ideas and acts of violence against religious and royal objects had already existed within the discourse of the new 'public sphere'; however, the combination of attacks on some tombs and images with the preservation of others, both under the auspice of different government commissions, codified the question of iconoclasm within the fabric of the State.

For some historians, this institutionalization of iconoclasm served to temper the 'fury' (to use Taussig's term) against images of the old regime within the mechanics of a new government. Greene writes that following the initial attack on St. Denis, 'the atmosphere became gradually more sympathetic' towards the royal tombs, and the idea of preserving some for their artistic value was proposed. Alexandre Lenoir, who had been present at the emptying of the royal tombs in 1793, was given permission one year later to transport some of the artwork from these tombs to a depot for protection and, eventually, exhibition. According to Greene, for whom 'many of these bodies had been exhumed by revolutionary mobs and subjected to indignities ... in a sense Lenoir rescued them', so that by 1795 he 'was pleading with the Comité d'instruction publique for permission to re-erect the tomb of François I – not to perpetuate the memory of the king, but because otherwise the pieces would get lost or decay, and it was important to preserve this "immortal monument which had taught French artists good taste and the proper style of design"'.[30] Lenoir's plans were approved by the Comité d'instruction publique in 1795 and by the National Convention in 1796 – following this approval, he was put in charge of the tombs and other displaced religious objects under the auspices of the new Musée des monuments français.

Greene's somewhat eulogistic account of Lenoir must be read with caution, in particular the description of him during the attack on one of the royal tombs in St. Denis: 'since the body was well preserved, he had had the pleasure of shaking the king's hand. "I took his hands with a certain respect, which I couldn't prevent, although I was a real republican." In the Middle Ages men collected the remains of saints and of the True Cross; in the Revolution they collected parts of famous men. This is undoubtedly evidence of the influence of the Enlightenment'.[31] As I have endeavoured to show, there is nothing 'undoubted' about the complex influences of Catholic, Calvinist, and Enlightenment thinking on the iconoclasm of the French Revolution. However, his description of the founding of a national museum of monuments as the culmination of an intensive administrative process goes some way to explaining the forces of political centralization which transformed the attacked objects. One of the aspects of this process was, according to Greene, the removal of monuments in the provinces to furnish the new museums of Paris. Unlike Geneva or Riyadh, Paris was already a capital city, but criticisms were increasingly made against Lenoir that the Musée des monuments français was 'robbing' churches in other cities in order to strengthen the cultural influence of Paris, to the extent that even monuments which had not been attacked were taken away from their original settings.[32]

This combination of administrative pronouncements, institutional permission to destroy or preserve objects, a belief in the difference between the 'true' art or symbols of the people and the false 'idols' of an *ancien régime*, and the increasingly centralizing influence of Paris over the provinces, many of which had at one time been independent from France, was brought into sharp definition when the target of destruction was an ostensibly political rather than religious object (that is, the object had no ostensible religious setting, such as an abbey or basilica). One such example, described in detail by Clay, was the attack in 1792 on an equestrian statue of Louis XV sculpted by Edme Bouchardon which stood between the Champs Elysées and the gardens of the Tuileries Palace. Like many other symbols of the divine unity between king and people which had been produced at the time,[33] the statue depicted a 'warrior leader ... bringing peace to Europe' on a triumphal chariot; 'positioned around the pedestal were allegorical figures that represented the king's virtues: strength, justice, love and peace'.[34] As with the attack on St. Denis, the destruction of this statue took place quickly, following legislative change: the National Assembly suspended the monarchy on 10 August, and one day later the Bouchardon statue was pulled down. However, as Clay notes, this event represented not one moment of fixed or final destruction, but rather part of a cumulative process that had built up over several decades. He argues that the popular discourse of the public sphere – that is, the public discourse of pre-revolutionary, royalist Paris – already contained a different account of the statue from its official signification, focusing in particular on the king's love affairs. Thus the signification of the statue on the public level was the opposite of the warrior king it was intended to depict. Clay writes, 'the common semiotic ground provided by shared knowledge of unofficial discourses about the king's libertinage, allowed Parisians to generate and disseminate new connoted meanings for Bouchardon's sculpture. At the level of discourse the statue was transformed into a signifier of bad kingship'.[35] This ongoing transformation of signs, as Clay terms it, became expressed – or *fixed* momentarily – in physical acts of violence once the news of Louis XVI's capture in 1791 filtered through to the public sphere:

> News of these events provided the semiotic ground for the discursive transformation of all royal signs into signifiers of royal betrayal. Many Parisians responded by ensuring that royal signifiers pointed visibly to the new meanings made available for them by shifting discourses. As Gustave Isambert noted at the time, people began 'effacing king, queen and royal from signs, smashing the arms of France and scraping-off *fleurs de lys*', signifying permanent rejection of the monarchy. The historian Tackett has written that, 'busts of kings were pulled over, and larger royal statues, too massive to be removed, were covered in black cloth'. The addition of funereal cloth materially transformed statues of kings, including Bouchardon's, into signs of the monarchy's end, its death.[36]

It will be noted that, for Clay, the covering of statues with black cloth is interpreted to be as much of a transformation of signs as effacing, smashing, or scraping, as it represents 'a moment in ongoing processes of sign transformation focused on the statue' which had begun 'before the sculpture was even erected', notably in the subversive arena of the public sphere, as described by Habermas, which 'drew upon, and fed into, the ever changing, competing discourses that provided

Parisians with shifting semiotic ground for interpreting and representing the statue's meanings'.[37] Under these terms, the destruction of the object is not the only significant component or category of iconoclasm. As with the removal of royal tombs from a religious context in St. Denis to a republican context in the new state museums, a great proportion of the iconoclasm of the French Revolution involved as much of what Rambelli and Reinders have categorized as 'theft, partial destruction, and negative cultural definition', as the 'total obliteration' of a site like Cluny. Thus Clay has included further types of iconoclasm where the physical transformation of the object involves an attack on its integrity, not necessarily its fabric – for example, the pouring of buckets of excrement over a stature of the king.[38]

This kind of approach to the relationship between iconoclasm of a religious and political, physical and symbolic nature takes the debate away from a narrative of mob vandalism and loss, and brings it closer to one of semiotic and critical analysis. It also informs the study of preservation, restoration, and the construction of national identity that took place in the years following the French Revolution. For example, the restoration of churches by Viollet-le-Duc in the nineteenth century, many of which had been damaged during the Revolution, was accused by some thinkers (notably Ruskin) of being an act of destruction in itself. Debating the difference between 'true' and 'false' architecture (and, by extension, what should be left to ruin and what should be preserved), Armi describes 'the easy but treacherous slide from preservation to restoration to reconstruction', adding that for Ruskin 'the *heritage* or craft of building – as seen in surviving traditions such as plastering – were, but never should be, confused with the actual *history* of architecture, as seen in the authentic character of an original: "It is impossible, as impossible as to raise the dead, to restore anything that has ever been great or beautiful in architecture"'.[39] Ruskin's association of some types of restoration with destruction, when considered in the light of Clay's idea of 'shifting semiotic ground' during the eighteenth century, brings the *iconoclasm–enlightenment* debate used by historians to describe the connection between Calvinists and anti-royalists into its inverted, nineteenth-century context: that of *restoration–regression*. The next chapter will examine this development in more detail.

To summarize: within the public sphere, it is evident that the transformation of signs reflected fluid processes of breaking and remaking objects for a range of social and individual reasons. However, in this brief chapter I have endeavoured to demonstrate that the French Revolution represented an institutionalization of this process, fixing it in the legal declarations of newly founded committees and other administrative bodies which gave permission for destruction or preservation to take place from the centralizing force of Paris over the provinces. On the institutional or administrative level, then, the transformation of signs was codified according to categories which had political impact: they gave administrative weight to the lexicon of the modern, political, liberal State. Thus even the preservation of certain works of art or broken tombs could be considered as being permitted not for their aesthetic value but rather their service to the State. As Idzerda notes, artists like Jacques-Louis David were members of the Monuments Commission. In this administrative role, David appealed to the National Assembly in 1790 'for the partial preservation of Louis XIV's statue in the Place Victoire, lest this "masterpiece" be lost to posterity'; later, however, 'David arranged that a statue of liberty be raised in the Place Victoire; before this statue the "attributes of royalty ... would be made into an enormous bonfire ... as an expiatory sacrifice"'.[40] Idzerda considers such developments in primarily Art Historical terms, as a case of the artist turning iconoclast. I consider them to be relevant also to the politics of iconoclasm. Like the Museum of French Monuments, the Louvre was a product of this politics, a new national museum within which the Monuments Commission and the Temporary Arts Commission could exhibit 'proscribed symbols'. This administrative conclusion of sign-transformation affected the object on both its cultural and political level – in the words of Idzerda, revolutionaries 'created a public institution called a "museum"; immure a political symbol in a museum and it becomes merely art – iconoclasm is thus achieved without destruction'.[41] According to the politics of iconoclasm, the act of institutionalization can be an act of destruction, if we accept Clay's position that an attack on the integrity and context of the object represents as much of a transformation of signs as its physical obliteration.

In this way, the iconoclasm of the French Revolution encapsulated many of the evolving terms that were beginning to constitute, following their emergence in the context of Calvinist image-breaking, the new lexicon of modernity and the State. It was institutionalized in the administrative mechanics of the new 'public sphere' – namely, the city. The city, its ruins, and its museums became the battleground of ideas over destruction and preservation, with cultural, religious, and political consequences which would intensify, as described by Burleigh's account of 'Earthly Powers', during the industrial changes of the nineteenth century until the mechanized crisis of modernity that is typically associated with World War I. Thus the question of iconoclasm was increasingly brought into the urban realm, where new dilemmas concerning art, preservation, and authenticity featured as prominently as the old struggles between religious and political power. This urban realm is the context from which we shall examine our next case of iconoclasm one hundred years after the French Revolution: the case of a bourgeois European city and its critics.

CHAPTER 4

The Bourgeois City and Iconoclasm: Venice

'There's nothing quite like a Venetian crowd', said Lord Marchmain. 'The city is crawling with Anarchists, but an American woman tried to sit here the other night with bare shoulders and they drove her away by coming to stare at her, quite silently; they were like circling gulls coming back and back to her, until she left'.

Evelyn Waugh, *Brideshead Revisited: the Sacred and Profane Memories of Captain Charles Ryder*[1]

The relationship between destruction, preservation, and transforming cultural identities that defined the iconoclasm of the French Revolution also influenced subsequent debates over history and heritage which took shape during the nineteenth century, including famous controversies such as the building of Haussmann's Parisian boulevards, the 'renovation' of mediaeval façades in the Cambridge colleges, and the 'preservation' of the Elgin marbles in London's British Museum. This debate took place not only in connection with the objects brought into the rapidly expanding national museums and art galleries, but also the design of street-plans, buildings, and monuments in the public sphere. The battleground of terminology – what is 'renovation' to some being 'desecration' to others – that accompanied much nineteenth-century urban development provided the foundations for a notion of heritage and preservation that operated on both the international as well as the individual state level, eventually influencing the creation of UNESCO-designated 'World Heritage Sites' in the twentieth century. Considering the global reach of this debate, then, the reader might question why I have chosen to focus on one particular city, Venice, in order to illustrate the international development of a changing iconoclastic narrative. My reference to Ruskin and Viollet-le-Duc in the previous chapter hinted at the course such a narrative was taking. In the early 1850s, Ruskin published *The Stones of Venice*, in which he described a 'decline' of the city that could be seen in its architectural changes. This notion of decline implied a golden (particularly mediaeval) age, when Venice represented a place of ideal cultural and political order: from Trapezuntius' comparison of the city with Plato's Republic in 1452 to the annual casting of gold rings into the Adriatic, a myth of Venice grew around the idea of a free city uniquely 'married' with the sea and, protected by the body of St. Mark, holding 'an apostolic status equal to that of Rome'.[2] Architecturally, its three main focal points were designed around a tripartite structure with religious signification that looked towards the Classical as well as the Catholic: San Marco, 'the place of eloquence' represented by Minerva; the Rialto, 'place of function', by Mercury; and the Arsenal, 'place of technique', by Vulcan. Palladio was involved with these plans of urban self-fashioning, which were never fully realized. Describing the significance of this urban organization, Cosgrove writes that 'in the innovations of the sixteenth century we may read the myth of Venice in its townscape'[3] – a link between architecture and ideal which was promoted by a wide range of writers from Boschini ('This island is truly a jewel / set in this crystal which surrounds it / where ebbing and flowing the waves beat. / Doesn't it look as if it were done with a paint brush?')[4] to Byron (who described the city as 'the greenest island of my imagination'), to Henry James, who wrote letters from the Palazzo Barbaro describing 'the Venice of one's dreams'.[5] This *mythology* of the city was reiterated to the extent that Venice has become widely recognized as a cultural icon, encouraging (and building its tourist trade upon) artistic pilgrimage.

By the nineteenth century, and with the impact of Napoleonic change, Venice had lost its independence as a city state and had become part of an imperial struggle between Italy and Austria. This political situation combined with an increase in both European tourism to the city, building on the earlier 'Grand Tour' reputation, and the sale of many palaces by their Italian families to wealthy foreigners. Faced with these changes, some of those writers who had previously promoted the city's mythology began to describe 'the quietude of Venice's decline'.[6] With a weaker naval base, and a movement of the local population and industry from the islands to the mainland at Mestre, the Venetian economy depended increasingly on the investment of tourists and foreign house-buyers. Accordingly, the myth of Venice began to be redefined around an aesthetic of crumbling stone, ruins, and decline – an image of the city that drew on popular notions of decay in the eighteenth-century 'capriccio', the work of artists like Hubert Robert, and ruins such as Tintern Abbey. Responding to this dichotomous image of Venice as either ideal city or idealized ruin, Henry James, a foreigner himself, warned against 'the stamping of poor Venice beyond repair as the supreme bugbear of literature'.[7]

This chapter will examine the image of Venice as an idealized city in a state of ruin: first, in the construction of a 'Venice' myth as cultural icon; second, in its so-called 'decline' due to political and cultural change, as well as the environmental circumstances of stone built on water; and, third, the emergence in the early twentieth century of a movement of iconoclasts – namely, the Futurists – who chose Venice as the target of their attacks against bourgeois European culture, proposing to fill its canals with the rubble of its razed palaces and churches. While the questions posed by this chapter are specific to Venice at the beginning of the twentieth century, the wider issues of destruction, preservation, and cultural identity both draw on the terms of the French Revolution and provide a context for the destruction of other cities like Warsaw and Dresden during World War II, the idea of universal heritage and the World Heritage Site, and attacks on internationally recognized artifacts such as the Bamiyan Buddhas. In this way, as well as building on the terms of the French Revolution in my previous chapter, this Venetian example informs the issues affecting my following chapters on Warsaw, Banja Luka, and present-day Mecca.

VENICE AS AN IDOL: WORSHIP AND PLUNDER

The construction of the myth of Venice involved separating the city as a site of poetry from an otherwise prosaic world. For Henry James, the American 'reality' was 'too large a mass for a mere mouthful: it is as if the syllables were too numerous to make a legible word'. He compared 'the illegible word' which 'hangs in the vast American sky ... as something fantastic and abracadabrant, belonging to no known language'[8] to 'Venice' – 'it is a pleasure to say the word'.[9] As 'nothing can be said here (Venice) that has not been said before',[10] the myth of the city is represented by its name, which 'characterizes all human process, all thought and action and emotion'.[11] As such, the word 'Venice' is 'translated' (if we continue to make use of Clay's terms) from a city on the Adriatic coast into a signifier for human artistry. For the myth-makers, this combination of city and artistry placed Venice as a supreme example of European civilization. For example, Ezra Pound's narrative in Canto XVII describes the 'hell mouth' of twentieth-century war in amphibious terms – a 'lake of bodies, aqua morta, / of limbs fluid, and mingled, like fish heaped in a bin'[12] – where Venice floats above both the sea and history:

> And thence down to the creek's mouth, until evening,
> Flat water before me,
>   and the trees growing in water,
> Marble trunks out of stillness,
> On past the palazzi,
>   in the stillness,
> The light now, not of the sun ...[13]

The reader will note that much of this poetic language applied to Venice mirrors that of the 'Word', representation, and artifice which has threaded through my study of iconoclasm. In this context of myth-making – what Zorzi describes as 'the weight of the representations of Venice' – 'the real city hardly counts: the physical Venice could well disappear and literary Venices would still be created'.[14] Zorzi's observation is particularly pertinent when considered alongside the political 'decline' of Venice in the nineteenth century, during which – for many of its mythologists – the physical city really did begin to disappear. Zorzi notes that after the fall of the Venetian Republic at the end of the eighteenth century, the architectural heritage of the city's palaces and churches was put into jeopardy by 'speculators' and antique-sellers, writing that 'the very walls of these palaces were plundered: the stucco work was chiseled off, the frescoes were torn down, the inlaid wooden doors were lifted off their iron hinges; whole buildings were razed and the bricks and stones were used as building materials'.[15] This situation, leading Ruskin to describe Venice as 'a heap of ruins', redefined 'a literary and visual myth' of the city, according to Perosa, which 'sowed the seeds and drew the outlines of what would quickly become the *topos* or conceit of "death in Venice"' – an image of the decaying city which would later feature in Thomas Mann's novella *Tod in Venedig*. Perosa writes that as Ruskin 'worked a totally ahistorical and moralized myth about her; by rationalizing her decadence, however, he would portray it – the decadence – as a wood-worm worming its way into, and corroding, the beauty of a lost Eden', adding that he deployed 'the lexicon, the very vocabulary, that would go into the making of so many literary deaths

Still from Nicolas Roeg, Don't Look Now *(1973)*

in Venice. Blight, stagnation, death, darkness, decline, and ruin, mark the end of Volume 1 of *The Stones of Venice*.[16] Thus the myth of Venice as the best example of human artistry, when considered according to the consequences of its political decline, was turned into the myth of Venice as the worst example of human nature, its reputation summarized by Taussig as a place 'for homosexual prostitution, cross-dressing, boys naked on gondolas, the sensualized "ghettoized Jew" as the culprit for syphilis, venereal diseases' – in short, 'the mysterious powers of pollution' that could be traced from the Merchant of Venice and his 'pound of flesh' to Ruskin's ruins,[17] as well as Mann's dying Gustav von Aschenbach, Nicolas Roeg's mystic sisters in 'Don't Look Now', and Ian McEwan's brutal end to *The Comfort of Strangers*.

For each of these artists, Venice hides a hidden, savage side of dirty canals, decay, and disease. Henry James remarked, in words not dissimilar to Benjamin's notion of a document of civilization's connection to a document of barbarism, that 'what strikes me is … the monuments and treasures of art, the great palaces and properties, the conquests of learning and taste, the general fabric of civilization as we know it, based if you will on all the despotisms, the cruelties, the exclusions, the monopolies and the rapacities of the past, but thanks to which, all the same, the world is less of a "bloody sell" and life more of a lark'.[18] For James, the question of 'cruelty' against the 'treasures' of Venice was understood through the 'diluting' process of those foreigners who 'unwittingly but none the less deplorably trifled'[19] – that is, in the desire to be part of the Venice-myth, typically through purchasing those artifacts which 'obscure' and 'consign to oblivion' the 'work' of the city,[20] the Venetian visitor transformed the city into a 'dishonourable place' of 'whores' and 'beggars': 'there is a great deal of dishonour about St. Mark's altogether, and if Venice, as I say, has become a great bazaar, this exquisite edifice is now the biggest booth'.[21] Ironically (or, perhaps, necessarily), James himself was one of those visitors, and in this way he recorded an anxiety not untypical of those writer-visitor-tourists who, in trying to capture the city, found that their time passed, in the words of Waugh's Charles Ryder, 'quickly and sweetly – perhaps too sweetly; I was drowning in honey, stingless'.[22]

These writers depicted Venice using the terminology of idolatry in both the cultural mind and the marketplace, in which, to borrow Mitchell's words on Marx, 'ideology and fetishism are both varieties of idolatry, one mental, the other material, and both emerge from an iconoclastic critique'.[23] Embodying this fetishism, the writer-tourist stands in St. Mark's piazza-'bazaar'. In response, the 'iconoclastic critique' asks the question:

> Why should it be beautiful at all? Why should Venice, aside from its situation, be a place of enchantment? One appears to be confronted with a paradox. A commercial people who lived solely for gain – how could they create a city of fantasy, lovely as a dream or fairy-tale? This is the central puzzle of Venice.[24]

It is this 'puzzle' which led Henry James to declare that the myth of Venice built on the 'bloody sell' until 'the tourist Venice is Venice',[25] connecting the mythology of artifice and reality with the fetishism of the idol and its purchase. As such, the debate over Venice's beauty and decline pointed towards a wider question of the fetishization of cultural icons and their monetary value – a question which connects the mythologists and critics of Venice to the issue of idols and iconoclasm.

These notions of Venetian artifice, representation, and value were described by writers like James and Pound in terms of noble, 'true' materials such as stone and gold, and the 'untrue' materials of money.

According to a tradition made famous in Shakespeare's *The Merchant of Venice*, much of the city was built through wealth gained by usury. For Ezra Pound's proto-Fascist poetic stance, this represented a crucial difference between Venice and other cities. For Pound, gold was regarded as the tangible material of myth, able to be physically moulded into the beautiful object, whereas usury originated from nothing and results in nothing; it is, in Pound's words, '*ex nihil*'. Gold implies the organic; usury implies inorganic corruption. Under these terms, as the myth of Venice represented the best example of good European culture and government, Pound's *Cantos* traced the decline of this moral Europe through the example of a usurious Venice. This echoed Ruskin's warnings in *The Stones of Venice*, which claimed that there were three 'thrones' which stood 'above all other' – Tyre, Venice, and England: 'of the First of these great powers only the memory remains; of the Second, the ruin; the Third, which inherits their greatness, if it forgets their example, may be led through prouder eminence to less pitied destruction'.[26] For Pound, the third of these 'thrones' had at its heart the Bank of England as the historical den of English usury. However, Canto XLV takes the capitalist legacy one step further, and associates the 'usura' of 'hell knows which Rothschild' with 'The Eunited States ov America'.[27] As Ruskin believed England to be the potential heir of Venetian ruin, Pound continued the usurious lineage from England to Roosevelt's America. For this reason, a rejection of world finance, usury, and foreign influence led Pound to describe Venice's 'light now, not of the sun' as, in Canto LXXVI, 'all the gold domes of San Marco' – a reflected light, 'dark and mysteriously vibrant with the swart glimmer of gold and ruby',[28] the focus of it being San Marco's gilded interior, the Pala d'Oro, and in 'somewhat Ruskinian terms ... "the jewel-box"' of Santa Maria dei Miracoli.[29] Precious materials are not condemned here, as they are hewn from the earth and therefore hold 'true' value: Canto LXXVI states that 'the crystalline, as inverse of water, / ... can be weighed in the hand'. Thus, as Ruskin traced the 'ruin' of Venice from the decline of an organic gothic order to the so-called modernity of the Renaissance, so Pound saw the same corruption in the shift from gold, a natural and tangible material, to usury, which the 'Bank creates ... *ex nihil*'.[30]

Ruskin acknowledged this difference between the wealth of gold and usury in Venice, when describing the inscription on the church of San Giacomo di Rialto (believed to be the first church of the city, and therefore bearing 'the first words that Venice ever speaks aloud'):[31]

SIT CRUX VERA SALUS HUIC TUA CHRISTE LOCO

HOC CIRCA TEMPLUM SIT IUS MERCANTIBUS
AEQUUM PONDERA NEC VERGANT NEC SIT
CONVENTIO PRAVA[32]

Blythe argues that this is a 'seminal edict' for the city, citing Ruskin's approval of 'the great command against usury ... the first recorded words of Venice herself'.[33] *The Merchant of Venice* was central to this understanding of the corrupting influence of usury. Blythe states that 'Ruskin saw the fall of the Venetian state as a change "from her days of religion and gold ducats" (public, Gothic, Antonio) to "her days of infidelity, and paper notes" (private, Renaissance, Shylock)'.[34] Again, this division of value presented gold within a framework of organic morality, and paper money within a scheme of usury, the inorganic, and corruption. In this way, the corruption of Venice was not associated with its gilded architecture, but with 'modern' finance – 'from Ruskin's point of view, the physical form of the money-document depends, like architecture, on social morality'.[35] A city is built with material, according to Pound's Canto XLV: 'came not by usura ... / no church of cut stone signed: *adamo me fecit*'.

This emphasis on the 'true' value of the city's architectural morality compared to the 'false' and foreign influence of usury had, inevitably, a political dimension – not least in the proto-Fascist and anti-Semitic elements to much early twentieth-century poetic description of Venice. Pound's earliest experiences of the city, when 'the gondolas cost too much that year', reflected his own sense of financial exclusion in Venice as a penurious young poet. To combat this exclusion involved as much the identification of a universal scapegoat for his poverty as the appropriation of Venice as an ideal place for writing poetry. As Shylock was meant to have refused to eat or drink with gentiles, but only lend money to them, 'making all men strangers',[36] so the perception of modern day usury was coined by Pound as 'JEW-sury' (echoing the link made between money-lending and the Rothschilds in Canto XLVI). This association of Jew, usury, and the ruined ideal of Venice was also promoted by other poets, notably in T.S. Eliot's depiction of Burbank with a Baedeker:

> A lustreless protrusive eye
> Stares from the protozoic slime
> At a perspective of Canaletto.

The smoky candle end of time

Declines. On the Rialto once.
The rats are underneath the piles.
The Jew is underneath the lot;
Money in furs ...³⁷

For both Eliot and Pound, then, the Jew corrupted the mythology of the poetic city in the same way that usury was supposed to have undermined the moral 'Stones of Venice'. Eliot described Burbank asking who 'clipped the lion's wings / And flea'd his rump and pared his claws?' (the lion being that of St. Mark), and in Pound's Canto XXV, usury has the answer: '1335.3 lire 15 groats to stone for making a lion'. Thus while Canto XVII established Venice as a place of mythology, transcending world history, by Canto XXI usury has corrupted the ideal city. Pound described how 'bringing in, thus, the vice of luxuria' (Canto XXVI), certain figures with 'credit emptied Venice of money' (Canto XXI) – consequently, Venice is described as having a *price*, like any other purchasable artifact, as credit and enumerated value replaced the organic construction of stone and gold on water.

In this way, the icon-idol of Venice was depicted in the years around World War I: jeweled, bourgeois, cosmopolitan, usurious, threatened by water, tainted by Jews, ruined by tourism, and an emblem of Europe's decline from the moral order of mediaeval cities to the decay of provincial towns contested by empires. This was the idea of Venice that existed in a certain cultural imagination at the beginning of the twentieth century, and was chosen by some groups at the time as the target of their iconoclastic rhetoric.

THE ICONOCLAST IN VENICE

Marinetti's 'Futurist Manifesto', published by both *Gazzetta dell'Emilia* and *Le Figaro* in February 1909, called for the 'Mythology and the Mystic Ideal' of old Europe to be broken, and 'enriched by a new beauty: the beauty of speed. A racing car whose hood is adorned with great pipes, like serpents of explosive breath – a roaring car that seems to ride on grapeshot is more beautiful than the Victory of Samothrace'. This 'new beauty', for Marinetti, is achieved by struggle, 'an aggressive character' in art, where poetry becomes 'a violent attack' used to 'glorify war – the world's only hygiene'. It is the aesthetic principle that gave the 'Futurist Manifesto' its iconoclastic rhetoric:

> We will destroy the museums, libraries, academies of every kind, will fight moralism, feminism, every opportunistic or utilitarian cowardice ...
>
> It is from Italy that we launch through the world this violently upsetting incendiary manifesto of ours. With it, today, we establish Futurism, because we want to free this land from its smelly gangrene of professors, archaeologists, ciceroni and antiquarians. For too long has Italy been a dealer in second-hand clothes. We mean to free her from the numberless museums that cover her like so many graveyards.[38]

As I have attempted to demonstrate, the wider context of these ideas of violence against European heritage was a post-Ruskinian notion of cultural decay – a notion which was reiterated by similar ideas of 'degeneration' (Max Nordau) and 'decline' or *Untergang* (Oswald Spengler). In the Italian context, works such as the operas of Puccini were increasingly labelled as 'effeminate', 'degenerate', and 'not art but artifice';[39] in 1912, Boccioni's 'Technical Manifesto of Futurist Sculpture' stated that 'the sculpture that we can see in the monuments and exhibitions of Europe affords us so lamentable a spectacle of barbarism and lumpishness that my Futurist eye withdraws from it in horror and disgust'. Echoing Marinetti's attack on Italy's 'second-hand clothes' and Torrefranca's attack on 'artifice', Boccioni claimed that 'we see almost everywhere the blind and clumsy imitation of all the formulae inherited from the past: an imitation which the cowardice of tradition and the listlessness of facility have systematically encouraged. Sculptural art in Latin countries is perishing under the ignominious yoke of Greece and of Michelangelo'. His response, like that of his fellow Futurist Marinetti, was to glorify speed, the machine, and new materials. In this way, his 'Unique Forms of Continuity in Space' expressed the belief that 'sculpture should give life to objects by rendering their extension into space palpable, systematic, and plastic, because no one can deny any longer that one object continues at the point another begins, and that everything surrounding our body (bottle, automobile, house, tree, street) intersects it and divides it into sections by forming an arabesque of curves and straight lines'.[40] On the political level, this artistic principle reflected a frustration that Italy was not competing in terms of industrial or technical advancement and colonial expansion compared to its European rivals, Britain, France, and Germany – a combination of aesthetics and politics which linked Boccioni and Marinetti to the ideas of Ezra Pound, D'Annunzio, and, ultimately, early Italian Fascism.

The 'Futurist Manifesto' responded to many of the cultural concerns about authenticity, artifice, and European decline that I have outlined in my brief section on the Venetian myth, with an iconoclastic rhetoric of destruction. As 'the aim of sculpture is the abstract reconstruction of the planes and volumes which determine form, not their figurative value', Boccioni argued, 'one must abolish in sculpture, as in all the arts, the traditionally "sublime" subject matter. Sculpture cannot make its goal the episodic reconstruction of reality. It should use absolutely all realities in order to reconquer the essential elements of plastic feeling'. The practical requirement of this 'reconquering', he believed, was to 'destroy the pretended nobility, entirely literary and traditional, of marble and bronze, and to deny squarely that one must use a single material for a sculptural ensemble'.[41] Likewise, Antonio Sant'Elia's *Manifesto of Futurist Architecture* claimed that 'we have lost our predilection for the monumental, the heavy, the static, and we have enriched our sensibility with a taste for the light, the practical, the ephemeral and the swift. We no longer feel ourselves to be the men of the cathedrals, the palaces and the podiums. We are the men of the great hotels, the railway stations, the immense streets, colossal ports, covered markets, luminous arcades, straight roads and beneficial demolitions'. In place of the destroyed objects of old Europe – that is, in place of the cities of churches and palaces – Sant'Elia proposed that 'we must invent and rebuild the Futurist city like an immense and tumultuous shipyard, agile, mobile and dynamic in every detail; and the Futurist house must be like a gigantic machine'.[42] From the principle of both Sant'Elia's 'rebuilding' and Boccioni's 'reconquering', according to Simonsen, the Futurists were 'trying to delineate a future world'.[43]

These ideas of the new European city were summed up in the Futurist declaration against 'past-loving Venice'. In 1910, Marinetti climbed to the top of the clock tower in the Piazza San Marco and addressed the crowds below through a megaphone, scattering thousands of leaflets containing the following words:

> We renounce the old Venice, enfeebled and undone by worldly luxury, although we once loved and possessed it in a great nos-

talgic dream. We renounce the Venice of foreigners, market for counterfeiting antiquarians, magnet for snobbery and universal imbecility, bed unsprung by caravans of lovers, jeweled bathtub for cosmopolitan courtesans, *cloaca maxia* of passéism.

We want to cure and heal this putrefying city, magnificent sore from the past. We want to cheer and ennoble the Venetian people, fallen from their ancient grandeur, drugged by a contemptible mean cowardice in the practice of their little one-eyed businesses.

We want to prepare the birth of an industrial and military Venice that can dominate the Adriatic sea, that great Italian lake.

Let us hasten to fill its little reeking canals with the shards of its leprous, crumbling palaces.

Let us burn the gondolas, rocking chairs for cretins, and raise to the heavens the imposing geometry of metal bridges and howitzers plumed with smoke, to abolish the falling curves of the old architecture.

Let the reign of holy Electric Light finally come, to liberate Venice from its venal moonshine of furnished rooms.[44]

As Simonsen notes, it is 'no wonder the performance caused a battle between the Futurists and Venetian "passéists"', adding that 'the incident is a good example of the Futurists' boastful and grandiose rhetoric, their calculated provocation and their modernist concern to refute the past'.[45] For Blum, the scattering of the leaflets was a 'prank', showing the 'playful, farcical side'[46] of what has elsewhere been described as the performance art of 'clowns'.[47] This element of farce, however, was accompanied by a call for less humouristic activities – namely, street-fighting in the ruins of the city – which, when coupled with the political terminology of urban 'reconquering', reflected not only the changing cultural identity of Venice but also an emerging Fascist identity among many artists in Italy. Thus James' description of Venice as a 'dishonourable' bazaar and Pound's description of Venice as an edifice of usury – both places of tourism, money, and plunder – was repeated by Marinetti's description of the city as a 'jeweled bathtub for cosmopolitan courtesans', where the rejection of the foreign, the bourgeois, and what Eliot depicted as 'Jewish' forces of corruption was increasingly accompanied by the militaristic language of domination. Marinetti called for the 'liberation' of Venice not just through the technology of the 'holy Electric Light' but also the artillery of the 'Howitzer' – a language from which, according to Simonsen, 'Futurism was part of a larger European tendency in which heroic indifference to danger and aggression became a valued component in the individual (male) character, creating a social environment in which war was anticipated and welcomed'.[48]

In this way, the aesthetics of the machine espoused by Marinetti, Boccioni, Severini, and Sant'Elia became part of a politics of war where a bourgeois European city like Venice was the frontline target. In the *Manifesto Concerning the Ethiopian Colonial War*, Marinetti claimed that 'war is beautiful because thanks to gas masks, terror-inducing megaphones, flame-throwers, and small tanks' the domination of man over the subject machine is proven[49] – an aesthetics of violence that led Walter Benjamin to respond that 'all efforts to aestheticize politics culminate in one point. That one point is war' and, ultimately, 'the apotheosis of war by Fascism'.[50] Expressed through the destructive rhetoric made by the Futurists against the Venetian icon-idol, this aestheticized concept of war became central to the twentieth-century politics of iconoclasm, and will be examined in the next chapter looking at attacks on cities during World War II. The fact that Simonsen suggests that such rhetoric was 'welcomed' on the popular level demonstrates the extent to which art, radical politics, and violence had become intertwined in cultural discourse during the years surrounding World War I. As Perloff asks: 'who among the ordinary Venetian citizens of 1910, a people abjectly serving the tourist trade from the richer countries of northern Europe, did not yearn to make Venice once again the capital of the great Adriatic Empire?'[51] – a notion of humiliation that goes some way to explaining why, 'for Marinetti and the other Futurists, the attack on Venice was of particular significance; more than any other city ... as the very symbol of the *passatismo* and *Amore* that threatened the destruction of the Italian nation'.[52] Thus the aesthetics of political violence against an 'enfeebled' Venice operated at the centre of a network of destruction which can be observed in other historical examples, including my previous case study of revolutionary Paris (enabling a comparison which, in the words of Perloff, is 'not inaccurate'):[53] the network of destruction, preservation, fetishism, urban reconstruction, and the State. In the next chapter, which examines cases of iconoclasm during World War II, I shall investigate some examples of the moment when a theory of Futurist-Fascist urban aesthetics became a reality, through the administration of Nazi rule, in the widescale destruction of European cities.

CHAPTER 5

World War II and Iconoclasm

The construction of the strategy of air war in all its monstrous complexity, the transformation of bomber crews into professionals, 'trained administrators of war in the air', the question of how to overcome the psychological problem of keeping them interested in their tasks despite the abstract nature of their function, the problems of conducting an orderly cycle of operations involving '200 medium-sized industrial plants' flying towards a city and of the technology ensuring that the bombs would cause large-scale fires and firestorms – all these factors, which Kluge studies from the organizers' viewpoint, show that so much intelligence, capital and labour went into the planning of destruction that, under the pressure of all the accumulated potential, it *had* to happen in the end.

W.G. Sebald, *On the Natural History of Destruction*[1]

In my previous chapter, I examined how a rhetoric of destruction against the city combined with the emergence of a machine aesthetic, and touched on the common ground between such an iconoclastic discourse and the politics of totalitarianism – specifically, in the relationship between Futurism and Fascism. This common ground remained primarily theoretical at the beginning of the twentieth century, confined to debates in Parisian art galleries, congresses in St. Petersburg, and Bavarian beer halls. With the rise of Bolshevism in Russia, Fascism in Italy, and National Socialism in Germany, however, debates over Europe's cultural 'decline' were accompanied by attacks against churches, large-scale rebuilding projects for the urban landscape, and, in the most extreme cases, the mass destruction of cities during World War II. This shift in the *extent* of destruction was linked to the development of weapons of mass destruction, an increase in territorial conflict following World War I, and the emergence of new, often totalitarian, states. As such, the iconoclasm of the twentieth century represented a dramatic culmination of those tensions surrounding issues of religious identity, cultural authenticity, universal heritage, and state formation, which I have described as evolving with the French Revolution.

Much has been written about the destruction of sites of religious and cultural significance in the totalitarian environment of Europe between 1920 and 1950. Notable examples include: the demolition of Moscow's Christ the Saviour Cathedral and other Russian churches under Stalin; the architectural ambitions of Adolf Hitler and Albert Speer (described by Erich Fromm as marrying 'Hitler's passion to destroy buildings and cities' with 'his passion for building');[2] the razing of Warsaw; the Nazi burning of Jewish sacred books on holy days; the obliteration of places of cultural importance during Nazism's territorial expansion; the use of new technologies to rationalize and increase the efficiency of destruction; the 're-Germanizing' of Slavic art; the theft of works of art to furnish the museums of Linz and Berlin; the British bombing of German cities, including the attack on Dresden; the rebuilding of European cities following the war, either as reconstructed Old Towns (Warsaw), as new modernist communities (Le Havre), or as suburban 'New Towns' loosely modeled on pre-war 'garden cities' (Stevenage); the A-bomb, Hiroshima, and Nagasaki; the redrawing of Europe's borders after the war, the deportation of whole German populations, and the cultural redefinition of their communities (Königsberg); the decay of the East Prussian churches under Soviet occupation; and the effects of widespread and often total destruction on the memory and self-identity of the communities involved. This chapter will provide a brief outline of these many and complex issues, considering them according to the terms of iconoclasm and political construction that I have introduced in the cases of Calvinism, Wahhabism, the French Revolution, and the debate over cultural 'decline' in the early twentieth century. It will examine the destruction of cultural and religious sites during World War II, notably in the case of Warsaw, and the effects that this destruction had on post-war rebuilding projects and the emerging notion of a 'World Heritage Site'.

First, to provide the military context for these issues, the question must be asked: to what extent is iconoclasm different from other 'conventional' types of destruction during a time of war? Responding to this question requires an acknowledgment of the cultural and religious significance of the destroyed object – a significance which makes easier the difficult task of understanding the intentions of the destroying party. If this significance is acknowledged, events like the German destruction of Warsaw, the British destruction of Dresden, and the Russian destruction of the villages of Kaliningrad Oblast can be considered within a different category from examples of attacked industrial targets, such as the German bombing of the Austin 'Shadow Factory' at Longbridge or the British bombing of Siemensstadt. As the same armies and air forces were involved in destroying targets of both cultural and industrial importance, it is clearly difficult to distinguish the iconoclasm of World War II from 'usual' military practice according to the terms of intentionality. However, the religious significance of the destroyed objects enables such a distinction to be made. In many cities, the church was the first building to be bombed; following the war, the church was sometimes the only building to be rebuilt. In the case of the City of London and Cologne, the streets of the Old Town were reduced to rubble by air raids, but the cathedral was left intact. This is not an insignificant detail. The symbolism of the sacred building in the destroyed city reflected a complex dialogue between military attacks on civilian targets to weaken morale, debates over universal heritage, and propaganda against the enemy. Cathedrals, the most recognizable symbols of cities, began to represent wider issues of cultural and political conflict. If, as McElligott notes, 'by the third decade of the twentieth century over two-thirds of Germans lived in towns and cities, and those who did not, found themselves inexorably sucked into an ever-widening urban vortex',[3] then to destroy the city was to attack the social framework of the entire population. To destroy the city's cathedral was to attack its symbolic framework.

In the case of Nazism, this renewed emphasis on choosing religious sites as military targets was intensified with a culture of racism and anti-Semitism. From the publication of *Eine Abrechnung* in 1925, Hitler (like Pound and some Futurists before him) had identified 'international Jewish world finance' as a single body that sought 'to carry out its long-desired plan for destroying Germany'.[4] This rhetoric of quasi-mythological destiny combined with military attacks on cities containing large Jewish populations. The Nazi attacks on the architectural fabric of cities like Warsaw focussed deliberately on the cultural and religious significance of the object and site which they were destroying, thus translating Ludendorff's notion of 'total war' into a wider holocaust. As such, the iconoclastic rhetoric against Europe's bourgeois cities at the beginning of the twentieth century and the aesthetics of the machine were developed, by World War II, into an expression of urban destruction designed to fashion state identity on the political, cultural, and racial level – a type of 'total' iconoclasm which was repeated, as I shall describe in my next chapter, in the Serbian concept of 'Christoslavism' and the attacks on Bosnian mosques in the 1990s.

ICONOCLASM AND WARFARE

Mass urban destruction through bombing was not new to World War II. The first airborne bomb was dropped on Venice in 1849 from Austrian balloons, and in 1911 the Italians launched the first air assault on Tripoli.[5] Technological advances in weaponry, notably the machine gun, tank, and aeroplane, reflected wider industrial developments within a growing urban population – a shift which led to an increase in the capabilities of mass destruction, culminating in the events of World War I.[6] This increase in technological capability was already evident in the power of the machine gun over armies like the Mahdist forces in Sudan, who during the Battle of Omdurman lost eleven thousand fighters compared to forty-seven on the British side.[7] Heavy artillery had always been used against urban targets, but during the nineteenth century more advanced guns enabled better penetration and damage against large swathes of cities. Likewise, the ability to raze a cathedral through ariel bombardment from distance rather than the costly task of occupation and burning was made easier with more powerful, more accurate heavy guns. During both the Franco-Prussian War and World War I, churches and buildings and monuments of historical importance were targeted and destroyed by the German forces. In 1870, Strasbourg Cathedral was hit by Prussian artillery and in 1914 German shells destroyed much of Reims Cathedral. For many historians, these attacks on religious buildings using increasingly powerful weapons with increasingly devastating effect began to stretch the boundaries of 'conventional' military practice. Lambourne notes that such attacks between Germany and France increased at the same time – that is, from the late nineteenth to the early twentieth centuries – as the emergence of a popular notion of architectural heritage and preservation in the museums of Paris and Berlin, and the developing self-identity of new nation states like Italy and Germany.[8] In this way, the crisis of interwoven notions of destruction, preservation, and statehood during a time of industrialized war reflected the same iconoclastic dilemma that I have described in previous chapters: one army's idea of destruction was another's idea of salvation. Consequently, when the Prussians attacked Strasbourg Cathedral, the French painted their own military inferiority in the colours of cultural superiority, stating that they would never commit such an act of architectural destruction[9] – despite the fact that Baron Haussmann was, at the same time, engaged in the process of razing much of mediaeval Paris in order to build the boulevards.

This interpretation of what destruction 'meant' became part of the rhetoric of the State. For example, in the case of Reims, Lambourne notes that the German shelling of the cathedral during World War I was depicted by the French as an attack on the national and cultural significance of the building's historical connection to royal coronations and the political and religious identity of France. The reader will note that such a claim ignores the events of 1793, as I have described them in my chapter on the iconoclasm of the French Revolution, when relics of royal and religious importance like the 'Sainte Ampoule' were broken in the name of the new French Republic. It could be said that while the exterior of Reims Cathedral was destroyed by the Germans, its interior had already been destroyed by France. For the French State during World War I, however, such nuances were ignored in order to depict the German attack on the building as an assault, in the words of the artist Fraipont, on 'the soul of France'. Thus, writes Lambourne, 'if the physical damage to the fabric of the building was the work of German shells, the rich wartime meaning acquired by Reims Cathedral was a product of French propagandists'.[10]

This response of state propaganda to attacks on buildings of religious significance during war emphasized the boundaries of 'conventional' (that is, 'tolerable' or 'rational' as opposed to 'intolerable' or 'irrational') military practice. World War II saw an increase in both these attacks and their corresponding depiction in propaganda accusing the enemy of breaking the 'rules' of war. In the words of Calame, 'extreme scenarios throw core issues into sharp relief. Violent inter-ethnic conflicts frequently result in destruction of the iconic built environment because it is a place where emblematic and psychologically potent associations can be exploited directly for purposes of widespread psychological demoralization within the ranks of an enemy population'.[11] However, this notion of 'demoralization' was also used to defend the destruction of an enemy's 'iconic built environment' as a part of conventional combat. For example, Strachan argues that the destruction of Dresden was 'legitimate', despite the huge number of human and architectural losses. He states that 'this was of course the consequence of Ludendorff's definition of total or totalitarian war: if entire nations were to be mobilised for the purposes of the war, then the peoples were potential and even legitimate targets ... killing civilians was still a means to an end, not an end in itself. This was not genocide. It was about winning the war, not about racial cleansing'.[12]

This makes use of a *means-end* justification for violence, typical of much 'Just War' theory, which echoes Weber's ideas on rationalization, where the irrational act is that which confuses the means for the end. By citing Ludendorff, Strachen arrives at the limits of such a rationality, established in a theory of warfare which is traced back to von Clausewitz's statement that war 'is not the action of a living force upon a lifeless mass (total non-resistance would be no war at all) but always the collision of two living forces'.[13] As a 'living' mass, then (albeit an unarmed and 'non-resistant' one), the civilian population of a city like Dresden was able to be considered a combatant. However, the means-end justification for the killing of civilians does not take into account von Clausewitz's implied notion of the inanimate object – an object such as, for example, Dresden's destroyed cathedral. On this level, Sebald disputed the idea that the destruction of Germany's cities was part of a rational military practice, describing 'Bomber' Harris as being 'in perfect sympathy with the innermost principle of every war, which is to aim for as wholesale an annihilation of the enemy with his dwellings, his history and his natural environment as can possibly be achieved':[14]

> The war in the air was war pure and undisguised. Its continuation in the face of all reason suggests that, as Elaine Scarry has put it in her extremely perspicacious book *The Body in Pain*, the victims of war are not sacrifices made as the means to an end of any kind, but in the most precise sense are both the means and the end in themselves.[15]

In this way, the debate over whether the building of religious or cultural significance was a legitimate target or not – that is, whether its destruction was a means or an end of war – was of central importance to the issue of iconoclasm during World War II, where the widescale destruction of cities remains a controversial subject to this day. As Thomas Mann's Serenus Zeitblom observed while writing about the life of Doctor Faustus, 'true, by the destruction of our cities from the air, Germany has long since become a theatre of war; but it still remains for it to become so in the most actual sense, a sense that we cannot and may not conceive'.[16]

Much of the debate over the destruction of cities during World War II has referred to battles that took place between the British and German armies, two apparently 'conventional' opponents. The more complex issue of German attacks on Jewish and Slavic sites transformed the notion of a means-end rationality to urban destruction. Those historians who have rejected the claim that the iconoclasm of World War II remained within 'conventional' boundaries point to the difference between attacks that occurred between 'Western' European armies and German attacks against the 'East'. Lambourne states that 'the cultural destruction of the Second World War was not an innovation in itself; the novelty lay in its greatly increased extent and in the technology used to cause such damage ... Nazi treatment of cultural property in eastern and western Europe differed; in eastern Europe, the policy was simply to destroy ... in western Europe the attitude was more one of respect for the cultural history of those countries'.[17] Following the logic of a means-end rationality, Lambourne's claim that the violence of the 'Western' campaigns during World War II differed categorically from that which took place in the 'East' indicates that the Nazi attacks on British cities remained within 'conventional' limits, whereas their attacks on Warsaw, Minsk, and Stalingrad went beyond rational boundaries into the realm of ethnic cleansing and Holocaust. Indeed, this distinction is affirmed by Borin's description of the Nazi destruction of Poland's libraries, where 'the situation itself was not unusual in that all through history, books, libraries, and the ideals inherent therein were among the first things to be destroyed in times of war. The difference in Europe during World War II was that the destruction was highly organized and a central part of the overall plan of annihilation. Books became "not only weapons to wage war but also the enemy to be tagged for obliteration"'.[18]

This process of 'organized annihilation' was concentrated in the attacks on churches and cultural sites in Poland. In contested cities like Danzig-Gdańsk and Posen-Poznań, symbols of Polish identity were burnt and broken; in Warsaw and Krakow, 'Germanic' art and artifacts were 'secured' and sent to Germany, including the altar made by the Nuremberg artist Veit Stoss (Wit Stwosz) in the fifteenth century for a commission from Krakow's Church of St. Mary.[19] 'Germanization' (that is, appropriation of an object for the German State) also affected libraries as well as churches and art galleries. Sroka writes that 'the Jagiellonian Library was spared because the Nazis turned it into the *Staatsbibliothek* that would support a future German university in Krakow. Also, Krakow was made into an important center of Nazi political, educational, and cultural administration of the territories of *General-gouvernement* (General Government)', adding that 'unlike Warsaw, Krakow was not a scene of major military operations'.[20] This transformation through the total or partial destruction of a Polish library, church, art gallery, or castle, brought the broken city under the domination of the German *Staat* (State) and *Volk* (people), demonstrating a political organization to iconoclasm which can be located within a wider study of the Holocaust.

The Nazi attack on Warsaw represented a seminal example of iconoclasm during World War II, because the extent and organization of its near-total destruction (on both the human and architectural level) goes beyond much of the means-end debate over rationality that has been applied to other examples of urban devastation. Clearly, this is not to present an uncomplicated narrative of influence from Hitler's anti-Semitic rhetoric in *Mein Kampf* to the removal of the Veit Stoss altar – recent Holocaust historians urge caution against drawing too direct and causal a line between the original intentions and the final acts of individual Nazis in such a complex and shifting situation as the campaign in the East.[21] However, the scale of the destruction of Warsaw and the technical practicalities involved in achieving this destruction are widely considered to have represented an ordered and administrated attempt at obliteration, like the gassing of Polish Jews, which differs on the categorical level from many of the chaotic village massacres of the *Einsatzgruppen*. This is why I have chosen to highlight the destruction of Warsaw rather than other examples of murder during the *Generalplan Ost*, as the technical practicalities required to demolish eighty per cent of the city represented an extreme example of the kind of administrated iconoclasm that was used in the service of German state identity. For this reason, while recognizing the historical importance of Dresden, Coventry, and other ruined cities during World War II, it is to the example of Warsaw that I shall now turn.

THE DESTRUCTION OF WARSAW

The scale of the attack on Warsaw (according to most reports, over eighty per cent of the city was razed), combined with evidence that its destruction had been planned before the war, sets it apart from other examples of iconoclasm that took place during World War II. While acknowledging the argument that the British bombing of German cities exceeded the limits of conventional warfare, it is almost certainly not the case that the British had pre-ordained such destruction as agreements were signed in 1939 between Britain and Germany not to target civilian areas or sites of cultural and historical importance. Despite these agreements between 'Western' powers, however, Warsaw was bombed by German aircraft at the outset of the war, resulting in significant architectural damage and human loss. As such, the case of Warsaw cannot be considered as part of the debate over the retributive air-raids that evolved between the Luftwaffe and the Royal Air Force. Warsaw was bombed not as an act of retribution, or even 're-Germanization' (as was argued by German nationalists in the case of a city like Danzig), but because it was considered, within the wider context of *Lebensraum* and ethnic cleansing, to be an icon of Jewish and Slavic culture.

The destruction of Warsaw can be identified as taking place in three key stages: first, during the initial bombing raids of 1939 and subsequent occupation of the city; second, during the Jewish Ghetto Uprising of 1943, which saw both the destruction of the Muranów district and the mass deportation of the Jews; and third, following the Warsaw Uprising of the Polish population and Home Army in 1944. As this final Uprising was crushed, the city paid a heavy price: on the human level, several hundred thousand people were deported, many of whom were sent to labour and extermination camps; on the architectural and cultural level, teams of special troops known as *Verbrennungs und Vernichtungskommando* ('Burning and Destruction Detachments') attacked the physical fabric of the city with flame-throwers and tanks, adding to the damage already inflicted during the Uprising by German artillery and Stuka bombing raids. By early 1945, the churches and palaces of the Old Town had been destroyed, together with almost the entire network of ancient streets – a fulfillment of the claims made by both Poland's Nazi Governor-General, Hans Frank, that 'Warsaw will get what it deserves – complete annihilation'[22] and Hitler, that Warsaw must be 'pacified': 'that is, razed to the ground'.[23]

This wholesale destruction of the city was not an act of spontaneous retribution that followed the uprisings. Before the war, plans had been drawn up to transform the city from the Polish capital into a provincial German town – a 'New German City of Warsaw' (*Neue deutsche Stadt Warschau*) designed by Friedrich Pabst in collaboration with Hubert Gross and Otto Nurnberger. The designs for this New Town (typically referred to as the 'Plan Pabsta' or 'Pabst Plan') were, according to some reports, first seen by Hitler in Würzburg in 1939. They presupposed the destruction of the Polish city in order to facilitate the building of the German town (*Abbau der Polenstadt und der Aufbau der deutschen Stadt*) in a style which, according to Gross after the war, would 'emboss' the stamp or 'image' of the German city on Warsaw to shape the urban landscape for both 'party' and 'State'.[24] These plans for the *Abbau der Polenstadt*, or destruction of the Polish city, contained a list of Warsaw's buildings destined for demolition, achieving 'a new variant of the German Warsaw predicted to leave one twentieth of the previous area – from Ujazdów to the Old Town. This plan envisaged the elimination of all sites with the exception of Warsaw's Belvedere Palace and the Old Town'.[25] The list of targets included, among other sites: the Royal Castle, the collection of manuscripts from the National Library of Poland, the Brühl Palace, the Saxon Palace, the Kotowski Palace, the Ostrogki Palace, and the churches of St. Alexander, John, Mary, Kazimierz, Hyacinth, and Martin. Thus the eventual destruction of these buildings during the Uprising in 1944, rather than representing a spontaneous act of retribution against Polish partisans, followed a pre-war plan for Warsaw's 'reconstruction' according to a model of the German state and colonization within the *Generalplan Ost*. The Warsaw Uprising represented the catalyst, not the cause, of the city's pre-destined destruction. Consequently, Himmler's 1944 statement that 'the city must completely disappear from the surface of the earth and serve only as a transport station for the Wehrmacht. No stone can remain standing. Every building must be razed to its foundation'[26] reflected longstanding plans for a provincial *Neue deutsche Stadt Warschau*.

This use of the term *Neue Stadt* was intended to echo the 'New Towns' that were built in both Germany and Great Britain before and after the war. In Britain, the ideal of the 'Garden City' in places like Letchworth and Welwyn was redefined in the post-war context by the New Towns Act of 1946, creating places like Bracknell, Redditch, and Stevenage; in Germany, the ideal of pre-war industrial New Towns such as the Stadt des KdF-Wagens bei Fallersleben (now known as Wolfsburg) was reaffirmed in the post-war construction of settlements like Eisenhüttenstadt. In this way, the Pabst Plan for Warsaw was intended to represent the same architectural ideals – albeit with the involvement of large-scale human suffering – as other provincial German towns at the time, established around a network of ordered, clean streets set on either side of a river and served by an axis of roads and a developed railway system. This principle of urban planning, connecting territorial organization (*Raumplanung*) with repopulation, modernity, and community, was applied to the Nazi New Towns as the self-fashioned heirs of the Anglo-Saxon model of Ebenezer Howard's 1898 diagram depicting the 'Social City'.[27] However, the German model differed from its English counterpart in the sense that while the latter encouraged a decentralizing of communities in the suburbs, the former posited a 'decisive break with what was increasingly portrayed as the "Anglo-Saxon model of decentralization"'. This 'break' was promoted in the 1937 exhibition organized by the Germans to rival the International Congress of Housing and Town Planning at the Paris World Fair. The exhibition, entitled *Reichsausstellung Schaffendes Volk*, approached the issue of *Lebensraum* or 'living space' for Germans by arguing that Anglo-Saxon decentralization was only appropriate for colonial empires with 'a world of empty space. Since Germany was "a country without space", territorial order had to proceed on different lines ... compromised by *the need for a settlement pattern that allowed centralization based on Nazi party structure*'.[28]

In this context, the Pabst Plan for a New Town of Warsaw responded to wider problems of housing and state or territorial organization in Germany during the 1930s, when the average apartment (*Volkswohnung*) measured about thirty square metres and the Nazi Party were struggling to match the supply of new houses with the demands of an increasing urban population.[29] The housing crisis of Germany, while officially portrayed by the Nazis as being similar to other European countries such as Great Britain and France and therefore given the appearance of industrial and infrastructural normality, was ideologically connected to the philosophy of *Lebensraum*, the politics of centralization, and the culture of destruction. Grunberger notes that the extermination of German Jews and the creation of a *Judenrein* Germany served partly to free up housing supply;[30] accordingly, the destruction of entire urban districts and the construction of New Towns like the *Neue deutsche Stadt Warschau* was promoted as meeting an infrastructural rather than a racist-ideological demand. Yet behind this image of the Pabst Plan as a kind of German garden city was the reality of removing the Polish population of Warsaw and destroying the architectural fabric of Polish identity. As well as the obliteration of the city's churches and palaces, the human cost was significant: regular Poles were transported through the Durchgangslager in Pruszków and other transit sites, the inhabitants of the Konzentrationslager Warschau were evacuated to Dachau and Ravensbrück, and the Jews were ghettoized before being sent to Treblinka.[31]

A further observation to make concerning the destruction of Polish cities is the way in which religious buildings and artifacts were targeted and destroyed on days of particular religious significance. For example, Borin's account of the destruction of Poland's Jewish libraries by so-called '*Brenn-Kommandos*' notes that 'the destruction of Torah scrolls and other religious books was especially difficult for the religious Jewish community, since according to orthodox religious law, it is imperative that these materials be treated with the utmost respect and reverence, and those who destroy such sacred documents are considered in violation of a divine command'. Describing the edict that 'the *sefer torah*, or any sacred book or writing, or anything which has served a holy purpose, which has become worn out, must not be burned but secreted', Borin writes that 'some Jews attempted to save Torah scrolls and other materials from the burning buildings but were either shot or thrown into the flames. In such a way the Great Talmudic Library of the Jewish Theological Seminary in Lublin burned while Nazis cheered and Jews wept'.[32] This deliberate targeting of objects of particular symbolic or iconic significance to the Jews, such as the destruction of the Jewish library in Lublin or the Warsaw Great Synagogue in 1943, mirrored a Nazi predilection for initiating pogroms on holy days. As with the churches chosen to be the first targets of bombing raids, Jewish religious artifacts were targeted for their symbolic value. It is worth noting that this systematic destruction by Germans of Polish and Jewish objects of iconic significance in Warsaw in 1944 took place at the same time as British-led bombing campaigns were razing the cities, churches, and museums of Germany itself. It is difficult for the historian to resist reading a certain irony in this wave of devastation: while German soldiers were engaged in icon-breaking in the East, their sisters, mothers, and children were witnessing the destruction of their own icons back at home.

REBUILDING THE RUINED CITY

As I have described the iconoclasm of World War II in terms of urban design as much as urban destruction, it is necessary to touch on the subject of the rebuilding of Europe's ruined cities after the war. The methods of reconstruction differed depending on the military circumstances of the city involved, the extent of destruction, the political situation of the country after the conflict, and the available finances to rebuild. Lambourne illustrates these differences of post-war reconstruction through three examples (Stuttgart, destroyed by the British and Americans; London, destroyed by the Germans; and Rouen, destroyed by the Americans), using Baedeker travel guides published at the time to give an indication of how the rebuilt city was perceived by other Europeans. For Stuttgart, Lambourne notes, tourist guides focused on the 'untouched' suburbs and the surrounding countryside, ignoring the devastated Old Town in order to emphasize a new, progressive Germany. In the 1951 Baedeker guide to London, it was suggested that the bombing of the city had some beneficial consequences inasmuch as it cleared space around St. Paul's Cathedral and helped both locals and tourists gain a better view of Wren's design. However, for Rouen in the 1949 *Guide Bleu*, the description of the reconstruction of the Old Town focused on the interior of the cathedral as it was before being damaged by bombs, implying that France and French culture had not been profoundly affected by the war.[33]

Lambourne writes that these different depictions of reconstruction reflected the political agendas of each country. In the case of Germany, Sebald also notes that post-war postcards of Frankfurt am Main made the rebuilding look, as in Stuttgart, as though 'the image of total destruction was not the horrifying end of a collective aberration, but something more like the first stages of a brave new world', adding that 'the now legendary and in some respects genuinely admirable reconstruction of the country after the devastation wrought by Germany's wartime enemies, a reconstruction tantamount to a second liquidation in successive phases of the nation's own past history, prohibited any backward view'.[34] This suggestion of a 'second liquidation' of a nation's cultural heritage was made frequently in connection with Modernist designs for the rebuilding of cities, and echoes a tradition of post-conflict conservatism that can be traced back, as I have endeavoured to show in Chapter 3, to the reconstruction of damaged buildings following the revolutions of the eighteenth and nineteenth centuries.

Cologne in Ruins: Cologne Cathedral, Central Station, and the destroyed Hohenzollernbrücke over the River Rhine during B-24 VE 'Trolley Missions' (1945)

I have suggested that the destruction of Warsaw was widely recognized as being of a different order from most other European cities attacked during World War II. It corresponds, then, that the rebuilding of Warsaw differed in some ways from the culture of Modernist development that influenced the post-war designs of cities like Coventry, Le Havre, or Magdeburg. The sculptor of the monument to the

Part of the model prepared to the plans of Donald Gibson (Coventry City Architect) for the post-war rebuilding of Coventry's bomb-damaged city centre (1945)

Warsaw Uprising, Nathan Rapoport, expressed this belief by asking, 'could I have made a stone with a hole in it ... and said "*voilà*! The Greatness of the Jewish People?" No, I needed to show the heroism, to illustrate it literally in figures'. Rejecting the aesthetics of abstraction which defined much post-war design, he continued, 'this was to be a public monument after all. And what do human beings respond to? Faces, figures, the human form. I did not want to represent resistance in the abstract; it was not an abstract uprising. It was real'.[35] Rapoport's words emphasize the perception that the artistic and architectural rebuilding of Warsaw needed to respond to the unique order of its destruction rather than general post-war ideals of the modern community: that is, while the abstract forms of 'brave new' cities like Stuttgart embraced universalism instead of a reconstruction of the architectural particulars of the city, Warsaw was to find its 'image' and 'face' again. At the same time, popular opinion in Warsaw expressed a desire to rebuild the Old Town exactly as it had looked before the war. To achieve this, paintings of the city by eighteenth-century Italian artists like Bacciarelli and Bellotta were used with other architectural documents (including many hastily drafted images of buildings put on paper by resistants during the Uprising) in the reconstruction of the Old Town – a situation which led to the concern that Warsaw was being fixed somewhat artificially in the image of the eighteenth century.

The decision to reconstruct Warsaw's Old Town according to its 'original' design had practical and political as well as aesthetic and cultural reasons. On the practical level, the rebuilding was achieved using the same stones as the destroyed buildings, as it was logistically too difficult to clear old rubble out or transport new stone in. Even in the case of Muranów, the site of the totally obliterated Jewish district, the original stone was used to build a post-war housing estate based on a Modernist design. Elzanowski writes that 'the material that underlies the district of Muranów is the spoil from the razing of the Warsaw Ghetto that took place following the Ghetto Rising of 1943. The blocks of flats that today stand upon it were built of rubble recovered and pulverised after 1945', adding that 'even though there are no visible ruins in Muranów, the entire district is literally made of them'.[36] In addition to these practical concerns, the decision to rebuild the Old Town in its pre-war image also had a political element. Rebuilding with the original stone supported claims for the reconstructed town's 'authentic' character, and promoted the idea of an unbroken Polish cultural identity surviving in the face of total war. Calame claims that 'rarely does a central government subsidize projects on principle; more often, reconstruction is tied to discernible political priorities. The simplest of these would be the belief that certain historic sites are strongly associated with patriotism and the national identity; when these monuments are threatened in war their rehabilitation strengthens morale during periods of transition. Middelburg, Warsaw, Coventry, Kuwait, and Dubrovnik all fall fairly cleanly into this category.'[37] To borrow Clay's terms again, it is evident that ruins, like other broken objects, are transformed into signifiers for a range of wider issues, including that of a contested political identity. On this level, the act of reconstructing a city like Warsaw could be considered as making use of the same organized elements of state self-fashioning (including propaganda and promotion) as the act of destruction. Calame continues, 'propaganda is the instrument of this promotion, and recovery projects that have benefited from media attention are generally more successful than those that do not ... positive publicity for the heroic effort of Warsaw's planners insured support for the reconstruction and ongoing preferential treatment for the city as an icon of Polish resistance'.[38]

The reader will note that when the 'heroic' Poles were rebuilding their 'icon' of an Old Town in the image of its eighteenth-century 'original', Warsaw was under Soviet occupation. As such, the question of reconstruction became a matter of contention and compromise between different political identities. Calame claims that the rebuilding of the Old Town was permitted as a concession on the part of the Soviet authorities in exchange for the construction of large socialist housing estates in the suburbs which surrounded the city. He writes that 'function-oriented goals of urban renewal frequently competed with the public's desire for restitution of cherished scales, monuments, and details. Professionals in charge of recovery had to balance these disparate agendas. Warsaw planners struck a rather rigid bargain; permission to replicate the historic urban core was effectively traded for the simultaneous development of the outer industrial bands according to updated economic models which completely reconfigured the functional zones of the city with minimal concession to preexisting patterns'.[39] Tung concurs with this position, arguing that 'for Communists, the rebuilding of Warsaw would be a tool for propaganda, the creation of a model city of social justice. For non-Communists living under Communist rule, recreating the historic core would be an act of symbolic moral resistance'. He portrays this in terms of fusion and collaboration, stating that 'through a fusion of disparate motives, the new metropolis would be a symbol of national pride, a city of accumulated memory, and a city of dreams'.[40] In this context of concession and collaboration, then, the rebuilding of Warsaw's Old Town according to the eighteenth-century models of Bacciarelli and Bellotta was able to be portrayed by the Communists as a political act because 'the nineteenth-century city was viewed as representative of the oppressive class structure of capitalism'.[41] Thus the ruins of the nineteenth-century 'capitalist' city were removed, and their political significance was transformed: in the southern district of Marszałkowska Dzielnica Mieszkaniow, the rubble was used to build a model socialist housing estate, and in the northern Old Town the streets were meticulously reconstructed in their eighteenth-century image. Through these dual claims of 'modernity' *and* 'authenticity', the authorities could legitimize their power through history.

In this chapter, I have attempted to demonstrate that the iconoclasm of World War II was defined as much by the designs for *construction* of a city like Warsaw – both in its pre-war Nazi 'Pabst Plan' and in its post-war Soviet rebuilding – as its *destruction* by the Germans following the uprisings of 1943 and 1944. The issues of centralized administrative organization, architectural authenticity, and cultural legitimacy which influenced both the breaking and the remaking of the Old Town made the case of Warsaw a central historical example of what I have termed the 'politics of iconoclasm'. Following the near-obliteration of the city in an attempt to implement the designs of a provincial German 'New Town', this politics of iconoclasm was also expressed in the treatment of the ruins of the city as transformative signs of Polish identity. Elzanowski argues that the political concession of allowing a rebuilt Old Town to be surrounded by newly built suburban housing estates did not accommodate the presence of ruins, despite the fact that over eighty per cent of the city had been reduced to rubble. This treatment of the ruin differed from other European cities following the war, where the remnants of attacked buildings were often preserved and used as monuments to the national memory in places like Coventry (St. Michael's Cathedral) and Berlin (the Kaiser Wilhelm Memorial Church). Elzanowski describes the declaration of Zachwatowicz (one of the leaders of Warsaw's reconstruction plans in 1946) that the ruins of the city were not like other 'romantic' ruins in Europe: 'ruins that were created as a result of twentieth-century war technology contain nothing romantic. Dynamiting a building folds it in upon itself like a house of cards; such a ruin has no picturesque qualities. [Through reconstruction] will we not create fakes? … The question of falsification is a subtle one … our national pride obliges us to rebuild'. For decision-makers like Zachwatowicz, according to Elzanowski, the post-war choice facing Warsaw 'was either "total reconstruction" or "total demolition"' in the sense that 'the enterprise of rebuilding could be summed up as a battle to control the politically dangerous and psychologically oppressive ruin. Whether it was by eliminating, caging or reproducing, the ruin needed to be tamed'.[42] This act of 'taming' the ruin led to a transformation of its symbolism, to the extent that Warsaw, according to the 'Warsaw Charter' of 1981, had become a city 'destroyed not only by war, but later also by the meeting of a contemporary urban doctrine with a totalitarian sociopolitical one'[43] – a notion of 'double destruction' which echoes Sebald's description of the 'second liquidation' of German culture following the Modernist rebuilding of its bombed cities.

In this way, the case of Warsaw represents a key example of the politics of iconoclasm in the twentieth century, and has informed the post-war debate over universal heritage, preservation, and the reconstruction of damaged sites of cultural and religious significance. Zachwatowicz articulated the tension at the heart of this debate when he rejected the notion of 'reconstruction' for fear of inauthenticity, yet declared 'rebuilding' to be a national obligation. Indeed, this tension reflects the complex identity of Warsaw itself, where the city, like Rome, is built from layers of broken stone, and where certain buildings have been preserved or removed according to their political interpretation – namely, the layers of a mediaeval Catholic, eighteenth-century baroque, nineteenth-century capitalist, twentieth-century Nazi, reconstructed eighteenth-century baroque, twentieth-century Communist and, today, twenty-first-century capitalist city. These layers reflect a history of continual construction existing alongside continual destruction, where the few ruins which are left standing are 'hidden and unstudied, they decay behind the façades of socialist realist housing or peek out from behind modernist blocks. They linger in courtyards, caged and obscured from the gaze of the various phases of the socialist and now the capitalist city'.[44] For this reason, Zachwatowicz's notion of an 'authentic' Warsaw is a problematic one, and led to controversy when the city was proposed for UNESCO World Heritage Site status in the 1970s. UNESCO demand that candidates for this status must meet the test of 'physical authenticity, defined in terms of design, materials, workmanship and setting' as a condition for inclusion. Despite the fact that the Old Town had been entirely rebuilt, Warsaw's unique circumstances of destruction and reconstruction (and its symbolic importance as a symbol of anti-Nazi resistance) meant that 'for three years the Committee discussed whether a reconstructed site could be considered to possess authenticity. In the end, the Committee inscribed Warsaw on the World Heritage List as an exception, adding that no other reconstructed sites would be considered'.[45] As such, the issue of symbolism influenced that of authenticity and universal heritage – a qualitative decision which subsequently affected the debate over post-war cases of objects (such as Mostar's Stari Most and the Buddhas of the Bamiyan Valley in Afghanistan) which were destroyed, rebuilt in total or in part, and categorized as sites of universal heritage. It is to these examples of the 'post-Warsaw' world that I shall now turn, beginning with the case of iconoclasm during the Balkan conflicts of the 1990s.

CHAPTER 6
The Balkan Wars and Iconoclasm

> In a context where ethnic identity is defined by the religious choices made by one's ancestors, it is religious buildings – mosques, churches, monasteries – that serve as the most potent markers of a community's presence. Thus it is not surprising that the destruction of houses of worship became one of the hallmarks of 'ethnic cleansing' in Bosnia.
>
> András J. Riedlmayer, 'From the Ashes: the Past and Future of Bosnia's Cultural Heritage'[1]

In the previous chapter, I examined how the iconoclasm of World War II took place within a context of territorial conflict and ethnic cleansing, and was used for the promotion of a range of connecting and opposing national identities. For a majority of commentators, including political decision-makers such as Bill Clinton and Margaret Thatcher, the territorial and ethnic conflicts of the Balkan wars during the 1990s represented a continuation of Nazism in Europe.[2] While this direct association has been refuted by many in the Balkans (not least those Serb partisans who fought under Tito against German occupation during World War II), it is evident that the proliferation of Serb attacks on mosques in Bosnia between 1992 and 1995 and Kosovo in 1999, which saw religious sites deliberately targeted and destroyed in order to redefine new territorial boundaries, echoed the particular combination of iconoclasm and *Lebensraum* that characterized much of Nazi-controlled Central and Eastern Europe. In this chapter, I shall examine the nature of the iconoclasm which occurred during the Balkan wars, focusing on the relationship between a notion of 'Christoslavism' and the Serbian State, and drawing on the example of the destruction of mosques in what is today called the Republika Srpska. As with my account of the reconstruction projects which followed the destruction of Warsaw, I shall examine the controversies surrounding those Ottoman-era mosques which were attacked by Serb forces and subsequently rebuilt with the aid of money from Saudi charitable organizations that have been described by many as 'Wahhabi'. First, in order to give a context to these iconoclastic events, I shall begin with a brief outline of the relationship between religion and Balkan state identity.

RELIGION AND BALKAN STATE IDENTITY

The religious context of the Balkans in the late twentieth century was defined by a complex combination of local, post-Ottoman, and Soviet influences which operated within a political structure of forced state unification based around a predominantly Serb identity following an acrimonious division of loyalties during World War II. These conditions were the source of frequent conflicts over the unclear demarcation of borders, ethnic enclaves within self-declared states (for example, the Republic of Serbian Krajina within the Republic of Croatia), and the presence of religious buildings catering for a minority – notably mosques – in areas with a hostile majority population. To a certain extent, these tensions were contained within a wider 'Yugoslav' identity under Tito and within the context of the Cold War, but after the dissolution of the Communist League of Yugoslavia following its fourteenth congress in 1990, they were newly expressed in claims of territorial independence. Seven years later, Huntington described the 'complexity of the post-Cold War world' as involving the 'movement back to a future of traditional power politics, the proliferation of ethnic conflict verging on anarchy, the clash of civilizations, and conflicting trends toward integration and fragmentation'.[3] Similarly, Liotta and Simons have argued, in the Balkan context, that 'until 1990, American policymakers could comfortably avoid thinking deeply about entrenched cultural or civilizational differences. The Cold War's bipolarity lessened the need to probe local quirkiness when developing policy ... But with bipolarity displaced by new world disorder and with multiculturalism now at the centre of American domestic debate, foreign policy analysts and others have found themselves suddenly having to dust off concepts like "culture", geography, and "civilizations" to explain the appearance and reappearance of particularized conflict'.[4] This allusion to 'particularized conflict' referred specifically to the Balkans, a region for which Liotta and Simons defined the key post-Cold War 'concepts' as *kin* and *religion*. In this way, historians of the Balkan conflicts in the post-Cold War world have tended to mirror a school of thought in the Sociology of Religion which argues that with the collapse of fixed twentieth-century state blocs, the world has witnessed a 'return to religion' along local and increasingly violent ethnic lines.[5] In the case of the Balkans, Hajdarpašić states that 'since the 1990s, escalating tensions across Croatia, Bosnia, Serbia and Kosovo invariably combined images of "alien Turks", "Muslims", and "Ottomans" as synonymous categories that stood in contrast to the "Serb", "Croat", and other apparently "native" Christian Balkan nations',[6] adding that 'religious divisions form one of the defining features of the recent depictions of Ottoman legacy in the Balkans'.

As with the erroneous sociological notion of a 'return to religion' or 'desecularization' in the post-Cold War world (a notion which ignores in the first place the problematic historical and politicized theory of 'secularization' to define 'modernity')[7] it is inaccurate to claim that the religious dimension to the Balkan conflicts was somehow new to the 1990s. Instead, it reflected what Hajdarpašić has described as the 'conflation' of long-standing religious and ethnic identities, combined with an explosion of territorial assertiveness following the collapse of previously established national boundaries. Hajdarpašić follows Todorova's *Imagining the Balkans* in arguing that the perception of an Ottoman identity as 'synonymous with Islamic or Turkish (and to a lesser extent Arabic and Persian) influences' was the product of a nineteenth-century Christian-nationalist rhetoric which defined the Ottoman Empire as 'a religiously, socially, and institutionally alien imposition on autochthonous Christian medieval societies', where 'the central element of this interpretation is the belief in the incompatibility between Christianity and Islam, between the essentially nomadic civilization of the newcomers and the ... settled agrarian civilizations of the Balkans and the Middle East'. The reader will note that these terms, echoing established notions of settled legitimacy and nomadic illegitimacy within the emerging identity of the modern State, mirror my description in Chapter 2 of the Saudi distinction between the 'idolatrous' beliefs of nomads and the image-breaking of an increasingly settled (*hadar*) and centralized community in Riyadh. This issue of centralization is of critical importance to my account of the politics of iconoclasm. It informs the relationship between nationalism and religious violence which underpinned, according to Hajdarpašić, the 'nation-building projects that emerged in the nineteenth century' and which 'constructed the new Balkan states on the existing double boundary of language and religion', boundaries which culminated in the association of mosques with notions of 'Ottoman' oppression.[8]

In this way, the increase in territorialism and nationalism across Central and Eastern Europe following the end of the Cold War has typically been defined, in the case of the Balkans, through the prism of religion – a historical perception which is also partly explicable by the fact that Yugoslavia was never considered a fully 'Soviet' territory. However, some historians have urged caution against the drawing of too uncomplicated a line of influence between the religious identities of Balkan communities and the ethnic violence of the 1990s. Malcolm argues that such a narrative is a reductive way of understanding the pluralism of Bosnian society and the traditionally secular identity of Bosnian Muslims. He claims that 'for many rural Muslims and the vast majority of urban ones, being a Muslim was reduced to a set of cultural traditions', giving the examples of Muslim names, circumcision, the eating of baklava, the celebration of Ramazan Bajram, and 'a preference for tiny coffee cups without handles, a sympathy for spiders and various other traditional practices, the origins of which are frequently unknown to those who practice them'.[9] For Malcolm, the fact that Bosnia's first elections in 1990 were split along religious lines reflected little more than the demographic situation of the country: that is, votes corresponded to a population of forty-one per cent Muslim, thirty-five per cent Serb, and twenty per cent Croat, leading President Alija Izetbegović to form 'in effect a government of national unity, constructed out of a formal coalition between all three major parties, and the government posts were shared out between them'.[10] This claim is significant inasmuch as Izetbegović is considered by some analysts of the Bosnian war to have promoted partisan Islamist interests among the Muslim population in order to resist Serb oppression. Refuting this claim, Malcolm argues that it was the Serbs, not Izetbegović, who disrupted the unity government through Milošević's support (using federal forces) of ethnic Serb separatists in the Knin region of Croatia.[11] Thus Malcolm, like the majority of historians examining the religious and ethnic conflicts of the former Yugoslavia, identifies the Serbs (both in Bosnia and Serbia proper), not the Bosnian Muslims, as being the agents responsible for redefining a pluralist Balkan society along exaggerated ethnic and religious lines.

By diminishing the historical role of religious conflict in Bosnian culture, and by emphasizing Serbian territorial claims as the driving force behind the violence of Yugoslavia's fragmentation, Malcolm engages with a wider debate over culpability for the ethnic cleansing that took place during the Balkan wars of the 1990s. Clearly, the large majority of scholarly and media opinion points to the Serbs as the party responsible for initiating the ethnic cleansing, and, in the words of Ramet, 'have identified variously "Belgrade" or "the Serbian side" or "Milošević and his henchmen" as bearing primary responsibility for the war', to the extent that 'for most analysts, including Norman Cigar, Thomas Cushman and Stjepan G. Meštrović, Reneo Lukić and Allen Lynch, James Sadkovich, Michael Sells, and Laura Silber and Allan Little, there is no doubt concerning the incendiary role played by Milošević and his associates'.[12] This issue of culpability — that is, the controversies over whether the first shot of the war was fired by a Muslim at a Serb wedding party or whether the Slovenian constitutional amendments of 1989 made war inevitable — while not in itself strictly relevant to my study of iconoclasm, nevertheless provides the terms of 'a Serbian tradition of violence fostered by ecclesiastical elites and cultural artifacts' which inform an examination of the destruction of mosques and sites of religious significance during the Balkan conflicts. The conflation of political and religious identity represented by the concept of Serbian 'Christoslavism' presupposed the identification of Bosnian Muslims as foreign Turks. Faced with the consequences of this conflation, historians of the Balkan wars 'have no alternative', according to Hajdarpašić, 'but to accept the nationalist projects as "realistic" political forces that are the unstoppable makers of Balkan history', thus drawing on an idea of 'the two-centuries-old, delayed, and long-interrupted process of the formation of modern European nation-states out of the ruins of the Ottoman Empire'.[13] It is this association of State and ruin, religion and ethnicity, which provides the context for my study of Balkan iconoclasm.

The 'ruins' of the Ottoman Empire, for Hajdarpašić, were 'not only "ruins" in the largely figurative sense of the fragments of a decaying political structure' but also '"ruins" in a more literal and more unsettling sense, as in the scattered heaps of rubble left behind the burnt houses or deliberately targeted Ottoman-era bridges, mosques, churches, graveyards, and other sites across the Balkans'. In this way, the literal breaking of post-Cold War Yugoslavia along religious and ethnic lines involved 'the nationalist destruction of the Ottoman architectural heritage in Bosnia and Kosovo during the 1990s'[14] — a political use of iconoclasm during the ethnic conflicts which not only permitted attacks on sites of religious significance but was legitimized through them. Furthermore, destructive acts against Muslims and mosques were legitimized not only by the self-fashioned concept of the Serbian State but also by elements within the Orthodox Church. In 1992, the 'Tigers of Arkan' – Željko Ražnatović's paramilitary group infamous for its atrocities against civilians – were blessed by an Orthodox priest during the singing of a Serbian 'renaissance' hymn before going into 'battle' in the Bijeljina region of Eastern Slavonia.[15] It should be noted that any collaboration between the Serbian nationalism of Milošević and the Orthodox Church was not without its own internal conflicts; Perica states that while Milošević 'did not remain indifferent to the appeal of the captivating myth and awakened tradition', 'the issue of restitution of Church property remained unresolved, Serbian historic and holy lands remained "unredeemed", and Church-State relations continued to be tense and even worsened after the war'.[16] However, those unresolved tensions which did remain between Church and State were subsumed within the political and ceremonial use of the symbols of Orthodoxy, often with the complicity of its clerics, to furnish what Sells has labelled a dominating sense of 'Christoslavism' in Serbian society.[17] Within this context, the October 1987 issue of the Serbian Orthodox Church Patriarchate's semi-official journal *Pravoslavlje* announced that the 'prevailing perspective' of the Church was to advocate the partitioning of Yugoslavia into two 'civilizational blocks', stressing that 'the two incompatible worlds sharply differ from one another in religion, culture, historical development, ethics, psychology and mentality, and therefore previous conflicts that culminated with massacres of the World War II could repeat'[18] – that is, advocating a territorial and cultural partitioning expressed through 'religious symbols, mythologies, myths of origin (pure Serb race), symbol of passion (Lazar's death), and eschatological longings (the resurrection of Lazar)', which sought revenge against 'the Christ killer, the race traitor, the alien' and the '"fundamentalist" next door' and through which, according to Sells, 'the ideology operated not only in speeches and manifestos, but in specific rituals of atrocity'.[19]

Sells describes a blood-libel myth which existed in some Serb narratives and which accused the Muslims, not the Jews, of being the killers of Christ, using the device of the passion play to connect the political struggles of the twentieth century with the fourteenth-century martyrdom of the Serb prince Lazar in Kosovo: 'in the passion play commemorating the battle of 1389, Lazar is portrayed as a Christ figure with disciples (sometimes explicitly twelve), one of whom is a traitor. The Turks are Christ-killers, and the Judas figure, Vuk Branković, becomes the ancestral curse of all Slavic Muslims'.[20] This association of ethnic destiny with the execution of Christ drew on another religious aspect to national identity – the idea that the Serbs were historically victims of Turkish atrocities, not vice versa. Indeed, the notion of Serbian victimhood intensified during the Cold War context of Tito's rule: for example, in 1969, a delegation of bishops complained to Tito that Christian property in Kosovo was being vandalized by Muslims, and on Good Friday, 1982, a group of Orthodox priests and monks appealed against the 'Turkish' desire to exterminate the Serbs and 'crucify' the Serb nation.[21]

This is the context in which political identity and religious imagery – a combination which Sells has described as a 'fundamental iconography'[22] – became an integral part of the self-fashioned Serbian notion of statehood during both the Bosnian and Kosovan conflicts. As Lazar was born near Novo Brdo in what is today delimited as Kosovo, such an 'iconography' (a term which reflects the fact that Lazar is considered to be a saint in the Serbian Orthodox Church as well as a prince of the Serbian nation) was particularly contentious within the debate over Kosovan history. By June 1989, according to Sells, the narrative of this history had been 'completely nationalized and appropriated', culminating in Milošević's initiation of a ceremony held in honour of the Serbian-Kosovan martyrs, focussed on an Orthodox cross with the Cyrillic 'S' at each side to signify *samo sloga srbina spasava* ('only Unity Saves the Serbs'). Malcolm describes the influence of such an ethno-religious iconography on this ceremony, as well as the complicity of members of the Orthodox Church:

> On 28 June 1989 several hundred thousand Serbs assembled at the battlefield site of Gazimestan, outside the Kosovar capital, Priština, to celebrate the six-hundreth anniversary of the Battle of Kosovo. For many weeks a ferment of national feeling had been created inside Serbia; the bones of Prince Lazar, who died at the battle, had been taken on a tour of the country, becoming an object of pilgrimage wherever they were. In the courtyard of the monastery at Gračanica (South of Priština), while people queued to pay their devotions to the Prince's bones inside, stalls sold icon-style posters of Jesus Christ, Prince Lazar and Slobodan Milošević side by side. At the ceremony on the battlefield Milošević was accompanied by black-robed metro-

politans of the Orthodox Church, singers in traditional Serbian folk costumes, and members of the security police.[23]

This ceremony, taking place in the context of the collapse of Communism in Central and Eastern Europe and one year before the breaking apart of Yugoslavia, demonstrated the extent to which the imagery of the State and the icons of the Church were connected within a single and dominant Serbian identity. Such icons permeated every level of society, including the domestic – one year after the ceremony at Gazimestan, as the dissolution of the Communist League of Yugoslavia was taking effect, pictures of Prince Lazar alongside posters of Slobodan Milošević could be seen in private homes throughout Kosovo.[24] It is within this context of conflating religious and political iconologies that the iconoclasm which took place in the Balkans between 1992 and 1995 can be understood.

ICONOCLASM DURING THE BALKAN WARS

Riedlmayer estimates that during the Balkan wars, 'more than one thousand of Bosnia's mosques, hundreds of Catholic churches and scores of Orthodox churches, monasteries, private and public libraries, archives, and museums were shelled, burned, and dynamited, and in many cases even the ruins were removed by nationalist extremists in order to complete the cultural and religious "cleansing" of the land they had seized'.[25] He provides a table, based on data from the Institute for Protection of Cultural, Historical and Natural Heritage of Bosnia and Herzegovina, to illustrate the losses: between 1992 and 1995, over eighty per cent of congregational mosques, forty-six per cent of small neighbourhood mosques, forty-eight per cent of shrines and mausolea, and thirty per cent of buildings built through religious endowments were attacked. As well as the partial destruction and disfiguring of these sites, many of them were completely obliterated without residue (if we are to make use of Rambelli and Reinder's categories of iconoclasm), the structure of the buildings taken apart into pieces and their foundations rooted up, turned over, and replaced by wasteland, tarmac, and, in some cases, car parks and rubbish dumps. Such an attempt at total obliteration, comparable to Chapman's description of the clearing (rather than the slashing and burning) of woodland in Anglesey by Roman troops or the systematic levelling of some districts in Warsaw's Old Town, had a clear objective: 'by burning the documents, by razing houses of worship and bulldozing graveyards, the nationalists who overran and "cleansed" hundreds of towns and villages in Bosnia were trying to insure themselves against the possibility that the people they expelled and dispossessed might one day return to reclaim their homes and properties'. As with the case of Warsaw, then, the use of iconoclasm as a tool of ethnic cleansing during the Balkan wars, together with the extent of its obliteration, has been described by analysts as being different from what could be called the 'collateral damage' of some cultural monuments during a time of 'conventional' warfare.[26]

This *absolutism* of destruction, where the objective is to remove totally any residue of another culture in order to push forward a territorial claim, has influenced the debate over the correct terminology used to describe attacks on buildings of religious and cultural significance during the Balkan wars. Reflecting the term used to describe the destruction of a people – genocide – some scholars have used the label 'urbicide' to explain the destruction of cities and their urban fabric. Coward argues, like Riedlmayer, that attacks on mosques during the Bosnian war were not a case of collateral damage but rather an example of the deliberate and wholesale destruction of the urban environment, or urbicide.[27] Key to this concept of urbicide is the connection between the city and human heterogeneity; Coward notes that the 'density of the urban population is important insofar as it gives rise to a greater frequency of encounters between these heterogeneous traditions and beliefs' and, as such, 'the destruction of urban life is the destruction of heterogeneity'.[28] Under these terms, to destroy the city is to destroy the fabric of the heterogeneous 'public sphere' – an idea which I have discussed in the previous chapter in connection with the bombing of German cities during World War II. This notion of 'killing the urban' is central to a politics of iconoclasm where the city is typically the battleground. As with the case of Riyadh's domination over Hijaz, described in Chapter 2, both the destruction and reconstruction of the Bosnian city operated through the forces of *centralization*, forces through which iconoclasm served 'the creation of homogenous Serb areas which could eventually be joined to other Serb areas, including Serbia itself, to create a greater Serbian state'.[29] For the politics of iconoclasm, such homogeneity becomes the urban tool to achieve what I have described in Chapters 1 and 2 as a territorial, religious, and cultural desire for 'unity'. Both homogeneity and unity require the clearing of the heterogeneous public sphere (as I have understood it to be through my discussion of Habermas in Chapter 3): this clearing is most readily achieved through acts of violence against the architectural fabric of the city. Hence Coward's connection between urbicide and genocide, and the fact that in today's legal environment, attacks on items of cultural heritage are considered under the rubric of war crimes.[30]

A key example of this process was the destruction of the Ferhadija mosque in Banja Luka, a building considered by local Muslims to be 'the very soul of the city',[31] and which was attacked by Serb forces in May 1993. To understand the significance of the destruction of this building, it is necessary to outline the context to Banja Luka's contested identity. For the majority of historical opinion, Banja Luka was an Ottoman town. According to Kiel, mediaeval Bosnia was populated by a number of 'quasi-urban' communities structured under the supervision of Saxon miners, most of which having populations of around two hundred inhabitants. Only nine of these communities had either a church or a monastery, leading Kiel to describe the towns of mediaeval Bosnia as among the smallest and least developed in Europe.[32] As such, the development of some of these communities under the Ottomans during the sixteenth century represented the emergence of a Bosnian urbanism. This was the case for all of Bosnia's major cities, including Tuzla, Mostar, Sarajevo and Banja Luka. The latter is described by Kiel as an Ottoman 'creation' in 1552 which, with the building of a mosque, bridge, baths, and market, grew into a newer site in 1580, becoming the most important provincial city of the Ottoman Empire's northern territories. It was during this time of urban development that the Ferhadija mosque was built, named after the Turkish governor of the city, and considered the second most important Bosnian mosque after Sarajevo's Husref Bey. For this reason, the mosque is viewed by many historians to represent the transformation of Banja Luka under the Ottomans from a small mediaeval settlement into a site of cultural and commercial importance[33] – a narrative rejected by those Serb nationalists who considered Banja Luka to be part of a wider Serbian, not Bosnian-Muslim, realm of political and cultural influence.

The Ferhadija mosque was attacked by Bosnian Serb troops, paramilitaries, and nationalist volunteers on 6–7 May 1993, following the Orthodox feast of St. George. During the night, the streets surrounding the mosque were sealed off and their residents kept indoors, before munitions were used to destroy the building with a series of explosions. Some of the foundations of the mosque withstood this initial attack, in particular the base of the minaret, and the Muslim community of Banja Luka appealed to its Serb mayor to preserve these remains – a plea which was refused for the reason of Health and Safety. The events which then followed this initial attack could be categorized, if we are to make use of the terms of Rambelli and Reinders, as an example of the total obliteration of any residue of the building: in the words of Reidlmayer, 'using more explosives and pneumatic drills, the remaining fragments of the ancient stonework were broken up into gravel, which was trucked off to a secret dump site outside the city limits to prevent it from ever being used in rebuilding the mosque'.[34] Following this, 'the municipal authorities in Banja Luka not only removed the rubble of Ferhadija and the other demolished mosques, they also deleted the mosques from the city's master plan', so the sites where the mosques once stood were transformed into public parks, making any reconstruction unlikely. Despite this systematic attempt at obliteration, however, the Dayton Accord of 1995 ordered the Serb authorities to rebuild Ferhadija and the several other mosques of Banja Luka which had been damaged or destroyed during the war, and to enable the Muslim refugee population to return to the city. This was ignored, and when it became the task of the Bosnian Commission to Preserve National Monuments (one of the few governmental bodies that was granted jurisdiction in both the Federation of Bosnia Herzegovina and the Republika Srpska) to take charge of the plans for the reconstruction of Ferhadija, the situation became embroiled in legal and procedural debates between both the Serb and Muslim communities. In 1999, the Human Rights Chamber published a report on the destruction of the fifteen mosques of Banja Luka in 1993 and the 'refusal to date of permission to reconstruct any of the destroyed mosques' (Case no. CH/96/29, The Islamic Community in Bosnia and Herzegovina v. The Republika Srpska) announcing that, according to Article 9 of the European Convention for the Protection of Human Rights and Fundamental Freedoms, the city's Islamic community had the right to reclaim their religious sites from the municipal authorities and that, crucially, the local government did not have the right to give new construction permits for those sites.[35] The report noted:

> Nothing remains on the sites of Ferhadija, Arnaudija, Hisečka and Novoselija. The witness had seen cars driving over the site of the Ferhadija mosque. At Novoselija (Behram Efendija) a garage has been built and heavy vehicles parked there. Buses occasionally park on the site of the Hisečka mosque. In the course of irrigation works in 1998 a remaining wall of the Arnaudija mosque was pulled down together with a drinking-fountain and a gate. Some ruins remain on the sites of the Še-

her and Stupnica mosques. On the site of the Gazanferija mosque two small mausoleums still remain.[36]

Despite these legal challenges made against the Serb authorities in Banja Luka, reconstruction of the Ferhadija mosque remained mired in dispute and delay. In 1998, the Serb mayor called the mosque 'a monument of the cruel Turkish occupation',[37] and on 7 May 2001 (the anniversary of its destruction), Serb nationalists disrupted a ceremony arranged to mark its rebuilding. In the words of Hajdarpašić, 'a massive organized protest blocked this event; thousands of Serb demonstrators marched around the empty Ferhadija site, many pelting the delegation of Bosnian Muslims and international community officials with stones, burning the nearby buses and cars, and shouting "This is Serbia" and "Kill the Turks". Dozens were seriously hurt and one person died from injuries sustained during the stoning'. A video of these events has been posted on the internet and can be watched on a site like YouTube: Mustafa Cerić, the Grand Mufti of Bosnia Herzegovina, is seen laying a foundation stone before being disrupted by young men who place the Serbian flag on the side of a building, while a crowd starts shouting 'Serbia! Serbia!', leaving a delegation of international guests hiding behind a locked door to avoid the stones being thrown. It is worth noting, for the sake of understanding the iconoclastic environment of 2001 with a degree of chronological clarity, that these events took place only two months after the destruction of the Bamiyan Buddhas and four months before the destruction of the World Trade Center in New York.

Since 2001, the situation of the mosque and its planned reconstruction has changed considerably. In 2003, the authorities of Republika Srpska accepted the conditions of reconstruction following the nomination of the Ferhadija site as a national monument. A governmental report by Bosnia and Herzegovina's Commission to preserve National Monuments declared the following (I shall quote the report at length):

> The Government of Republika Srpska shall be responsible for ensuring and providing the legal, scientific, technical, administrative and financial measures necessary to protect, conserve, display and rehabilitate the National Monument of the Ferhad paša (Ferhadija) mosque and graveyard in Banja Luka.
> ... The building of the Ferhad paša – Ferhadija – mosque in Banja Luka shall be reconstructed on its original site, in its orig-

inal form as to proportions, volume and décor, with the identical horizontal and vertical dimensions, and the use of original or the same type of material and original building methods, on the basis of evidence preserved *in situ* or found elsewhere.

... All original fragments of the demolished building found on the site or on other sites to which they were removed after the demolition of the building must be assembled, registered, photographed and reintegrated into the reconstructed building.[38]

At the time of writing, this reconstruction is still ongoing; photographs from the internet which were taken in August 2011 show the rebuilt mosque nearing completion, surrounded by tarpaulin, scaffolding, and cranes. Many of the legal controversies surrounding the case of Ferhadija remain unresolved, in particular the matter of reparative money from the Serb authorities to Banja Luka's Muslim community. These legal issues are also accompanied by a cultural debate over the 'authenticity' of the rebuilt building. In terms which echo the questions asked over the authenticity of Warsaw's reconstructed Old Town and its legitimacy as a UNESCO World Heritage Site, the decision to use, by necessity, 'the same type of material' through 'original building methods' instead of the original stone itself has led to some criticism over the building's status as a 'National Monument of Bosnia'. On this level, as with the case of Warsaw's Old Town, the issue of symbolism has influenced that of authenticity and universal heritage, with the stated objective of the reconstruction being to achieve peace between the Serb and Muslim communities. According to a UNESCO report of 2010, the Commission's work to preserve national monuments seeks 'to promote a collective Bosnian cultural heritage. In this context of memory "competition", practices of patrimonialization (heritagization) show the expression of group memories whose aim is often to assert precedence at a specific site. The uses and misuses of the past reveal the tensions within the system of spatial and temporal markers of identity'.[39] Thus, through its breaking and remaking, the significance of Ferhadija has been transformed from a symbol of ethnic conflict and iconoclasm into an icon of the new Bosnian state. It remains to be seen how the finished building will meet the state's future symbolic intentions.

WAHHABISM AND THE RECONSTRUCTION OF OTTOMAN MOSQUES

Within this context of reconstruction and the debate over the visual limits of religious and political identity, it is necessary to describe, as a kind of *coda* to this chapter on Balkan iconoclasm, another controversy which has emerged since the end of the conflicts. This controversy involves a number of Ottoman-era mosques which had been destroyed by Serb forces in both Bosnia and Kosovo and which were subsequently rebuilt through money channeled via Saudi Arabian organizations, in addition to the building of new, Saudi-funded mosques and religious schools in Bosnian towns. The influence of these Saudi funds on local communities has been labelled by many commentators as 'Wahhabism', pointing to the removal of some decorative features and the white-washing of walls within the rebuilt mosques, the destruction of gravestones in cemeteries, and the increase among the Bosnian Muslim population of wearing beards and the Islamic veil – neither of which were particularly in evidence before the Balkan conflicts. In order to account for the complexities of this situation, as well as its relationship to the politics of iconoclasm, I shall end this chapter with a brief examination of the 'Wahhabi' influence during and following the Balkan wars. This, in turn, will introduce the key themes of my next chapter: namely, the influence of an international culture of iconoclasm on the political identity of certain Muslim countries today, and the relationship between this identity and the label of 'Wahhabism' according to the historical terms I have described in Chapter 2.

Following other scholars, I have described the ethnic and political identity of many Serbs during the 1980s and 1990s as being fashioned through a heightened sense of religious heritage and the promotion of 'Christoslavism'. Likewise, for some historians, texts such as Izetbegović's *The Islamic Declaration* (first published in 1970 and republished in 1990) reflected – and influenced – an intensification of religious identity within Bosnian Islamic culture. However, Malcolm urges caution against viewing *The Islamic Declaration* as unequivocal proof of an increasingly Islamist element to Muslim self-identity in Bosnia before the war. He argues that the book constitutes 'a general treatise on politics and Islam, addressed to the whole Muslim world; it is not about Bosnia and does not even mention Bosnia', and 'some of the arguments in this treatise which have been described as "fundamentalist" are simple statements of orthodox belief with which any sincere Muslim would agree'.[40] Furthermore, Sells notes that 'when Izetbegović became President of Bosnia in 1989, the vast majority of Bosnians had never read *The Islamic Declaration*'.[41] According to Malcolm's historical account, Bosnian Muslims continued to live during the 1980s within a tradition of pluralism, supporting his claim that when Izetbegović became President, he ruled over a multiethnic government which reflected the demographic situation of the country. Concurring with the majority of historical opinion, then, this account maintains that Bosnian pluralism was broken by the pressures of Serb nationalism and militarism, and it was with these pressures that it became increasingly replaced, or defended, by a wider and more forceful notion of Islam.

As with the debate over Serb culpability, such claims of a 'switch' in collective Bosnian Muslim self-identity are too dependent on intangibles and accusations to be readily verifiable; what is evidently the case, however, is that with the outbreak of ethnic hostilities, Izetbegović made the controversial decision to invite foreign fighters (in particular, Arab *mujahideen*) to support the Muslim community against attacks from Serb military and paramilitary forces. Huntington refers to this situation in *The Clash of Civilizations* as an Islamic call for 'significant assistance from its civilizational kin' which 'was particularly prevalent among Muslims'.[42] The reader will note from my description of the kind of Serbian Christoslavism promoted by ceremonies like that of Gazimestan that the conflation of ethnic and religious identity during a time of war was not unique to Islam. Nevertheless, it is clear that the large number of foreign *mujahideen* who came to Bosnia during the wars of the 1990s had an impact on the cultural and religious practices of the local Muslim community. Many videos of these fighters in combat, marching, and calling for *jihad* can be found on the internet through a search for 'Mudzahedini + Bosna' or 'Mujahideen + Bosna'. One example shows grainy footage of an interview with 'Abdul Ibrahim', a twenty-one year old Birmingham University medical student from Golders Green in London, who is filmed with an AK-47 raised in his hand and his head covered by a scarf, while stating to the interviewer that 'what we lack here [Bosnia] is Muslims who are prepared to suffer and sacrifice ... I watch the TV and tears roll down my face when I see the Muslims in Bosnia, Muslims in Palestine, Muslims in Kashmir, and then I come here and you feel a sense of satisfaction. You feel that you are fulfilling your duty, you feel that you are doing what the Prophet Muhammad (*s.a.a.w*) and his companions did fourteen hundred years ago ... this is a nice holiday for us, where you meet ... you meet some of the best people you ever met in your life, people from all over the world, people from

Brazil, from Japan, from China, from the Middle East, from America ...'.⁴³ A large number of such fighters, many of whom were accused of atrocities against captured Serb and Croat soldiers (leading to the indictment for war crimes of the Bosnian military commander, Rasim Delić) returned home once the war had finished, but some also stayed in Bosnia, joining local mosques, marrying local women, and becoming active within local Muslim communities.

Alongside this small but vocal change to the Muslim population of post-war Bosnia was the expensive dilemma of restoring or reconstructing those mosques which had been damaged or destroyed during the conflict. In Banja Luka and much of Republika Srpska, this responsibility fell to the Serb authorities, as I have described in the case of Ferhadija; however, for much of the Federation of Bosnia and Herzegovina and subsequently Kosovo, foreign organizations were invited to help fund the reconstruction projects. Riedlmayer writes that 'in general, international aid agencies and non-sectarian organizations concerned with heritage protection have tended to shy away from projects that involve religious structures, in the mistaken belief that the reconstruction of houses of worship is a "sensitive issue", which it is best to avoid or postpone for the sake of postwar reconciliation', noting that 'by keeping their distance from such projects, the secular organizations have also left the field open to sectarian sponsors, among them Islamic fundamentalist aid agencies from the Arab world that have their own radical agendas and have little interest either in the preservation of heritage or in the promotion of interreligious and intercommunal harmony in Bosnia'.⁴⁴ Such 'sectarian sponsors' were identified chiefly as Islamic relief agencies from Saudi Arabia, a group of charitable organizations which were responsible for the reconstruction of over a hundred mosques in Bosnia.

This combination of the influence of Arab *mujahideen* during the war and the Saudi funding of rebuilt mosques after the war led, perhaps inevitably, to the accusation that 'Wahhabism' was beginning to influence local Bosnian Islamic culture in the late 1990s. Numerous articles exist on the internet – without either peer reviewing, the corroboration of independent witnesses, or the formal channels of publication, they are often impossible to verify – which describe the 'Wahhabi' rebuilding of Ottoman mosques in the Balkans as representing a second wave of iconoclasm following their initial destruction by Serb forces, from Zulficar's article 'Alerte aux iconoclastes!' to Naegele's 'Saudi Wahhabi Aid Workers Bulldoze Balkan Monuments' and Schwartz's 'Islamic Fundamentalism in the Balkans'. In these articles, organizations like the 'Saudi Joint Relief Committee for Kosovo' are accused of rebuilding Balkan mosques according to a 'Wahhabi' style by whitewashing their walls and removing the vestiges of their original Ottoman decoration. Schwartz, a long-term opponent of Saudi Wahhabism, describes the story of the 'reconstruction' of the Imperial Mosque in Sarajevo, where Saudi workers 'turned what had been a beautiful, balanced complex of buildings, which seemed to invite entry, into something not much different from a parking garage in a Western city' and where the Bosnian authorities could do nothing to oppose this as 'they [the Saudis] have the money and they are going to do what they want'. He supports these claims with another story: 'in October 1999, the Bosnian weekly *Dani* published an extremely revealing interview with Kemal Zukic, director of the Center for Islamic Architecture in Sarajevo. The interviewer asked Zukic about the wall decorations in the Begova mosque ... He answered, "There were several layers of paintings, so that in the end we were in a quandary about which layer merited preservation ... The biggest contribution came from a Saudi donor ... Parts remain but most of the walls are now blank"'.[45]

In addition to the debate surrounding these reconstructed mosques, where the decision over which 'layer merited preservation' reflects UNESCO's description of 'memory competition' and 'heritagization', commentators like Bilefsky in *The New York Times* have also written about the controversy over a number of new constructions funded by Saudi Arabian organizations, including 'more than half a dozen new madrasas, or religious high schools, [which] have been built in recent years, while dozens of mosques have sprouted, including the King Fahd, a sprawling $28 million complex with a sports and cultural center'. Bilefsky draws a cultural conclusion from these developments, noting that 'before the war, fully covered women and men with long beards were almost unheard of. Today, they are common', and describes the influence of Saudi Arabia in terms of 'Wahhabism', providing a potted history: 'Muharem Bazdulj, deputy editor of the daily *Oslobodenje*, the voice of liberal, secular Bosnia, said he feared the growth of Wahhabism, the conservative Sunni movement originating in Saudi Arabia that aims to strip away foreign and corrupting influences. Analysts say Saudi-financed organizations have invested about $700 million in Bosnia since the war, often in mosques. Wahhabism arrived via hundreds of warriors from the Arab world during the war and with Arab humanitarian and charity workers since, though sociologists here stress that most Bosnian Muslims still believe that Islam has no place in public life'.[46] Such a generalized use of the term 'Wahhabism' is common in Bosnia today; for example, the October 2011 attack by the Serbian Muslim Mevlid Jašarević on the American Embassy in Sarajevo was described in the local media as an act of 'Wahhabism' – demonstrating that the label is now being used within popular discourse as a shorthand reference to pan-Islamist extremism rather than the specific historical conditions which I have presented in Chapter 2 of this book.

Conscious of the dangers of inaccuracy when describing local Islamic extremists as 'Wahhabis', some critiques are emerging of this post-war Bosnian narrative. On the cultural level, films like Jasmile Žbanić's 'Na Putu' ('On the Path') examine the complexities of the labels of religious and cultural identity in Bosnia today through the prism of Wahhabism. In relation to the rebuilding of mosques, while Donia acknowledges that 'Wahhabis have won control of several schools and mosques in a number of towns in Bosnia Herzegovina', he states that 'it is tempting to see new and rebuilt Middle Eastern style mosques as manifestations of Wahhabism, but Wahhabis have intruded into only a few such mosques, leaving the correlation between modern mosque architecture and Wahhabist influence subject

Graves at Hadum Mosque in Gjakova, Kosovo (2011)

to doubt'.[47] This is also the case for some reconstructed religious buildings; indeed, a visit today to some of those mosques rebuilt with Saudi funds demonstrates that the narrative of the Wahhabi destruction of Ottoman heritage is problematic. For example, Schwartz has claimed that the mosque in Gjakova in Kosovo had its graves destroyed by Saudi 'Wahhabis': 'at the end of July 2000, Saudis who had taken over the refurbishment of the Hadum mosque complex in Gjakova, dating from 1595 and devastated by the Serbs during the 1999 war, suddenly turned up in the old Ottoman cemetery inside the walls and began removing its centuries-old gravestones'.[48] However, the reader should not therefore assume that this event amounted to a total obliteration of the site comparable to Medina's Janat al-Baqi. A visit to the site in the autumn of 2011 finds a graveyard still full of headstones, albeit slightly overgrown with nettles and weeds.

In this way, it is clear that the mosque which was rebuilt by Saudi Arabian charitable organizations is as contested an iconoclastic object as the mosque which was destroyed by Serb soldiers: that is, it is a symbol of the claims and counter-claims of ethnicity, territory, religion, the relationship between local and international culture, the State, and the concepts of universal heritage and human rights. For examples like both Ferhadija and Gjakova, the lack of clarity over these contested claims creates a lacuna within which political self-fashioning takes shape. Central to these contested claims is the perceived influence of an international Wahhabism over the iconoclastic climate of the early twenty-first century. Thus my next, and final, chapter will examine this label of Wahhabism and its relationship to acts of image-breaking which have taken place over the last ten years.

CHAPTER 7
Islamic Iconoclasm Today

> The eventual transport of Western journalists to the site to record the void left by the Buddhas' destruction suggests that the intended audience for this *communiqué* was neither divine nor local but global: for all its recidivist rhetoric, this was a performance designed for the age of the Internet.
>
> Finbarr Barry Flood, 'Between Cult and Culture: Bamiyan, Islamic Iconoclasm, and the Museum'[1]

2011 marked the tenth anniversary of the destruction of the Bamiyan Buddhas in Afghanistan, an event which brought the issue of iconoclasm to the wider attention of both the public and the media. Two months after this event, the ceremony for the reconstruction of the Ferhadija mosque was disrupted by Serb nationalists; six months afterwards, the World Trade Center was hit by Boeing 767 jet airliners which had been hijacked by Islamic extremists, the majority of whom were Saudi Arabians; following George W. Bush's decision to invade Iraq in 2003, statues of Saddam Hussein were toppled in what was described by *The New Yorker* as an 'act of iconoclasm';[2] during the sectarian conflicts which followed the removal of Saddam, a number of important Shiite mosques and shrines were attacked by Sunni extremists, including the Imam Ali Mosque in Najaf by two car bombs in 2003, the al-Askari Mosque in Samarra by explosives in 2006 and by rockets or explosives in 2007, and the golden-domed Imam Abbas Mosque in Karbala by a car bomb in 2007; in 2005, the Danish newspaper *Jyllands-Posten* published a series of caricatures depicting 'The Face of Muhammad' (*'Muhammeds ansigt'*), leading to attacks against the Danish embassies of Iran, Lebanon, Pakistan, and Syria; these were followed by a series of cartoons of Muhammad in the French journal *Charlie Hebdo*; in 2007, suspected pro-Taliban militants attacked an ancient rock carving of a seated Buddha located near Janabad, Pakistan; in 2011, both before and after the fall of Hosni Mubarak, Coptic churches in Egypt were targeted by Islamic extremists, leading to sectarian conflict in that country; in 2004 construction began on the Abraj al-Bait complex of hotels and shopping malls in central Mecca, which in its completion in 2012 measured as the world's largest concrete structure containing the world's second-tallest tower, situated around two hundred metres from the Kaaba, and which involved the destruction of several existing buildings of historical significance; and, finally, the rise of ISIS in Iraq and Syria since 2013 has led to the destruction of numerous religious and cultural sites in those countries. The global scale of these examples has led some observers to describe the first years of the twenty-first century, following the attack on the Buddhas of Bamiyan, as a newly iconoclastic era.[3] Through the case studies in Part II of this book, however, I have attempted to demonstrate that this is not the case: these recent events of image-breaking, while seeming to represent a new phenomenon to many in the media, are part of a complex and long-standing tradition of iconoclasm in Christianity, Islam, and the emerging identity of the modern State.

In this chapter, I shall attempt to account for these recent events within their wider context, by comparing the destruction of the Bamiyan Buddhas to the construction of Abraj al-Bait through an analysis of the terms of international 'Wahhabism' as they have been outlined in the previous chapter. Such a comparison draws on the historical framework of the politics of iconoclasm – that is, the relationship between attacks on images, the construction of the visual domination of the State, and the emergence of self-fashioned, charged labels. My deconstruction of a 'Wahhabi' label which depends on the narrative of 'a long, culturally determined, and unchanging tradition of violent iconoclastic acts', acknowledges, in the words of Flood, that 'the conception of a monolithic and pathologically Muslim response to the image, which substitutes essential tropes for historical analysis, elides the distinction between different types of cultural practices'.[4] As such, a deconstructive critique of the 'Wahhabi' label enables a wider account of the iconoclastic environment today to be elicited from the specifics of a study of different types of 'Islamic' practice and, in turn, other types of 'Christian' and 'political' image-breaking such as those described by Flood as occurring during the Protestant Reformation and the French Revolution. Thus the following chapter, as with my previous case studies, accords with Flood's advice against depicting the present-day Muslim iconoclast as an abstract or ahistorical actor, because the comparison which I make between one iconoclastic event and another (specifically, between that of Bamiyan and Mecca) is achieved through a critique of the historicized label of Wahhabism.

THE BAMIYAN BUDDHAS

In March 2001, the two large standing Buddhas of the Bamiyan valley in Afghanistan were destroyed by the ruling Taliban regime. The exact details of this destruction were unclear at the time, leading to accusations between rival factions over who was responsible. Some reports claimed that local Shiite Hazara were forced by outside Sunni (also labelled as Deobandi and Wahhabi) Taliban to destroy the statues. Other reports claimed that the attacks were carried out by local Taliban fighters under orders from Mullah Omar; some argued that Omar himself was reluctantly following orders from Osama bin Laden. As such, within this web of claims and counter-claims, the destruction of the Buddhas reflected the complex levels of tribal, Islamic, Pashtun, and Arab identity that defined the conflict in Afghanistan. During an interview in a 2005 documentary by Christian Frei, one inhabitant of the network of caves next to the statues claimed that 'the Taliban initially attempted to hack away at the Buddha and the frescoes adorning the niches. And then ... they attacked the statues with tanks, grenades and anti-aircraft missiles ... the Taliban placed large quantities of mines, grenades and bombs at the feet and shoulders of the statues and ignited the whole lot. The torso of the giant figure, however, remained intact. Only after around twenty days of senseless attacks at the beginning of March 2001, were specialists flown in to blow up the two giant Buddhas professionally'.[5] Other reports echoed this claim that initially the Taliban coerced locals into abseiling from the cliffs and defacing the statues,[6] and when this strategy failed, they detonated the Buddhas themselves with high explosives in a series of spectacular attacks, captured on video and subsequently broadcast by Frei.

Intrinsic to these differing claims over responsibility for the attack was a debate over whether it constituted an act of religious or political violence. On the religious level, Flood argues that 'the opposition to figuration in Islam is based not on Quranic scripture but on various Traditions of the Prophet, the Hadith',[7] and focuses on the issue of historically and locally contextualized acts of iconoclasm to refute the generalized idea that the Taliban destroyed the Buddhas because they were Muslims – as he notes, Muslims had lived alongside the Buddhas for centuries.[8] He depicts the act of destruction as something distinct, not symptomatic to Islam, and emphasizes the difference 'between *instrumental* iconoclasm, in which a particular action is executed in order to achieve a certain goal, and *expressive* iconoclasm, in which the desire to express one's beliefs or give vent to one's feelings is achieved by the act itself', where 'the use of decapitation and defacement by Muslim iconoclasts represents not expressive iconoclasm but a type of instrumental iconoclasm, for it permitted the licit survival of preexiting images'.[9]

While I have concurred with Flood that iconoclasm is not symptomatic to Islam, the reader will note that his claim that the opposition to figuration is not based on Quranic scripture differs from my own exegetical analysis of *tawhid* and *shirk* in Chapter 2 of this book. On this subject of the difference between scripture and its interpretations, Elias examines the relationship between the theology of iconoclasm in its scriptural context (in both the Qur'an and *The Book of Idols*) and its expression in local Islamic traditions, by comparing responses to the destruction of the Bamiyan Buddhas in Western (namely, English-language), Afghan (Pashtun), and Pakistani (Urdu) literature. Echoing Flood's claim that the destruction of the Buddhas was an 'aberration and not part of a universal Muslim attitude towards idols and images', Elias argues that 'there is no clear Islamic condemnation paralleling the Biblical ban of the second commandment'.[10] However, he deviates from Flood's description of the attack as an act of instrumental iconoclasm, writing that 'the Taliban's destruction of the Bamiyan Buddhas must be seen within the context of Muslim historical memory in which intolerance of idols can easily, if erroneously, be seen as woven into mores of proper Muslim behaviour'.[11] On this level, the difference between the international and local responses to the destruction of the Buddhas is of critical importance. Elias notes that descriptions of the attack in the majority of the Western media presented 'the Taliban's incomprehensible irrationality … out of keeping with the will of the Afghan people', where the Taliban were considered to be neither real Afghans nor real Muslims. However, he adds that 'significantly absent in the coverage of the events in Western-language publications is any indication that commentators had read the local press'.[12] Elias identifies a different account of the attack seen through the prism of localism; for example, when the events of early 2001 are considered according to the *Hijri* calendar and the context of the *Hajj*, it becomes clear that Western offers to 'save' the statues by transporting them away from Afghanistan and preserving them in a foreign museum were made during Eid al-Adha – a festival which commemorates, for many Muslims, Ibrahim's sacrifice and the opposition to idols. As such, Elias highlights the paradigmatic misunderstanding that occurred between the Taliban and international organizations like UNESCO during negotiations over the fate of the statues.[13] He provides an examination of the Pakistani press (noting that there was not an equivalent printed media in Afghanistan at the time) and, in doing so, uncovers an explicitly religious response to the debate over the Bamiyan Buddhas, including anger expressed at the destruction of the Babri mosque in 1992 and popular support for the actions of the Taliban's 'iconoclasm as a religious duty'. In this way, Elias concludes that 'the Taliban's public statements should be seen in the context of Pakistan's Urdu press, where they seem the least irrational'.[14]

In addition to this religious context, the attack on the Bamiyan Buddhas was also justified as a political retaliation to food shortages following the UN sanctions imposed on Afghanistan in 2000. The Taliban had been threatening to destroy the Buddhas for several months, following diplomatic negotiations between countries which considered them a legitimate regime and appealed to Islamic law to preserve the statues, and other countries which appealed to the idea of a universal cultural heritage. Asked about the destruction of the Buddhas during an interview with Charlie Rose on American television, the Taliban envoy Sayed Rahmatullah Hashemi responded by saying that Afghan children were dying while international scholars were discussing the state of the statues, adding 'if you are destroying our future with economic sanctions then you have no right to protect our heritage' – a stance he reiterated during an interview on America's National Public Radio.[15] On the Taliban's response to the sanctions, Elias writes that 'the very fact that money was offered to save the statues transformed them from artifacts into idols since they were now being venerated more than human lives, and this reverence necessitated their destruction'.[16] This notion of the 'transformation' of 'artifact into idol' echoes the debate over the relationship between cultural heritage, fetishization, and the politicization of the museum which I have described in Chapters 3 and 4. In the case of the Bamiyan Buddhas, Flood makes this relationship explicit:

> Mullah Omar made clear the perceived relationship between iconolatry and the museum. Faced with the threat to destroy the Buddhist icons, Western institutions offered to purchase the offending items, in effect legitimizing the practice of looting Afghan antiquities from which some had benefited in the preceding decades. In an attempt to save some artifacts, Philippe de Montebello, the director of the Metropolitan Musuem of Art in New York, pleaded with the Taliban, 'Let us remove them so that they are in the context of an art museum, where they are cultural objects, works of art and not cult images'. The response of Mullah Omar was telling, although its significance was missed at the time. The Mullah replied on Radio Sharia by posting the rhetorical question to the international Muslim community: 'Do you prefer to be a breaker of idols or a seller of idols?'.[17]

Under these terms, the object of local heritage is transformed, through the cultural colonialization or fetishization of the museum artifact, into an idol of the Western imagination: as Flood concludes, 'within this epistemological tradition, the origins of both the Bamiyan Buddhas and the museum as an institution lie in the same foundational stratum of classicism on which the universalizing values of the Enlightenment were constructed. It was precisely as a reaction to the hegemonic, economic, and political power of this Enlightenment tradition that the destruction of the Buddhas was undertaken'.[18]

On the social and political level, it is also important to note the effect of years of civil war on Afghanistan, during which it was possible to find large trucks being moved at the feet of the Buddhas and munitions being stored in the surrounding caves, threatening the structural integrity of the statues. In this environment of disorder and poverty, the late 1990s also saw a spate of theft and looting; indeed, the main museum at Kabul, having already been damaged during the civil war, had its pre-Islamic artifacts destroyed by the Taliban at the same time as the attacks at Bamiyan took place. Clearly, when analysing such events, it is futile to attempt to distinguish the 'religious' motive from the 'political' act. The attacks during the 2011 Arab Spring on the Egyptian Museum in Cairo have also demonstrated this problem of categorization: the uncertainty over whether they were carried out by thieves, protestors, opportunists, Muslim Brotherhood members, plain-clothed security forces, or a combination of all these factions shows that attempts to label such violence as *either* primarily Islamist *or* political risks misrepresenting a complex situation. As Elias notes, 'the Taliban's destruction of the Buddhas was neither part of a preconceived plan based on an uncompromising and anachronistic view of Islam, nor was it a petulant political reaction to their rejection and isolation by the world community'. Rather, a complex 'discursive process' shaped both the religious and the political dimensions to the Taliban's 'self-understanding'.[19] The evidence of Bamiyan shows that such moments of destruction are complex and hybrid acts that combine religious and political elements, as well as local (in this case, Hazara) and external (Taliban). Furthermore, within the religious and the political are other divisions: Shia and Sunni, Sunni and Deobandi, Deobandi and Wahhabi, Pashtun and Afghan, socialist and nationalist, ruling and ruled. The destruction of the Buddhas at Bamiyan serves as an extreme example of how such a network of conflict resists Western categorization and how Western observers must be cautious in their accounts of Islamic iconoclasm.

With caution, then, we can approach those connections between iconoclastic events which have been made in the post-Bamiyan environment of the so-called 'War on Terror', from attacks by ISIS on Shiite and Christian shrines in Iraq to the publication of caricatures of Muhammad in *Charlie Hebdo* and the assault on New York's World Trade Center, where predominantly Saudi *mujahideen* destroyed what *Der Spiegel* called 'the ultimate icon of capitalism', and what Habermas labelled, during an interview alongside Derrida, 'an icon in the household imagery of the American nation'.[20] These examples, despite crossing both geographical and cultural boundaries, can be considered in the post-Bamiyan world as comparable features of iconoclasm today. To examine such boundaries further, I shall now turn to another example: namely, the demolition of the eighteenth-century Ottoman Ajyad fortress in Mecca to make room for the construction of the Abraj al-Bait complex of hotels, shopping malls, and luxury apartments next to the Masjid al-Haram, 'the Sacred Mosque' – and, by extension, the label of Wahhabism which has been applied to this event.

ABRAJ AL-BAIT

The name Abraj al-Bait means 'The Towers of the House', referring to a cluster of skyscrapers that are situated about two hundred metres from the Kaaba (the 'House'). These have transformed the skyline of Mecca, the central tower reaching a height of six hundred metres, adorned with the world's largest clock face – a visual statement designed to establish 'Mecca Time' as an alternative to the Greenwich Meridian.[21] Over the past decade, pilgrims performing the *Hajj* have worshipped under large cranes dwarfing the minarets of the Masjid al-Haram. Today's finished construction, financed by the King Abdul Aziz Endowment, contains luxury hotels and studios for these pilgrims, shopping malls and restaurants including Western brands such as Top-Shop, Starbucks Coffee, and Hardee's Charbroiled Burgers, a prayer area for several thousand people, a convention room, a four-storey parking area for almost a thousand vehicles, and dozens of elevators which transport guests staying in the hotels of the Clock Tower directly to the mosque, enabling, in the words of the Fairmont Hotel's website, 'easy access' to prayer from 'the opulent and elegant comfort of the rooms', the more expensive of which overlook the Kaaba itself.[22]

For many Muslims, the construction of this 'beacon for pilgrims'[23] is a source of pride for the *ummah*, bringing Mecca into the twenty-first century and providing a spectacular frame for the Kaaba as the epicentre of a new world designed to shift the concept of time and space from the colonial and Christian legacy of Greenwich to the Islamic context of the Masjid al-Haram. For the inhabitants of the city, Abraj al-Bait is portrayed as evidence of Mecca's economic strength during a time of global financial crisis; in the words of the city's mayor, Osama al-Bar, the price of real estate in Mecca continues to increase, to the extent that the monetary value of its land per square metre is among the highest in the world. A monorail system has been designed to transport the city's ten million visitors a year from outlying sites of pilgrimage such as Arafat, Mina, and Muzdalifah to the Masjid al-Haram, which will also connect with a proposed high-speed rail service running from Mecca to Medina.[24] These plans, ostensibly designed to facilitate and rationalize the movement of pilgrims during the *Hajj*, are part of what is described by the authorities as a wider 'vision' of King Abdullah bin Abdul Aziz for the infrastructural and social future of Saudi Arabia, where the construction of Abraj al-Bait is mirrored by similar developments such as the Rawabi Rumah project in Riyadh and the 'King Abdullah Economic City' of a 'Jeddah Gate' to the country. In the words of the chairman of one of the key

Abraj al-Bait, with the Kaaba in foreground, Mecca (2011)

construction companies involved in these developments, Emaar Properties, 'We are thankful to The Custodian of the Two Holy Mosques King Abdullah bin Abdul Aziz Al Saud, His Royal Highness Crown Prince Sultan bin Abdul Aziz Al Saud and His Royal Highness Prince Meshal Bin Abdul Aziz Al Saud for their trust in Emaar. It is our honour to partner in the growth of Saudi Arabia through projects such as King Abdullah Economic City, Jeddah Gate and Al Khobar Lakes, and serviced residences at Abraj Al Bait in the Holy City of Makkah'[25] – a statement which, as well as demonstrating the geographical reach of these developments from Jeddah in the west to al-Khobar in the East, also encompasses a range of culturally and historically diverse identities, from Hijaz to the Eastern Province, within the centralizing orbit of a Saudi Riyadh.

The proximity of a skyscraper to the Kaaba which includes a shopping mall containing Western food chains and clothing brands and depends financially on a Saudi endowment that affects all pilgrims has caused controversy within the international Muslim community. According to Ali al-Ahmed, the director of the opposition Institute for Gulf Affairs in Washington, 'Mecca is becoming like Las Vegas, and that is a disaster', adding that 'it will have a disastrous effect on Muslims because going to Mecca will have no feeling. There is no charm anymore. All you see is glass and cement'.[26] On the architectural level, the construction of Abraj al-Bait involved the demolition of the eighteenth-century Ottoman al-Ajyad fortress, an event which prompted Istemihan Talay, Turkey's Culture Minister, to appeal to UNESCO over a 'cultural massacre' where, he claimed, 'the destruction of the al-Ajyad fort, part of the common cultural heritage of humanity, is an act equivalent to the destruction of the Bamiyan Buddha statues in Afghanistan'.[27] The Speaker of the Turkish Parliament, Murat Sokmenoglu, echoed these sentiments by describing the demolition of the fortress as an example of 'a Muslim country's destruction of another Muslim country's historic heritage'. This comparison of the construction of Abraj al-Bait to the destruction of the Bamiyan Buddhas, in the context of both the Saudi King Abdul Aziz Endowment and the Saudi origins of bin Laden before his affiliation with the Taliban, informs the debate over contemporary Islamic 'iconoclasm' on both the religious and political level. In response to the petitions of Turkey, the Saudi Minister of Islamic Affairs, Saleh bin Abdul Aziz al Ash-Shaikh (it should be noted that the Saudi name 'al Ash-Shaikh' refers to the descendants of Muhammad ibn Abd al-Wahhab and is typically associated with religious authority), stated that 'no-one has the right to interfere in what comes under the state's authority',[28] emphasizing the political influence of the Saudi 'custody' over the heritage of Mecca and Medina. Religiously, this influence is claimed to be, in the words of al Ash-Shaikh, 'in the interest of Muslims all over the world'. Such a combination of enforced state authority with international religious impact has angered many Muslims, who increasingly refer to the construction of Abraj al-Bait as an example of 'Wahhabi' iconoclasm in Saudi Arabia today, accompanying other cases which include the destruction of the tomb of the mother of

Muhammad, Aminah bint Wahb, the house of the first Caliph, Abu Bakr, and the house of Muhammad's wife, Khadijah, the latter of which was reportedly replaced by a public toilet.[29]

In this way, an examination of internet sources exposes the extent to which a range of Muslim voices are expressing anger over the 'Wahhabi' destruction of sites of religious and cultural significance within the context of the construction of Abraj al-Bait. However, this use of the label 'Wahhabi', typically intended to be a term of insult similar to its present-day Balkan equivalent (as described in the previous chapter), depends on often unverified accusations and, as such, does not operate within the historical framework of the concept of *tawhid* which I have described in Chapter 2 of this book. Instead of establishing a notion of contemporary Wahhabism around such accusations, then, a more accurate method of assessing the relationship between the prohibition of the worship of shrines, tombs, and images and the social organization of Saudi Arabia, as well as its influence over the wider international Muslim community performing the *Hajj* in Mecca, would be to consider how both the religious and political dimensions of iconoclasm are combined in legal pronouncements issued today through so-called 'Wahhabi' *fatwas*. Describing such *fatwas* as 'mechanisms by which modern Saudi state muftis cope with clashes between Wahhabi idealism and the reality of an evolving society',[30] al-Atawneh argues that they enable a 'mutually-beneficial partnership between the muftis and the government' to make practical decisions in response to the dilemmas of 'modernity' – for example, the *fatwa* which permitted American troops to be based on Saudi Arabian soil during the first Gulf War.[31] On the subject of iconoclasm, al-Atawneh provides a list of translated *fatwas* which respond to questions about worship, ceremonies, images, and associationism. I shall quote some of them at length, because they encapsulate wider issues concerning both image-breaking and the control of local Saudi and international Islamic practice:

Fatwa No. 11104: Coming of Age Celebrations

Query
In South Africa, we celebrate the coming of age at 21 for males and females; we recite verses of the Qur'an, cook various foods and give the young men and women a key. What is the Islamic ruling on this matter?

Response
What you have described regarding this celebration and the recitation of the Qur'an upon the coming of age at 21 has no basis in *Sharia*, rather, it is a forbidden innovation and an imitation of the Christians in your country ... The Prophet [said] 'whoever shall imitate a particular nation/people will be considered as part of them'.

Fatwa No. 6166 (Query 4): Placing Flowers on the Grave of the Unknown Soldier

Query
Is placing a wreath of flowers on the grave of the Unknown Soldier like the actions of people who glorify their saints to the extent that they worship them?

Response
This act is a forbidden innovation and excessive glorification of the dead, resembling the actions of those who over-glorify their saints. It is liable to lead to the building of domes over these graves ...

Fatwa No. 2036: Creating Likenesses

Query
What is the ruling regarding the creation of likenesses in Islam?

Response
Basically, the depiction of any being or creature that possesses a soul is prohibited, whether it is sculpted, drawn on paper, cloth, a wall, etc. ... Such an act competes with Allah, the Creator. Additionally, such likenesses are liable to be seductive, including pictures of: actresses, naked women, so-called beauty queens, and others.[32]

On the religious level, these *fatwas* respond to a changing Saudi society and international *ummah* with guidance designed to promote constancy and unity. Politically, they represent a process of centralization where the legal sphere is not independent of the State: in the words of al-Atawneh, 'in modern-day Saudi Arabia, the muftis have undergone a long process of centralization that reached its zenith in 1971, when an unprecedented number of senior muftis were co-opted by the new state *ifta* agencies', and where 'these official, senior muftis are subordinate to the direct authority of the King, who is entitled to appoint as well as to dismiss them according to his will'. In this way, the State has 'influence in several spheres simultaneously, primarily in legal, ethico-social and religious affairs by issuing relevant *fatwas*',[33] where the implementation of *Sharia* becomes an expression of political control. Socially, this process of centralization or state control reflects al-Rasheed's claim that both the Saudi leadership and the Wahhabi *mutawwaa* have historically represented the interests of Najdi settled or *hadar* communities within what al-Azmeh has described as the 'vortex' pulling towards Riyadh at the expense of provincial, local, and nomadic communities. In the words of al-Dakhil, the nomadic identity is deemed 'contradictory' to *Sharia*, and 'after the restoration of *tawhid* and the realization of a central state', Wahhabism became defined as a 'powerful, political urban movement in the state-formation process',[34] where religious dialogue (that is, in its legal articulation, the *fatwa*) combined with processes of social control or 'statehood'.[35] Under these terms, then, the construction of Abraj al-Bait can be considered an act of state centralization over the 'innovations', 'seductions', idolatry, and local practices of the provinces – in other words, an example of the politics of iconoclasm.

These points of connection, while unpalatable to many Saudis, provide the terms with which to analyse the processes of centralization and construction implicit in King Abdul Aziz's 'vision' for Saudi Arabia today and, by extension, the control of the international *Hajj* and the destruction of pilgrimage sites, shrines, tombs, and images. Indeed, it is the international impact of Saudi centralization which leads many observers to consider the label 'Wahhabism' to be an appropriate way of describing acts of iconoclasm which extend beyond geographical and cultural boundaries. Clearly, a scholarly account of iconoclasm today must seek to avoid the accusations and rumour which feed on internet forums in many tales of destruction in Saudi Arabia, Afghanistan, and the Balkans. As Knysh states in his study of the Soviet war in Afghanistan and the role of Saudi *mujahideen*, the label 'Wahhabism' should be avoided as 'a rhetoric of fear' through which academics and journalists hold a 'firm belief in the unproblematic heuristic value and self-sufficiency of the categories in question', regardless of whether 'we are dealing with a "real" organized movement, a catch-all name for Islamic political activism, or a bugbear of the philistine imagination shocked by acts of "Islamic" terror'.[36] From the media reports of Mevlid Jašarević's attack on the American Embassy in Sarajevo to unverified stories of image-breaking in Mecca and descriptions on internet forums of 'Wahhabi' and 'Taliban' soldiers arresting visitors to Jabal al-Lawz, a place considered by some evangelical Christians to be the Mountain of Moses, it is evident that the generalized label of 'Wahhabism' within popular discourse has resulted, in the words of Sardar, in the reduction of Islam today to a set of signs and symbols which have more to do with the Western imagination than theological accuracy.[37]

Beyond the rhetoric of fear and reduction, however, these widely held terms of contemporary 'Wahhabism' provide the historian of iconoclasm with an account of an international discourse of image-breaking which has exceeded, since the destruction of the Bamiyan Buddhas, the boundaries of nation, culture, and local community – a discourse which connects the role of Saudi funding organizations and *mujahideen* in Bosnia to Saudi *mujahideen* in Afghanistan, the destruction of the World Trade Center, the construction of Abraj al-Bait, and the attack on the Bamiyan Buddhas, which, in the words of Elias, 'recast the traditionally isolationist Taliban as part of an international Muslim movement'.[38] Thus, while on the local level the construction of Abraj al-Bait involves a political vision for Saudi Arabia and the centralization of its provinces, the construction of skyscrapers around the Kaaba also represents on an international level the domination of this vision over the *ummah*, provoking a wider debate concerning the global and the local, the constructed and the destroyed, the religious and the political, that literally faces many Muslims making their pilgrimage today. In this way, the historian of Islamic iconoclasm cannot ignore the popular discourse which is redefining the problematic label of 'Wahhabism' for the digital age.

Conclusion

> That powerful tendency toward uniformity of life, which today so immensely aids the capitalist interest in the standardization of production, had its ideal foundations in the repudiation of all idolatry of the flesh.
>
> Max Weber, *The Protestant Ethic and the Spirit of Capitalism*[1]

In Part I of this book, I identified a set of terms embedded within two historical prototypes – Calvinism and Wahhabism – and, in Part II, I considered the development of these terms through a series of case studies: from Revolutionary Paris to Bourgeois Venice, totalitarian Europe, the Balkan conflicts, and the changes facing Muslim pilgrims to Mecca today. With these terms, I have attempted to account for the relationship between religion, violence, and the culture of image-breaking in Christianity and Islam by suggesting a connection between the destruction of icons and the construction of the modern State. This relationship, which I have entitled 'The Politics of Iconoclasm', can be observed in a network of comparable acts across a range of cultural and geographical boundaries, and defines the influence of a perceived legacy of the Protestant Reformation and the French Revolution on examples of image-breaking in Christian and Islamic communities in both Europe and the Middle East.

Increasingly, this network is being debated by journalists today who seek historical answers to their questions on the links between religious violence and political or civil society. Since the attack on the World Trade Center in 2001, much has been written in the media suggesting points of comparison that can be made between different and dramatic iconoclastic events, including the destruction of the Bamiyan Buddhas in 2001, the caricatures of Muhammad published in *Jyllands-Posten* and *Charlie Hebdo*, the construction of the Abraj al-Bait complex of hotels and shopping malls next to the Kaaba between 2004 and 2012, the pulling down of the gold-coloured sculpture of a fist crushing an American fighter jet in Muammar Gaddafi's Bab al-Aziziyah compound during the Libyan civil war of 2011, the desecration in 2012 of shrines in Timbuktu, and the recent destruction of sites throughout Syria and Iraq by ISIS. In this book, through the terms of my prototypes and their development in my case studies, I have attempted to provide the historical and theoretical context with which such comparisons might, with the appropriate degree of caution, be made.

How does the theoretical context of a politics of iconoclasm outlined in this book inform the present-day debate over religion, violence, and the culture of image-breaking? First, following the work of scholars like Clay, Calame, and Charlesworth, it refutes a depiction of image-breaking which is associated with Réau's notion of the spontaneous violence of a vandalistic mob, and instead considers iconoclasm according to the organizational structure of the State. As Calame and Charlesworth note, 'much has been written about "wanton" destruction of historic fabric in wartime' through 'indictments' which 'patronize with familiar platitudes: senseless losses, ignorant perpetrators, universal values, and so forth'. Rejecting these terms of senselessness and ignorance, they seek the 'larger political program' within which image-breaking operates: 'whether the iconoclast's target is the Rokeby Venus, the Buddhas of Bamiyan, or the Manhattan skyline, the same dynamics of vulnerability, resentment, and antagonism apply and may be used to both contextualize the violence and rationalize the motives lying behind it ... In the case of cities subjected to wholesale attack, the purposeful destruction of historic structures is commonly part of a larger political program asserting competitive, and historically subordinated, values and priorities'.

In this book, I have attempted to provide such a 'contextualization' through the comparative examination of certain examples within Christianity and Islam. Central to the difference between senseless mob violence and a controlled political program is the distinction which I have made between the iconoclastic rhetoric of a charismatic individual (for example, John Calvin, Muhammad ibn Abd al-Wahhab, Filippo Tommaso Marinetti, or Hubert Gross, among others) and the acts of destruction perpetrated by groups of followers *interpreting* the rhetoric of iconoclasm, often without any living connection to the charismatic individual (for example, the 'Calvinists' in England, the 'Wahhabis' in Bosnia, or the *Brennkommandos* in Warsaw). It is this gap between theories of the 'True God', 'unity' or *tawhid*, and 'purity' within an iconoclastic rhetoric, and the acts of image-breaking committed in the name of these theories, which separates the political program from the senseless mob, enabling degrees of self-fashioning to take shape where the State appropriates the rhetoric of iconoclasm to achieve unity and purity on the territorial and social level.

I have argued that this appropriation or 'rationalization' of a religious and philosophical concept of unity (as I have described in my prototypes of Calvin and ibn Abd al-Wahhab) and its translation into a political expression of centralization according to the image of the State (as I have described in my case studies of Paris, Venice, Warsaw, Banja Luka, and Mecca) typically occurred during times of conflict, territorial expansion, and war. In this way, the machines which achieved the realization of icon-destruction were the machines which defined the rationalization of state-construction – in particular, the aeroplane, which was both the symbol of the Futurist aesthetic of speed and the tool for the destruction of a city like Dresden. The paradox inherent within such a symbol reflects, in the words of Fromm, 'the secret principle of a society in which the conquest of nature by the machine constitutes the very meaning of progress',[2] and where, 'with the increasing productivity and division of labour, the formation of a large surplus, and the building of states with hierarchies and elites, large-scale destructiveness and cruelty came into existence and grew as civilization and the role of power grew'.[3] This paradox of modernity, where violence and progress are seemingly inseparable within the mechanisms of the State, has represented a key question for much post-Marxian philosophy, and has been described as a 'dialectic of Enlightenment' within which, according to Adorno and Horkheimer, 'technology is the essence of this knowledge. It does not work by concepts and images, by the fortunate insight, but refers to method'[4] – a notion of *technicality* which is at the heart of the State's appropriation of image-breaking.

In addition to its expression through the machine, the politics of iconoclasm was also articulated through a lexicon of modernity which evolved, according to Skinner, during the post-Calvinist context of Reformation, Renaissance, and Revolution. New terms took shape during the sixteenth and seventeenth centuries – notably, those of the 'Modern', the 'State', 'Reason' (and, by extension, Foucault's notion of 'Madness', or *déraison*), the 'Secularized', and 'Iconoclasm', each of which gave philosophical and political legitimacy to those movements, the '–isms', acting in the name of certain charismatic individuals. In this way, the politics of iconoclasm refers to the organization of Calvin-

ism, Wahhab*ism*, or Futur*ism*, and does not depend on either a psychological account of mob violence or a theological account of Calvin or ibn Abd al-Wahhab. On this level, I have attempted in this book to provide a critique of the term 'Iconoclasm'; it should be noted, however, that this does not represent an especially new intellectual endeavour, as the deconstruction of other terms within the lexicon of modernity has featured as an important part of recent critical theory. On the 'Modern', for example, Latour has referred to the Hobbesian combination of science and society which created 'the double contradiction that is modern, the contradiction between the two constitutional guarantees of Nature and Society on the one hand, and between the practice of purification and the practice of mediation on the other'.[5] This critique of the absolutism, or tyranny, of a constitutional account of nature and reason is reflected, for Asad, in the domination of the 'Secular' through which 'it is not merely that the object of violence is different; it is that the secular myth uses the element of violence to connect an optimistic project of universal empowerment with a pessimistic account of human motivation'[6] – an *ontology* of violence, according to Milbank, which inhabits the gap (as I have called it) or the 'space in which there *can be* a "secular", or secular knowledge of the secular' and which Milbank states 'is just as fictional as all other human topographies'.[7]

These critiques of the lexicon of modernity reflect the paradox (what Latour has labelled the 'iconoclash' and Clay the 'semiotic turn') at the heart of the politics of iconoclasm, where the processes involved in the destruction of the sacred image or site are the same processes involved in the construction of a model of the State. As such, this book has referred not only to attacks which have taken place during a time of war, but also to urban planning during a time of peace. The city is the *locus* of iconoclasm: in addition to my case studies of Warsaw's reconstructed Old Town and Mecca's Abraj al-Bait, other examples of the politics of iconoclasm can be found in theoretical projects such as Le Corbusier's 1925 'Plan Voisin' to replace the historic Marais district of Paris with a grid of high-rise residential buildings situated around a central transport hub, and, on a more complex level, in realized projects such as Donald Gibson's plans for the rebuilding of Coventry after World War II.

Indeed, such examples provide the context from which future studies on the relationship between iconoclasm and urban design might proceed. The relationship between these plans for the construction of a city and the techniques involved in its destruction reflects the paradox of violence and progress which is inherent in the term 'Iconoclasm' and the wider lexicon of modernity. Thus Sebald's account of the Allied bombing campaigns on Germany describes 'the transformation of bomber crews into professionals', 'trained administrators of war in the air'[8] who decided that, 'once the material was manufactured, simply letting the aircraft and their valuable freight stand idle on the airfields of eastern England ran counter to any healthy economic interest', even if the German cities had surrendered[9] – a notion of the *supremacy* of technique which echoes Fromm's claim that the bombers were more 'concerned with the proper handling of their complicated machine'[10] than the urban destruction which those machines caused. This 'technicalization of destruction', in the words of Fromm, ensures that 'once this process has been fully established there is no limit to destructiveness because nobody destroys: one only serves the machine for programmed – hence, apparently rational – purposes',[11] a combination of destruction and technical progress which leads, according to Adorno and Horkheimer, to a kind of levelling or abstraction of the world around us.[12] The case of 'Little Boy' and Hiroshima is perhaps the most extreme example of this process.

Under these terms, then, my account of the politics of iconoclasm can be considered as part of a wider critique of the lexicon of modernity and its role within the construction of the State. As Latour argues, the narrative of modernity does not allow for the fact that 'society is neither that strong nor that weak; objects are neither that strong nor that weak';[13] instead, 'it is the modern Constitution which makes them strong and weak and translates nature and society into facts to be either upheld or broken within a discourse of either purity or hybridization'.[14]

Latour asks the question in *Pandora's Hope*: 'Why is it that associations of humans and non-humans always become, once clarified, rectified, and straightened out, something so utterly different: two opposing sides in a war between subjects and objects?'[15] In Part I of this book, I have attempted to give the historical and theological context to this 'war', where the politics of iconoclasm forces an opposition between the 'true' object, the 'authentic' object, the 'ruin', and the 'fake', and where, once this distinction has been made, objects and buildings are either preserved or pulled down. The cases which I have provided in Part II of this book, including the examples of Cluny, Venice, Warsaw, Banja Luka, and Mecca, each represent this process of opposition.

From these all-consuming narratives of 'purity' and 'authenticity', 'unity' and 'modernity', permission is given for some ruined objects to remain standing. It is through permission that their cultural value is determined. Thus cultural value becomes subject to political power, and the broken image becomes used for the purposes of propaganda: it is through this prism that the reader might consider the condition of ruined German-Lutheran churches in the Russian-controlled Kaliningrad Oblast, or the abandoned mosques which populate the empty villages of the Golan Heights, or the way in which the ruins of Nimrud became a weapon in the hands of ISIS.

In each of these cases, the broken image has been made subject to the permission and the power of the State – a process of self-fashioning through which the politics of iconoclasm claims the contested object as its own.

Notes

INTRODUCTION

1. Martin Amis, *Koba the Dread: Laughter and the Twenty Million* (London: Jonathan Cape, 2002), 58.
2. *Iconoclasm: Contested Objects, Contested Terms*, eds. Stacy Boldrick and Richard Clay (Aldershot: Ashgate, 2007).
3. Alain Besançon, *The Forbidden Image: an Intellectual History of Iconoclasm*, trans. Jane Marie Todd (Chicago: University of Chicago Press, 2000), 65.
4. Exodus 20: 3–5.
5. Exodus 32: 7–8.
6. Thomas Hobbes, *Leviathan* (New York: Norton, 1977), 90.
7. Besançon, *The Forbidden Image*, 69.
8. Qur'an 2: 92–93.
9. Qur'an 4: 153–155. The 'killing of the Prophets' refers to the execution of Isa (Jesus).
10. Qur'an 2: 163.
11. Ron Geaves, *Aspects of Islam* (London: Ashgate, 2005), 41.
12. Qur'an 2: 132, 2: 134, 2: 135.
13. Qur'an 2: 105.
14. Qur'an 3: 67.
15. Qur'an 2: 164–165.
16. Qur'an 53: 19–20, 23: 'Have you then considered al-Lat, and al-Uzza / and Manat, the other third? ... They are but names which you have named – you and your fathers – for which Allah has sent down no authority'.
17. Qur'an 5: 116.
18. Qur'an 9: 28.
19. For an account of the controversy surrounding this restoration, see Loren Partridge, *Michelangelo: The Last Judgement – A Glorious Restoration* (New York: Abrams, 2000).
20. John Paul II, 'Celebration of the Unveiling of the Restoration of Michelangelo's Frescoes in the Sistine Chapel', *Vatican Homilies*, 1994, http://tinyurl.com/john-paul-michelangelo

21 Augustine uses this term when debating the resurrection of the body in Book 22, Chapter 14 of *Concerning the City of God Against the Pagans*, trans. Henry Bettenson (London: Penguin, 1972), 1055.
22 John 14: 8–10.
23 Genesis 1: 24–27: 'God created man in his own image', and Genesis 5: 1: 'God created man, in the likeness of God he made him'.
24 John Paul II, 'Letter to Artists', *Vatican Letters*, 1999, http://tinyurl.com/john-paul-artists
25 J.H. Lupton, *St. John of Damascus* (London: Society for Promoting Christian Knowledge, 1882), 51–52. The orthodox tradition has maintained a distinction since the early Church between the dramatization of worship and idolatry. This distinction draws on 'the doctrine of the prototype, which had originated with St. Basil and which stated that the honour given to an image does not rest on that image but passes to what the image represents, that is, its prototype' (see Bryan D. Mangrum, introduction to *A Reformation Debate: Karlstadt, Emser, and Eck on Sacred Images. Three Treatises in Translation*, eds. Bryan D. Mangrum and Giuseppe Scavizzi [Toronto: Dovehouse, 1991], 8). This echoes Jerome's 'classic justification of such cults, that the relics were not worshipped in themselves, but were an aid to the veneration of martyrs' (see Jonathan Sumption, *Pilgrimage: An Image of Mediaeval Religion* [London: Faber, 2002], 22). For Christian pilgrims, according to Davies, 'even when the destination is the tomb of a saint, the Christo-centric nature of the devotion is not lost because all the saints are only of importance as so many examples of different ways to imitate their master' (see J. G. Davies, *Pilgrimage Yesterday and Today: Why? Where? How?* [London: SCM, 1988], 2).
26 Exodus 25: 17–22.
27 Numbers 21: 9.
28 John 1:14.
29 Graham Ward, 'The Beauty of God', in John Milbank, Graham Ward, and Edith Wyschogrod, *Theological Perspectives on God and Beauty* (London: Continuum, 2003), 38.
30 Lupton, *St. John of Damascus*, 54–55.
31 'De fide Orthodoxa', in St. John of Damascus, *On Holy Images: Followed by Three Sermons on the Assumption*, trans. M.H. Allies (London: Thomas Baker, 1899).
32 See Ian Wilson, *The Turin Shroud* (London: Penguin, 1979).
33 Lupton, *St. John of Damascus*, 17.
34 Simon Coleman and John Elsner, *Pilgrimage Past and Present: Sacred Travel and Sacred Space in the World Religions* (London: British Museum Press, 1995), 6.
35 Coleman and Elsner, *Pilgrimage*, 8.
36 Sumption, *Pilgrimage*, 22.

37 See, for example, Walter Rye, *A History of Norfolk* (London: Elliot Stock, 1885), 172–173, on '*The Image of Our Lady of Walsingham*: There were relics, of course, such as the coagulated blood of the Virgin, and an unnaturally large joint of the apostle Peter's forefinger, while another attraction was the "wishing well". Evidence of miracles were ever at hand, such as a house not built by hands, which was placed by divine power over the wells'.
38 Sumption, *Pilgrimage*, p. 29.
39 Lee Palmer Wandel, *The Eucharist in the Reformation: Incarnation and Liturgy* (Cambridge: Cambridge University Press, 2006), 29–31.
40 Léonide Ouspensky, *La Théologie de l'Icône dans l'Église Orthodoxe* (Paris: Cerf, 1980), 12. My translation.
41 John Paul II, 'Unveiling'.
42 2 Corinthians 5: 1.
43 Matthew 21: 13.
44 Andreas Karlstadt, 'On the Removal of Images' (1522), in Mangrum and Scavizzi, *A Reformation Debate*, 20.
45 Behind these attacks, according to McGrath, 'a paramount historical contingency was the presence of the Catholic duchy of Savoy and its allies on the very doorstep of the city. If the Reformation was to succeed, the major political and military threat posed to its progress by this duchy had to be neutralized'. See Alister E. McGrath, *A Life of John Calvin: A Study in the Shaping of Western Culture* (Oxford: Blackwell, 1990), 84.
46 Quentin Skinner, *The Foundations of Modern Political Thought. Volume One: The Renaissance* (Cambridge: Cambridge University Press, 1978), x. Skinner refers to this method as turning 'from history to historical semantics'.
47 Skinner, *The Renaissance*, x.
48 Arthur C. Danto, *Narration and Knowledge* (New York: Columbia University Press, 1985), 73, 90.
49 For example, see Coleman and Elsner, *Pilgrimage*, 57: 'the doctrines of the Wahhabis have been compared with those of Calvinist Puritanism in Christianity because of their asceticism and suspicion of all forms of idolatry'. Samuel P. Huntington also makes this connection when discussing 'The Islamic Resurgence' in *The Clash of Civilizations and the Remaking of World Order* (New York: Simon and Schuster, 1997), 111: 'in its political manifestations, the Islamic resurgence bears some resemblance to Marxism, with scriptural texts, a vision of the perfect society, commitment to fundamental change, rejection of the powers that be and the nation state, and doctrinal diversity ranging from moderate reformist to violent revolutionary. A more useful analogy, however, is the Protestant Reformation. Both are reactions to the stagnation and corruption of existing institutions; advocate a return to a purer and more demanding form of their religion; preach work, order, and discipline;

and appeal to emerging, dynamic, middle-class people'. From a journalistic perspective, see John Humphreys, 'The Real Battle is for the Heart of an Arab Child' in *The Sunday Times*, February 16, 2003, who claims that to 'the Wahhabi Muslims of Saudi Arabia ... Osama bin Laden is an Islamic Calvinist'.

50 For the sake of consistency, I will give dates according to the Common Era (CE) rather than the Islamic Hijrah (AH).

51 Muhammad ibn Abd al-Wahhab, *Kitab al-Tawhid*. I use a recent edition published with a commentary by Allamah Abd al-Rahman al-Sadi, *Kitab al-Tawhid* (Birmingham: al-Hidaayah, 2003), 45. The original text can be found in Vol. 1 of *Muallafat al-Shaykh al-Imam Muhammad ibn Abd al-Wahhab* (Riyadh: Jamiat al-Imam Muhammad bin Saud al-Islamiyah, 1977).

52 Ahmad Dallal, 'The Origins and Objectives of Islamic Revivalist Thought, 1750–1850', *Journal of the American Oriental Society*, 113, no. 3 (1993): 351.

53 Jean Louis Burckhardt, 'Materials for a History of the Wahábys', in *Notes on the Bedouins and Wahábys* (Reading: Garnet, 1992), 108–110.

54 Saudi 'centralization' of this kind around the Najdi capital involved an aggressive expansionism to unify nomadic and Hashimite Arabia. One historian states that centralization was central to the Wahhabi identity, writing that the Wahhabis 'decreed all territory identified for absorption by the expanding Saudi polity as *jahaliyyah* [pre-Islamic, or pagan] ... geographical territory to be subjugated, socio-political territory to be linked to the House of Saud in a tributary fashion, and of course religious territory defined by the diversity of local cults whose centralization and homogenization under the title of *Shariah* was a cultural precondition for political centralization' (Aziz al-Azmeh, *Islam and Modernities* [London: Verso, 1993], 99).

55 Max Weber, *Economy and Society: an Outline of Interpretive Sociology*, trans. Ephraim Fischoff (Berkeley: University of California Press, 1979), 623–627.

56 Bryan S. Turner, *Weber and Islam* (London: Routledge, 1998), 55.

57 Wolfgang Schluchter, 'Hindrances to Modernity: Max Weber on Islam', in *Max Weber and Islam*, eds. Toby Huff and Wolfgang Schluchter (London: Transaction, 1999), 69.

58 Max Weber, *The Protestant Ethic and the Spirit of Capitalism*, trans. Talcott Parsons (London: Routledge, 2001), 55–56.

59 Karl Jaspers, *Leonardo, Descartes, Max Weber: Three Essays*, trans. Ralph Manheim (London: Routledge, 1964), 238–240.

60 Weber, *The Protestant Ethic*, xxx.

61 Henry Chapman and Benjamin Geare, 'Palaeoecology and the Perception of prehistoric Landscapes: some Comments on visual Approaches to Phenomenology', *Antiquity*, 74 (2000): 317.

62 Oliver Rackham, *The History of the Countryside: the Classic History of Britain's Landscape, Flora, and Fauna* (London: Phoenix, 2000), 71–72.
63 Richard Clay, 'Bouchardon's Statue of Louis XV: Iconoclasm and the transformation of Signs', in Boldrick and Clay, *Iconoclasm*, 94.
64 David Morgan, 'The Vicissitudes of Seeing: Iconoclasm and Idolatry', *Religion*, 33, no. 2 (2003): 174.
65 See Chapter Five in Fabio Rambelli and Eric Reinders, *Buddhism and Iconoclasm in East Asia: A History* (London: Continuum, 2012).
66 Carlos Eire, *War Against the Idols: The Reformation of Worship from Erasmus to Calvin* (Cambridge: Cambridge University Press, 1989), 7.
67 David Knowles, *Bare Ruined Choirs: The Dissolution of the English Monasteries* (Cambridge: Cambridge University Press, 1976), 17.

CHAPTER 1

1 John Calvin, *Institutes of the Christian Religion*, trans. Henry Beveridge (London: James Clarke, 1962), Book 1, Chapter 11 (in this edition, volume 1, page 91). I shall henceforth cite this text by volume and page number (in this case, 1: 91).
2 This inscription, seen during a research visit to Geneva in September 2006, was kindly translated by Eleanor Brooke. The Latin reads: QUUM ANNO 1535 PROFLIGATA ROMANI ANTICHRISTI TYRANNIDE ABROGATISQUE EIUS SUPERSTITIONIBUS, SACROSANCTA CHRISTI RELIGIO HIC IN SUAM PURITATEM ECCLESIA IN MELIOREM ORDINEM, SINGULARI DEI BENEFICIO, REPOSITA: ET SIMUL PULSIS FUGATISQUE HOSTIBUS URBIS IPSA IN SUAM LIBERTATEM, NON SINE INSIGNI MIRACULE, RESTITUTA FUERIT: SENATUS POPULUSQUE GENEVENSIS MONUMENTUM HOC PERPETUAE MEMORIAE CAUSA FIERI ATQUE HOC LOCO ERIGI CURAVIT: QUO SUAM ERGA DEUM GRATITUDINEM AD POSTEROS TESTATAM FACERET
3 Bruce Gordon, *The Swiss Reformation* (Manchester: Manchester University Press, 2002), 150.
4 Stephen Greenblatt, *Renaissance Self-Fashioning: From More to Shakespeare* (Chicago: University of Chicago Press, 1984), 2.
5 These concerns were examined by the Reformation historian Trevor-Roper in his work on the death of Adolf Hitler. Trevor-Roper was employed by British intelligence in 1945 to write a report on what had happened to Hitler's body, in order to dispel the myths that were beginning to circulate. He did this by visiting the bunker in Berlin and interviewing Nazi prisoners. His description of the conflicting accounts of Dönitz, Späth, and Mory, is pertinent to my historiographical concerns:

'Anyone who undertakes an inquiry of such a kind is soon made aware of one important fact: the worthlessness of mere human testimony. It is a chastening thought to a historian to consider how much of history is written on the basis of statements no more reliable than those of Admiral Doenitz, Dr Spaeth and Carmen Mory. If such statements had been made and recorded with reference to the disputed death of the Czar Alexander I in 1825, plenty of historians would have been ready to take them seriously. Fortunately in this case they were made by contemporaries, and it was possible to check them. The English historian James Spedding said that every historian, when faced with a statement of fact, must ask himself the question: Who first said so, and what opportunities had he of knowing it? Subjected to this test, much of historical evidence is found to dissolve.' Hugh Trevor-Roper, *The Last Days of Hitler* (London: Macmillan, 1995), xxi.

6   Antoine Fromment, *Les actes et gestes merveilleux de la cité de Genève nouvellement convertie à l'Evangille, faictz du temps de leur Reformation et comment ils l'ont receue, redigez par escript en fourme de Chroniques, Annales ou Hystoyres commençant l'an MDXXXII* (Geneva: Jules Guillaume Fick, 1854), 144. My translation.
7   Psalm 115: 2–5, 8.
8   Fromment, *Actes et Gestes*, 145.
9   Eire, *War against the Idols*, 145.
10 Fromment uses the phrase 'ces petis enfants faysans tel bruict contre les Prebstres et se ioyans de leurs marmousets'. I am taking 'se ioyans de leurs marmousets' to mean 'se *moquant* de leurs marmousets' and the 'marmousets' to mean 'children' or 'boys' – in this context, the altar boys.
11 Fromment, *Actes et gestes*, 145–146. I have used 'false gods' for both 'ces petis dieux' and 'les dieux blancz'. The term refers to the hosts for communion and not the images within the cathedral, although the sense is the same – the hosts are idols. Additionally, the words of the crowd – calling upon God to save himself if he is truly present in the host – invert the orthodox accusation traditionally made against iconoclasts that those who destroyed images of Christ were guilty of desecrating the body of Christ. For example, the sixteenth-century advocate of icons Hieronymus Emser described an image of Christ that had been painted (according to the *Apocrypha*) by Nicodemus and which was kept in the house of a Beiruti Jew. Echoing the anti-Semitism of his time, Emser writes that this image was spat at, had nails driven into it, and a spear thrust into its side, making a deliberate connection between the attacked image and the crucified body that can be traced back to the anti-iconoclastic cartoons of ninth-century Byzantium. See Hieronymus Emser, 'That One Should Not Remove Images of the Saints from the Churches Nor Dishonour Them, and That They Are Not Forbidden in

Scripture' (1522), in Mangrum and Scavizzi, *A Reformation Debate*, 48–49.
12. Eire, *War against the Idols*, 147.
13. D. S. Chambers, *Popes, Cardinals, and War: The Military Church in Renaissance and Early Modern Europe* (London: I.B.Tauris, 2006), 146–147.
14. Chambers, *Popes, Cardinals, and War*, 156.
15. See T. H. L. Parker, *John Calvin: A Biography* (London: J. M. Dent, 1975), 54–55, describing Geneva's 'geographical situation that was the cause of her precarious political position throughout the century. Once again we must put from our mind the modern Geneva, one of the cities of Switzerland. In 1536 Geneva, this walled fortress, was a republic, squeezed between the Swiss cantons, the Duchy of Savoy, and the Kingdom of France. Lacking suburbs, and with only some four or five tiny and scattered acres in the surrounding countryside to call her own, she was an island, at first in the territory of Savoy and then of her ally Bern'.
16. McGrath, *A Life of John Calvin*, 84.
17. McGrath, *A Life of John Calvin*, 84. McGrath also points out another contingency: the city's economic decline in wealth and influence after the emergence of a trade fair at Lyon, and the subsequent shifting of Medici patronage west from Geneva to this new location (86).
18. McGrath, *A Life of John Calvin*, 123.
19. Henri Heyer, *Guillaume Farel: An Introduction to his Theology*, trans. Blair Reynolds (Lewiston: Mellen, 1990), 6–9.
20. Edgar Bonjour, *A Short History of Switzerland* (Oxford: Clarendon, 1952), 142.
21. John T. McNeill, *The History and Character of Calvinism* (New York: Oxford University Press, 1954), 9, 14.
22. Bruce Gordon, *The Swiss Reformation*, 150.
23. Carlos Eire, *War against the Idols*, 129.
24. Bruce Gordon, *The Swiss Reformation*, 151.
25. Carlos Eire, *War against the Idols*, 136. Eire details an inventory of the objects destroyed during this time of organized and legislated iconoclasm (152–153).
26. Carlos Eire, *War against the Idols*, 137, 154.
27. Edgar Bonjour, *A Short History*, 164.
28. T. H. L. Parker, *John Calvin*, 56–57.
29. Carlos Eire, *War against the Idols*, 151.
30. Carlos Ginzburg, *The Cheese and the Worms: The Cosmos of a Sixteenth-Century Miller* (London: Penguin, 1992), 28.
31. John Calvin, 'Preface' to *Commentary on the Book of Psalms*, vol. 1, trans. James Anderson (Edinburgh: Calvin Translation Society, 1845–49), 12.
32. William J. Bouwsma, *John Calvin: A Sixteenth Century Portrait* (New York: Oxford University Press, 1988) 18–19.

33 See 'Vita Calvini' in *Ioannis Calvini Opera quae supersunt omnia*, vol. 23, eds. G. Baum, E. Cunitz, and E. Reuss (Braunschweig: C.A. Schwetschke und Sohn, 1863 – 1900), 125.
34 The first edition of the *Institutes* was published in Latin in 1536, and later revised in 1539, 1543, 1550, and 1559 (the year from which my working edition has been translated into English), with a French version published in 1560. It should be noted that the word 'Institutes' has been questioned as a suitable translation for the Latin *Institutio*. Höpfl writes that 'until recently it was the common practice in English-speaking countries to render the title of the book as *Institutes*, on the analogy of the *Institutes* of Justinian ... of late, the more ambiguous *Institution* has again come to be preferred. The most current meaning of the term in Calvin's time was "education", "instruction", perhaps even "primer", and the earliest translations of Calvin took that to be Calvin's meaning, or simply reproduced the word ... It seems likely that the *Institutio* of the title was an elegant play upon words, the point of which was to indicate that the contents of the work were not only "instruction" in the commonplaces of the Christian religion, but also an account of that religion as "instituted" or founded by Christ, as opposed to its current, man-made deformations'. See Harro Höpfl, *The Christian Polity of John Calvin* (Cambridge: Cambridge University Press, 1982), 20. Höpfl uses *Institution* accordingly. However, as almost all other literature refers to the *Institutes*, for the sake of consistency I shall not follow his lead.
35 Calvin, *Institutes*, 1: 9.
36 Calvin, *Institutes*, 1: 11.
37 Calvin, *Institutes*, 1: 101.
38 Calvin, *Institutes*, 2: 310.
39 Calvin, *Institutes*, 1: 91.
40 Calvin, *Institutes*, 1: 91.
41 Calvin, *Institutes*, 1: 92.
42 Calvin, *Institutes*, 1: 91.
43 Calvin, *Institutes*, 1: 91–92.
44 Calvin, *Institutes*, 1: 96.
45 Calvin, *Institutes*, 1: 94.
46 Calvin, *Institutes*, 1: 94–95. My italics.
47 Calvin, *Institutes*, 1: 94.
48 Calvin, *Institutes*, 1: 99.
49 Calvin, *Institutes*, 1: 100.
50 Calvin, *Institutes*, 1: 103.
51 Calvin, *Institutes*, 1: 106.
52 Calvin, *Institutes*, 1: 51.
53 Calvin, *Institutes*, 1: 52.

54 See, for example, Giovanni Pico della Mirandola, *On the Dignity of Man*, trans. Charles Glenn Wallis (Indianapolis: Hackett, 1998). This realignment of the human position in the world was reflected in architectural changes at the time, replacing the cruciform axis of the Gothic church with a series of spheres often based around the human body. Filippo Brunelleschi's Duomo at Florence would be an example of this kind of 'humanist' architecture. For Calvin, however, the new architectural alignment was to emphasize the Word of God rather than the human body. On the general subject of Calvinism and Humanism, see Quirinus Breen, *John Calvin: A Study in French Humanism* (North Haven: Archon, 1968). Breen's thesis is that 'the study of [Calvin's] early life reveals a cross-section in miniature of French humanism as such. First because it is obvious that, up to 1532 at least, he is wholly identified with it ... Moreover, his conversion did not alter his mental "set"' (ix – x). For Breen, Calvin's commentaries on Seneca and the Bible are connected by a common intent: 'the Reformation may indeed be considered to have made, in Calvin, a significant break-through with respect to an age-old question of religion and culture ... Humanism was to Calvin no passing fancy; his heart was in it' (165, 166). See also Richard A. Muller, 'John Calvin and later Calvinism: the identity of the Reformed tradition', in *The Cambridge Companion to Reformation Theology*, eds. David Bagchi and David C. Steinmetz (Cambridge: Cambridge University Press, 2004), 131, on the wider influence of Humanism on Calvin's theological thinking: 'Zwingli was a humanistically trained exegete who had little contact with either a monastic or a scholastic theological training. Bucer was a theologically trained Dominican who had studied at Heidelberg. Capito studied medicine, law, and theology at Freiburg and held strongly humanistic views concerning languages and method of study and exposition ... Farel came out of the humanistic and reformist circles of the University of Paris and the so-called "circle of Meaux"' – a bishopric east of Paris. See also David Nicholls, 'Heresy and Protestantism, 1520–1542: Questions of Perception and Communication', *French History*, 10, no. 2 (1996): 182–205, and Guillaume Briçonnet and Marguerite D'Angouleme, *Correspondance (1521-1524); I, Années 1521-1522* (Geneva: Droz, 1975). This view is contrary to that held by Höpfl, who states that 'the *De Clementia Commentary* [of Seneca] was the beginning and also the end of Calvin's projected career as a humanist scholar. Less than a year after its publication he was an exile living in Basel in straitened circumstances and under the name "Martianus Lucianus"'. See Höpfl, *The Christian Polity of John Calvin*, 19.
55 Calvin, *Institutes*, 1: 88.
56 Calvin, *Institutes*, 1: 93.
57 Calvin, *Institutes*, 1: 97.
58 Calvin, *Institutes*, 1: 97.

59 Calvin, *Institutes*, 1: 101.
60 Calvin, *Institutes*, 1: 88.
61 Calvin, *Institutes*, 1: 37, 40.
62 Calvin, *Institutes*, 1: 41.
63 Calvin, *Institutes*, 1: 48.
64 Calvin, *Institutes*, 1: 126. For an overview of Calvin's Trinitarian theology, see 1: 117–119.
65 Calvin, *Institutes*, 1: 409.
66 Calvin, *Institutes*, 1: 123. The original verse from 1 Corinthians 6: 19 is 'What? Know ye not that your body is the temple of the Holy Ghost, which is in you, which ye have of God, and ye are not your own?'
67 T.H.L. Parker, *John Calvin*, 39–40.
68 On the connection between Catholicism and universality or unity, see F.E. Peters, *Judaism, Christianity, and Islam: The Classic Texts and their Interpretation* (Princeton: Princeton University Press, 1990), 339.
69 Calvin, *Institutes*, 1: 118.
70 John Calvin, *Commentary on the Gospel according to St. John. 1–10*, trans. T.H.L. Parker (Edinburgh: Oliver and Boyd, 1959), 7.
71 Calvin, *Commentary on John*, 8–9.
72 Calvin, *Commentary on John*, 8–9.
73 I am grateful to Eleanor Brooke for explaining the differences between *verbum* and *sermo* to me.
74 Calvin, *Institutes*, 1: 104.
75 Calvin, *Institutes*, 1: 100.
76 T.H.L. Parker, *John Calvin*, 59.
77 John Calvin, *Commentaries*, ed. Joseph Haroutunian (London: SCM, 1958), 79.
78 Calvin, *Institutes*, 1: 81.
79 Calvin, *Institutes*, 1: 65.
80 Calvin, *Institutes*, 1: 68.
81 Calvin, *Institutes*, 1: 14.
82 Calvin, *Institutes*, 1: 14.
83 T. H. L. Parker, *John Calvin*, 35.
84 Höpfl, *The Christian Polity of John Calvin*, 25.
85 See Ulrich Zwingli, *Commentary on True and False Religion* (Oslo: Labyrinth Press, 1981).
86 Calvin, *Institutes*, 2: 281.
87 Calvin, *Institutes*, 2: 281.
88 Calvin, *Institutes*, 2: 305.
89 Calvin, *Institutes*, 1: 48.
90 Eire, *War against the Idols*, 307.
91 Calvin, *Institutes*, 2: 305. His italics.
92 Florimond de Rémond, *L'Histoire de la naissance, progrèz et décadence de l'hérésie de ce siècle*, vol. 7 (Paris: Guillaume de La Noue, 1605), 1393.

93 See Alastair Duke, 'Perspectives on International Calvinism', in *Calvinism in Europe, 1540–1620*, eds. Andrew Pettegree, Alastair Duke, and Gillian Lewis (Cambridge: Cambridge University Press, 1996); see also Menna Prestwich (ed.), *International Calvinism 1541–1715* (Oxford: Clarendon, 1985); and Graeme Murdock, *Beyond Calvin: The Intellectual, Political and Cultural World of Europe's Reformed Churches* (London: Palgrave, 2004).
94 Calvin, *Institutes*, 1: 8. My italics.
95 Calvin, *Institutes*, 1: 76.
96 Calvin, *Institutes*, 1: 412.
97 Calvin, *Institutes*, 2: 306.
98 Calvin, *Institutes*, 1: 12.
99 David C. Steinmetz, 'The Theology of John Calvin', in *The Cambridge Companion to Reformation Theology*, 123.
100 Calvin, *Institutes*, 1: 4. Calvin is here referring to the Anabaptists.
101 Calvin, *Institutes*, 1: 4–5. On the subject of whether Calvin was trying to curry favour with the King of France in his address, see Höpfl, *The Christian Polity of John Calvin*, 20–21. Höpfl believes 'that Calvin was extremely sensitive to the lumping together of evangelicals and Anabaptists, a popular and serviceable weapon of Romanist polemic, particularly in the year after the "Kingdom of Christ" of Jan of Leyden at Münster had achieved its own apocalypse'. Hence 'the usual fulsome titles: "most puissant and most illustrious monarch", "most Christian King"'.
102 Calvin, *Institutes*, 1: 5.
103 Calvin, *Institutes*, 1: 47.
104 Höpfl, *The Christian Polity of John Calvin*, 28–29.
105 Calvin, *Institutes*, 1: 105.
106 Calvin, *Institutes*, 2: 131.
107 Calvin, *Institutes*, 2: 651.
108 Höpfl, *The Christian Polity of John Calvin*, 43, 152.
109 Calvin, *Institutes*, 2: 652.
110 Steinmetz, 'The Theology of John Calvin', 118, 129.
111 William R. Stevenson, Jnr., 'Calvin and Political Issues', in Donald K. McKim, *The Cambridge Companion to John Calvin* (Cambridge: Cambridge University Press, 2004), 173.
112 Stevenson, 'Calvin and Political Issues', 177.
113 Stevenson, 'Calvin and Political Issues', 179.
114 Calvin, *Institutes*, 2: 657. Breen's study of Calvin and humanism makes a distinction between these forms of government within the thinking of the time – 'Humanism is aristocratic, the Reformation democratic. The genius of the one is secular, that of the other religious' – and claims that Calvin's *Institutes* bridged the two. See *John Calvin: A Study in French Humanism*, p. ix. Höpfl develops this distinction between aristocracy and

democracy, introducing a further difference between aristocracy and monarchy: 'A clear preference for an aristocratic, or better still a mixed, form of civil polity was therefore on record by 1543. But this preference, which was subsequently restated and reinforced, had always to compete with a theological *parti pris* to the effect that in forms of polity, whatever is, is right. And although Calvin had enlisted "experience" in support for the mixed polity, the reflections of the philosophers which he had just adduced did not argue unequivocally in favour for aristocracy against monarchy, for each form has its characteristic defects ... Calvin at one time or another entertained hopes about Duke Christopher of Würtemberg, Protector Somerset, Edward VI and Elizabeth I of England, King Sigismund of Poland'. He adds, 'it would be prudent not to bring the term "democracy" into this discussion at all, since in its modern use it is entirely ambiguous as between the legitimacy of a whole system of rule and the authorization of particular persons to occupy positions within a pre-existent system'. See *The Christian Polity of John Calvin*, 155, 156, 159.

[115] Calvin, *Institutes*, 2: 660.
[116] Calvin, *Institutes*, 2: 669.
[117] Calvin, *Institutes*, 2: 670. My italics.
[118] Calvin, *Institutes*, 2: 657.
[119] Calvin, *Institutes*, 2: 673.
[120] Stevenson, 'Calvin and Political Issues', 174.
[121] Calvin, *Institutes*, 2: 675.
[122] Duke, 'Perspectives on International Calvinism', 2.
[123] Harro Höpfl, 'Introduction' to *Luther and Calvin on Secular Authority* (Cambridge: Cambridge University Press, 2005), xxi.
[124] On the connection of clergy and commerce, see Weber, *The Protestant Ethic*, 9: 'As a matter of fact it is surely remarkable, to begin with quite a superficial observation, how large is the number of representatives of the most spiritual forms of Christian piety who have sprung from commercial circles ... Especially Calvinism, wherever it has appeared, has shown this combination'; and 10: 'it is characteristic and in a certain sense typical that in French Huguenot Churches monks and business men (merchants, craftsmen) were particularly numerous among the proselytes, especially at the time of the persecution'.
[125] See Weber, *The Protestant Ethic*, 5: 'the rule of Calvinism ... as it was enforced in the sixteenth century in Geneva and in Scotland, at the turn of the sixteenth and seventeenth centuries in large parts of the Netherlands, in the seventeenth in New England, and for a time in England itself, would be for us the most absolutely unbearable form of the ecclesiastical control of the individual which could possibly exist'. Certainly Calvin, when addressing the English Protector Somerset in bellicose terms on 'the persons who persist in the superstitions of the

Roman AntiChrist', stated that they 'deserve to be repressed by the sword which is committed to you, since they not only attack the King, but strive with God, who has placed him upon a royal throne'. See John Calvin, 'Letter to the Protector Somerset' (1548), in *Letters of John Calvin selected from the Bonnet Edition* (Edinburgh: The Banner of Truth Trust, 1980), 92.

[126] Höpfl, *The Christian Polity of John Calvin*, 131–137; and William G. Naphy, 'Calvin's Geneva', in *The Cambridge Companion to John Calvin*, 36.

[127] McGrath, *A Life of John Calvin*, 98.

[128] *Letters of John Calvin*, 45. On the organization of parishes in Geneva, see E. William Monter, 'Historical Demography and Religious History in Sixteenth-Century Geneva', *Journal of Interdisciplinary History*, 9, no. 3 (1979): 400: 'after the Reformation, the city simplified its structure from seven to three major parishes: the Cathedral of St. Pierre; St. Gervais on the right bank of the Rhône; and La Madeleine, near the downtown commercial centre. The parish of St. Germain in the upper city was intermittently active after the Reformation, specifically from 1557 through 1570. Calvin's Geneva also possessed two foreign-language refugee churches, the short-lived English church (1555–1560) and the long-lived Italian church (from 1554 until the nineteenth century). Records of both baptisms and marriages are remarkably complete; exactly the same standards were used in 1550 as in 1599, or for long afterwards'.

[129] *Letters of John Calvin*, 37, 38.

[130] Höpfl, *The Christian Polity of John Calvin*, 31–32.

[131] Steinmetz, 'The Theology of John Calvin', 128.

[132] Naphy, 'Calvin's Geneva', 30.

[133] Naphy, 'Calvin's Geneva', 30.

[134] Naphy, 'Calvin's Geneva', 25.

[135] Monter, 'Historical Demography and Religious History in Sixteenth-Century Geneva', 399–400. On the general subject of Calvin and political society, see his *Studies in Genevan Government, 1536–1605* (Geneva: Droz, 1964).

[136] Monter, 'Historical Demography and Religious History in Sixteenth-Century Geneva', 401.

[137] Eire, *War against the Idols*, 161.

[138] Ole Peter Grell, 'Merchants and Ministers: the Foundation of International Calvinism', in *Calvinism in Europe*, 255.

[139] Mark Valeri, 'Religion, Discipline, and the Economy in Calvin's Geneva', *Sixteenth Century Journal*, 28, no.1 (1997): 127.

[140] Monter, 'Historical Demography and Religious History in Sixteenth-Century Geneva', 402.

[141] Monter, 'Historical Demography and Religious History in Sixteenth-Century Geneva', 402.

142 Monter, 'Historical Demography and Religious History in Sixteenth-Century Geneva', 405.
143 Monter, 'Historical Demography and Religious History in Sixteenth-Century Geneva', 404.
144 McGrath, *A Life of John Calvin*, 86.
145 Höpfl, *The Christian Polity of John Calvin*, 129, 130.
146 Monter, 'Historical Demography and Religious History in Sixteenth-Century Geneva', 408.
147 Monter, 'Historical Demography and Religious History in Sixteenth-Century Geneva', 409. My italics.
148 On the subject of a 'Calvinist' diaspora beyond Geneva, see Ole Peter Grell, 'Merchants and Ministers', 258: 'it is my contention that the social experience of exodus and diaspora, which Reformed merchants endured to an even greater extent than most of their coreligionists, was of paramount importance in providing Calvinism with an international character'. Weber describes the spread of Calvinism in *The Protestant Ethic*, 53–55. For Duke, 'Perspectives on International Calvinism', it was the Catholics who, ironically, helped this 'formation of a Calvinist, or more properly Reformed, international' by creating ghettos, as 'the experience of exile confirmed the Reformed character of the *émigrés*. Few of the dissidents would ever have encountered confessional Calvinism before they left their native cities ... many of those who fled only became Calvinists after they had gone into exile. Except in the case of Emden for Dutch speakers and Geneva for francophones, differences of language and of confession not only set, but kept the members of these stranger churches apart from the native populations ... The Reformed leadership fostered the *esprit de corps* among the local strangers as well as a sense of belonging to a wider Calvinist fraternity' (5, 6).
149 These acts in the Netherlands, most of which took place in 1566, were called the *Beeldenstorm*. For examples of their being designated 'Calvinist', see P.M. Crew, *Calvinist Preaching and Iconoclasm in the Netherlands, 1544–1569* (Cambridge: Cambridge University Press, 1978); see also Philip S. Gorski, *The Disciplinary Revolution: Calvinism and the Rise of the State in Early Modern Europe* (Chicago: Chicago University Press, 2003), which seeks to connect the rise of Dutch 'Calvinism' with early 'state' formation and Weber's idea of 'capitalism'.

CHAPTER 2

1 Al-Azmeh, *Islam and Modernities*, 106–107.
2 The lack of source material also makes difficult the task of locating ibn Abd al-Wahhab's *Kitab al-Tawhid*. See Michael Cook, 'On the Origins of Wahhabism', *Journal of the Royal Asiatic Society*, 2, no. 2 (1992): 191,

and Ibrahim Fasih al-Haydari al-Baghdadi, *Unwan al-majd fi tarikh Baghdad wa-l-basra wa-najd* (Baghdad: Dar Manshurat al-Basri, 1962), 228.
3   Interview with Natana Delong-Bas in *Al-Sharq Al-Awsat* (December 21, 2006).
4   Al-Wahhab, *Kitab al-Tawhid*, 23. The choice of English words translated from the Arabic (for example, 'associationism' for *shirk*) are my own.
5   For example, the *fitnah* referred to in Qur'an 2: 190–193.
6   The label 'Wahhabi' is believed to have emerged as a British accusation against certain Indian Islamists under the guidance of Sayyid Ahmad, and is recorded in W.W. Hunter's *The Indian Musalmans: Are they Bound in Conscience to Rebel against the Queen?* (London: Trubner, 1871). See also the statement by the Saudi ambassador to the United Kingdom, Ghazi bin Abdulrahman Al-Qusaibi, on 'Saudi Arabian Myths' at the University of Westminster, London (July 9, 2002): 'I must start by frankly admitting that Saudi Arabia has always been an extremely efficient factory for the production of myths … We Saudis – and this may shock you – consider Wahhabism a myth. No so-called Wahhabi ever accepted to be called a Wahhabi. The term was coined by the enemies of the reformist movement of Shaikh Muhammad bin Abdul-Wahhab and soon gained wide currency. We will continue to refuse the label in the hope that one day the outside world will listen, as it did when it stopped the earlier common practice of referring to Muslims as Muhammadans. I will quote directly from the *Encyclopedia Britannica* (15th edition): "Members of the Wahhabi call themselves *Al-Muwahhidin*, 'Unitarians', a name derived from their emphasis on the absolute 'oneness of God' (*tawhid*). They deny all acts implying polytheism, such as visiting tombs and venerating saints; and advocate a return to the original teachings of Islam as incorporated in the Qur'an and Hadith." This', concludes al-Qusaibi, 'is a concise and precise statement'. Ghazi bin Abdulrahman Al-Qusaibi, 'Saudi Arabian Myths', 2002, http://tinyurl.com/saudi-myths
7   Al-Azmeh, *Islam and Modernities*, 106.
8   Daniel Saunders, *A Journal of the Travels and Sufferings of Daniel Saunders, Jun, Mariner on board the ship* Commerce, *of* Boston, *SAMUEL JOHNSON, Commander, which was cast away near* Cape Moribot, *on the coast of* Arabia, *July 10, 1792* (Hudson, NY: Ashbel Stoddard, 1805), 40.
9   Saunders, *Journal*, 70.
10 Alexei Vassiliev, *The History of Saudi Arabia* (London: Saqi, 1998), 70.
11 Nikki R. Keddie, 'The Revolt of Islam, 1700 to 1993: Comparative Considerations and Relations to Imperialism', *Comparative Studies in Society and History*, 36, no. 3 (1994): 469, 472.
12 See Fouad al-Farsy, *Saudi Arabia: A Case-Study in Development* (London: Kegan Paul International, 1982), 30–36, promoted by the Saudi Ministry of Information.

13 Madawi al-Rasheed, 'Durable and non-durable Dynasties: The Rashidis and Saudis in Central Arabia', *British Journal of Middle Eastern Studies*, 19, no. 2 (1992): 144–145.
14 Jean Louis Burckhardt, *Travels in Arabia, comprehending an Account of those Territories in Hedjaz which the Muhammadans regard as Sacred* (London: H. Colburn, 1829), 118.
15 Such claims are described by al-Rasheed in a chapter on the teaching of history to Saudi school-children. See Madawi al-Rasheed, *A History of Saudi Arabia* (Cambridge: Cambridge University Press, 2002), 192.
16 Albert Hourani, *A History of the Arab Peoples* (London: Faber, 2002), 101–102.
17 Hourani, *History*, 108.
18 Al-Rasheed, *History*, 8, 15.
19 Suraiya Faroqhi, *Pilgrims and Sultans: The Hajj under the Ottomans, 1517–1683* (London: I.B.Tauris, 1994), 9–10.
20 Faroqhi, *Pilgrims and Sultans*, 99. A comparison of the costs involved in projects in both Istanbul and Hijaz shows that in 1585, repairs financed by the Sultan's Council on the grain stores in Medina, the outer wall of the courtyard of Muhammad's mosque, and sixty-three hospices for poor pilgrims amounted to around 92,000 gold pieces. In 1571, 60,000 gold pieces were spent on cleaning the water pipes and adding new ones from Arafat to Mecca. 'The costliness of building in Mecca and Medina', Faroqhi explains, 'as opposed to less out-of-the-way regions becomes apparent when we compare these figures to the building expenses of … the Süleymaniye complex – six colleges of law, religion, and medicine, a hospice, a hospital and a public kitchen, as well as the magnificently decorated mausolea of Süleyman the Lawgiver … 896,383 Ottoman gold pieces' (98).
21 Faroqhi, *Pilgrims and Sultans*, 164.
22 Joshua Teitelbaum, *The Rise and Fall of the Hashimite Kingdom* (London: Hurst, 2001), 12.
23 Hourani, *History*, 249.
24 Keddie states that 'it remains a dramatic and puzzling fact that, after many centuries in which such large-scale revolutionary *jihad* movements were quite infrequent, there was a sudden concentration of them in a period of about a century. It seems unlikely that this is a coincidence'. She argues that this local revivalism was due to the differing levels of authority being defined – in the absence of established state structures and kept fluid within the new movements of European trading routes – through the singular polity of Islam ('The Revolt of Islam', 467–469).
25 Hourani, *History*, 252–253.
26 For a recent edition of this text, see Husayn ibn Ghannam, *Tarikh Najd* (Beirut: Dar al-Shuruq, 1994).

27 Uthman ibn Bishr, *Unwan al-Majd fi Tarikh Najd* (Riyadh: Matbuat Darat al-Malik Abd al-Aziz, 1982), vol. 1, 35.
28 Muhammad ibn Abdallah ibn Humayd, *al-Suhub al-wabila ala daraih al-hanabila*, eds. Bakr Abdallah Abu Zayd and Abd al-Rahman ibn Sulayman al-Uthaymin (Beirut: Muassasat al-Risala, 1996), vol. 2, 675-676.
29 See, for example, Abu Ammaar Yasir Qadhi's commentary to *Kitab Kashf al-Shubuhat* (Birmingham: al-Hidaayah, 2003), 67.
30 Natana J. Delong-Bas, *Wahhabi Islam: from Revival and Reform to global Jihad* (London: I.B.Tauris, 2007), 17.
31 Delong-Bas, *Wahhabi Islam*, 14–15.
32 Louis Alexandre Olivier de Corancez, *The History of the Wahabis from their Origin until the end of 1809*, trans. Eric Tabet (Reading: Garnet, 1995), 5.
33 Ibn Abdallah ibn Humayd, *al-Suhub al-wabila ala daraih al-hanabila*, vol. 2, 679.
34 Robin Bidwell's 'Introduction' to Burckhardt, 'Materials', outlines these claims. Note also that Abd al-Wahhab b. Ahmad Barakat al-Shafii al-Azhari al-Tandatawi's text *Kitab Rad al-Dalala wa Qam al-Djahala* was written as a refutation of a letter that ibn Abd al-Wahhab had sent to religious scholars in Basra *before* his pact with the al-Saud family in al-Diriyyah.
35 Ibn Bishr, *Unwan al-Majd*, vol. 1, 7.
36 Samer Traboulsi, 'An Early Refutation of Muhammad ibn Abd al-Wahhab's Reformist Views', *Die Welt des Islams*, 42, no. 3 (2002): 376.
37 Al-Rasheed, *History*, 16–17. Al-Rasheed refers to Abu Hakima's 1967 description of Muhammad al-Saud's promise to ibn Abd al-Wahhab of perpetual sanctuary, where in return he was told by the preacher that if he performed *jihad* against the unbelievers he would become leader of the Muslim community.
38 John Voll, 'Muhammed Hayya al-Sindi and Muhammed ibn Abd al-Wahhab: An Analysis of an Intellectual Group in Eighteenth-Century Madina', *Bulletin of the School of Oriental and African Studies*, 38, no. 1 (1975): 33, 32.
39 Voll, 'An Analysis', 34.
40 Dallal, 'Origins and Objectives', 342.
41 Dallal, 'Origins and Objectives', 342.
42 Traboulsi, 'An Early Refutation', p. 373, 388.
43 Al-Wahhab, *Kitab al-Tawhid*, 33.
44 Al-Wahhab, *Kitab al-Tawhid*, p. 55.
45 Al-Wahhab, *Kitab al-Tawhid*, p. 56.
46 Qur'an 112: 1.
47 Dallal, 'Origins and Objectives', 351. Ibn Abd al-Wahhab also stated that 'if you wish to know the proof that these same pagans that the Prophet fought used to testify to all this, then recite these verses to he

who asks for proof: "Say: Who gives you sustenance from the Heavens and Earth? Or who controls hearing and sight, and who brings the living out of the dead, and who arranges (every) matter?" They will respond, "Allah"'. See *Kitab Kashf al-Shubuhat*, 81.
48   Al-Wahhab, *Kitab al-Tawhid*, 40.
49   Al-Wahhab, *Kitab al-Tawhid*, 51.
50   Dallal, 'Origins and Objectives', 351.
51   Al-Wahhab, *Kitab Kashf al-Shubuhat*, 99.
52   Al-Wahhab, *Kitab al-Tawhid*, 45.
53   Sahih al-Bukhari, Vol. 8, Bk. 77, No. 597.
54   Al-Wahhab, *Kitab Kashf al-Shubuhat*, 78.
55   Qur'an 71: 1–28.
56   Qur'an 71: 1–28.
57   Al-Wahhab, *Kitab Kashf al-Shubuhat*, 82–92. See also another of al-Wahhab's texts on *tawhid*, recently translated by Ismail Raji al-Faruqi and published in Philadelphia as *Three Essays on Tawhid* (Philadelphia: North American Trust Publications, 1979), 24: 'The associationists of our own day are worse and hence more guilty than those of pre-Islamic times. For, the ancient ones used to commit *shirk* in prosperity and return to genuine faith in adversity, whereas the present-day associationists are constant in their unbelief, regardless of prosperity or adversity. Evidence for this is in the verse: "And when they ride in barks [in stormy seas] they address their prayers to Allah in complete sincerity, but relapse into *shirk* when they reach the shore" [Qur'an 29: 65]'.
58   Al-Wahhab, *Kitab al-Tawhid*, 44.
59   Al-Wahhab, *Kitab al-Tawhid*, 262.
60   See Qur'an 8: 34–40: 'Why should Allah punish them while they hinder men from *al-Masjid al-Haram* [Mecca], and they are not its guardians? None can be its guardians except the pious, but most of them know not. / Their prayers at the house [*al-bait*, meaning the Kaaba] was nothing but the whistling and clapping of hands. Therefore taste the punishment because you used to disbelieve. / ... Allah may distinguish the wicked from the good, and put the wicked one over another, heap them together and cast them into Hell. / ... and fight them until there is no more *fitnah* [disbelief and polytheism] and the worship will all be for Allah alone'.
61   On the subject of this 'fight', Delong-Bas stresses that ibn Abd al-Wahhab used the word *qital* rather than *jihad*, indicating that changing the behaviour of the *kufir* is more important than killing them: 'it is also important to note that permission to fight was given only in cases in which the people in question were actively engaged in worship of created beings and objects' (see *Wahhabi Islam*, 64). See also al-Wahhab, *Three Essays on Tawhid*, 19, which indicates that the meaning of the 'fight' against the *mushrikun* denotes separation rather than killing: 'For

ten years, the Prophet called men to *tawhid*, after which he was raised to heaven where the five *salawat* were instituted. He performed the *salat* in Makkah for three years, after which he was commanded to emigrate to Madinah. *Al Hijrah* (the emigration) means self-removal from the land of *shirk* to the land of Islam. *Al Hijrah* is a duty eternally imposed by Allah on all Muslims to remove themselves from the land of *shirk* to the land of Islam ... The evidence that emigration from the land of *shirk* is a normative *sunnah* is the Prophet's saying: "Emigration will not stop unless repentance stops; repentance will not stop unless the sun rises from the West"'.

62 Ignac Goldhizer, *Muslim Studies (Muhammedanische Studien)*, trans. Barber and Stern (Chicago, Albany: Aldine, 1966), vol. 1, 209.
63 See Qur'an 15: 80–84: 'The dwellers of *al-Hijr* [translated as 'the rocky tract', and taken to mean Madain Saleh] denied the Messengers. / And We gave them Our Signs, but they were averse to them. / And they used to hew out dwellings from the mountains, feeling themselves secure. / But torment overtook them in the early morning'.
64 See A.R. al-Ansary, *Qaryat al-Fau* (Riyadh: University of Riyadh, 1981).
65 Toufic Fahd, *Le Panthéon de l'Arabie occidentale avant l'Hégire* (Paris: Paul Guethner, 1968), 249.
66 Alexander Knysh, 'The Cult of Saints in Hadramawt: An Overview', in *New Arabian Studies*, eds. R.B. Serjeant, R.W. Bidwell, and G. Rex Smith (Exeter: University of Exeter Press, 1993), Vol. 1, 145 ff.
67 G. R. D. King, 'Islam, Iconoclasm, and the Declaration of Doctrine', *Bulletin of the School of Oriental and African Studies*, 48, no. 2 (1985): 270.
68 King, 'Islam, Iconoclasm, and the Declaration of Doctrine', 267.
69 King, 'Islam, Iconoclasm, and the Declaration of Doctrine', 268–269.
70 Delong-Bas, *Wahhabi Islam*, 66–67: 'ibn Abd al-Wahhab addressed these local customs by referring to early Muslim history – namely, the deaths of Muhammad and some of his Companions – because it was during this time that the question of shrine and dome buildings over tombs came to a head for the early Muslim community. According to the historical record, Muhammad was buried in his house underneath the apartments of his favourite wife, Aisha. This house was later converted into a mosque. After a time, the tribe that controlled the mosque sought to expand it. This was opposed by some, who claimed it should not be done because this was also the location of Muhammad's tomb. The tribe in control responded that it had no intention of expanding the chamber where Muhammad was buried but simply wanted to expand the mosque. In reviewing the record, ibn Abd al-Wahhab agreed with the decision to expand the mosque because it was confined to the mosque. There was to be no embellishment or expansion of Muhammad's tomb. However, he remained concerned about the precedent that the construction of such a mosque set for future generations. He

noted that Muhammad himself had feared that people would come to his grave to worship him. Consequently, he instructed his followers not to place his grave above ground so that it could not be taken for a mosque ... Muhammad had expressly forbidden people to build graves within their homes or make graves places of celebration, even in the case of his own ... ibn Abd al-Wahhab expanded his discussion into a broader analysis of Muhammad's general opposition to shrines and mausoleums. The *Hadith* record Muhammad's declaration that all images should be wiped out and all high graves levelled to the ground so that no-one could use these images or graves as objects or sites of worship or claim that any human being has the power to grant them souls and life. Ibn Abd al-Wahhab's own commands to destroy elaborate tombs therefore stemmed from Muhammad's similar actions'.

71 Al-Farsy, *Saudi Arabia*, 36.
72 Burckhardt, 'Materials', 111.
73 Burckhardt, *Travels*, 191–192.
74 Muhammad Bari, 'The Early Wahhabis and the Sharifs of Makkah', *Journal of The Pakistan Historical Society*, 3 (1955): 93–95.
75 Al-Rasheed, *History*, 20–22.
76 Burckhardt, *Travels*, 104–105.
77 Bari, 'The Early Wahhabis'. On the travels of Ali Bey and his references to the political 'agitation' affecting Mecca, see *Travels of Ali Bey in Morocco, Tripoli, Cyprus, Egypt, Arabia, Syria and Turkey, between the Years 1803 and 1807, written by Himself* (London: Longman, Hurst, Rees, Orme, and Brown, 1816), vol.1, 219, 244.
78 H.J. Brydges, *An Account of the Transactions of his Majesty's Mission to the Court of Persia, in the years 1807–1811 ... to which is appended, A Brief History of the Wahauby* (London: J. Bohn, 1834), 8.
79 Brydges, *An Account*, 34.
80 Burckhardt, 'Materials', 100.
81 While both these sources were open to the theology of ibn Abd al-Wahhab, it should be noted that ibn Bishr also described the attack by Saud, 'his victorious army, famous pedigree horses, and all *the settled people and bedouin* of Najd' on Shiite shrines and individuals in Karbala, present-day Iraq, killing 'most of the people in the markets and houses. One cannot count their spoils'. See *Unwan*, vol. 1, 121–121. My italics.
82 Brydges, *An Account*, 109.
83 Al-Azmeh, *Islam and Modernities*, 106.
84 Burckhardt, 'Materials', 108–110.
85 Muhammad Asad, *The Road to Mecca* (London: Muslim Academic Trust, 1998), 23.
86 See Burckhardt, 'Materials', 96, which argues that the 'government of the Wahábys may be very briefly defined, as a Muselmán Puritanism'.

87 Jerzy Zdanowski, 'Military Organization of the Wahhabi Amirates (1750–1932)', in *New Arabian Studies*, vol. 2, 131.
88 Zdanowski, 'Military Organization of the Wahhabi Amirates', 132.
89 The first conquest of Hijaz by Saud in 1803 was crushed, briefly, by the Ottomans under Mehmed Ali 1818, who in turn was unable to retain control over the desert region of Najd. After a period of re-galvanization from 1820–1870, the second Saudi territory experienced infighting between its many fraternities, prompting the rise of the rival al-Rashidi family in 1891 until Abd al-Aziz (Ibn Saud) who, from exile in Kuwait, reclaimed Riyadh in 1902 with a band of nomadic fighters, the *ikhwan*. By 1925 he had unified the majority of the Arabian peninsula and, at the third attempt, the Saudi claim to Hijaz was realized. Ibn Saud routed the al-Rashidis in Riyadh, and the Hashimites in Mecca. After resolving the borders of Arabia and eliminating the threat of a rebellious *ikhwan*, in 1932 he declared the new country to be called – after his family and with the agreement of the British – The Kingdom of Saudi Arabia. The Hashimites fled, their sons being given by the British mandate the rule over the fledgling countries of Jordan and Iraq.
90 Aziz al-Azmeh, *Muslim Kingship: Power and the Sacred in Muslim, Christian, and Pagan Polities* (London: I.B.Tauris, 1997), 73.
91 Al-Azmeh, *Muslim Kingship*, 76–77.
92 Al-Azmeh, *Islam and Modernities*, 108. My italics.
93 Al-Azmeh, *Islam and Modernities*, 109.
94 Paul Dresch, 'Arabia to the End of the First World War', in *The New Cambridge History of Islam. Vol 5: The Islamic World in the Age of Western Dominance*, ed. F.H. Robinson (Cambridge: Cambridge University Press, 2010), 138–139.
95 Delong-Bas, *Wahhabi Islam*, 37.
96 Al-Rasheed, *History*, 23.
97 Al-Rasheed, *History*, 206–207. It should be noted that al-Rasheed, a social anthropologist at King's College London, is the grand-daughter of the last Rashidi amir.
98 Ernest Gellner, *Muslim Society* (Cambridge: Cambridge University Press, 1981).
99 Ira M. Lapidus, 'The Evolution of Muslim Urban Society', *Comparative Studies in Society and History*, 15, no. 1 (1973): 27.
100 Lapidus, 'The Evolution of Muslim Urban Society', 29–30.
101 Weber, *Economy and Society*, 1226.
102 Gregory Nowell, 'Hyper-Conservative Modernization: The United States, Saudi Arabia, and Poland'. Paper presented at the International Studies Association, Montreal, March 17, 2004.
103 Keddie, 'The Revolt of Islam', 471.
104 Al-Rasheed, *History*, 49.
105 Al-Rasheed, *History*, 39. My italics.

[106] Al-Azmeh, *Islam and Modernities*, 110. See also al-Rasheed, *History*, 22: 'The expansion of the first Saudi-Wahhabi emirate resulted in the creation of a political realm with fluctuating boundaries. The descendents of the al-Saud, legitimized by the Wahhabi leadership, provided a permanent political leadership in accordance with the oath of 1744. However, there were no mechanisms other than raids to ensure durability of either the polity or its boundaries, and tribal confederations retained their ability to challenge Saudi-Wahhabi authority. Withdrawing the payment of *zakat* and organising counter-attacks on groups and territories within the Saudi-Wahhabi sphere of influence were recurrent challenges'.
[107] It should be noted that the Saudi government now has a 'Department of *Zakat* ': http://www.dzit.gov.sa
[108] Al-Rasheed, *History*, 57.
[109] Vassiliev, *History*, 267.
[110] Joseph Kostiner, 'Transforming Dualities: Tribe and State Formation in Saudi Arabia', in Philip S. Khoury and Joseph Kostiner, *Tribes and State Formation in the Middle East* (London: I.B.Tauris, 1992), 227.
[111] Talal Asad, *Formations of the Secular: Christianity, Islam, Modernity* (Stanford: Stanford University Press, 2003), 198–199.
[112] Al-Azmeh, *Muslim Kingship*, 113.
[113] Al-Azmeh, *Muslim Kingship*, 120.
[114] Vassiliev, *History*, 256.
[115] Lawrence Paul Goldrup, *Saudi Arabia: 1902–1932: The Development of a Wahhabi Society* (unpublished doctoral dissertation, University of California, Los Angeles, 1971), 397.
[116] Vassiliev, *History*, 159.
[117] Gary Troeller, *The Birth of Saudi Arabia* (London: Routledge, 1976), 220–221.
[118] Al-Rasheed, *History*, 192–193.
[119] Al-Rasheed, *History*, 194.
[120] Al-Rasheed, *History*, 188. Al-Rasheed notes that some anthropologists have resisted this account, particularly the claim made by S. al-Torki and D. Cole in *Arabian Oasis City: The Transformation of Unayzah* (Austin: University of Texas Press, 1989), 233, that the role played by merchants and urban Najdis before the birth of ibn Abd al-Wahhab shows 'the indigenous process of state formation in Najd predates the present Saudi Arabian state by several centuries'.
[121] Al-Azmeh, *Islam and Modernities*, 39.
[122] Al-Rasheed, *History*, 51; see also al-Azmeh, *Islam and Modernities*, 107.
[123] Calvin, *Institutes*, 2: 669.

CHAPTER 3

1. Hobbes, *Leviathan*, 90.
2. Michael Burleigh, *Earthly Powers: Religion and Politics in Europe from the Enlightenment to the Great War* (London: Harper Collins, 2005), 46.
3. Dale K. van Kley, *The Religious Origins of the French Revolution: from Calvin to the Civil Constitution, 1560–1791* (New Haven: Yale University Press, 1996), 24.
4. Stanley J. Idzerda, 'Iconoclasm during the French Revolution', *American Historical Review*, 60, no. 1 (1954): 16. My italics.
5. Nathaniel S. McFetridge, *Calvinism in History* (Edmonton: Still Waters, 1989), 66–67.
6. Hilaire Belloc, *The French Revolution* (London: Butterworth, 1941), 229–230.
7. Belloc, *The French Revolution*, 224, 230.
8. Besançon, *The Forbidden Image*, 190.
9. Anne Betty Weinshenker, 'Idolatry and Sculpture in *Ancien Régime* France', *Eighteenth-Century Studies*, 38, no. 3 (2005): 489.
10. Weinshenker, 'Idolatry and Sculpture in *Ancien Régime* France', 488.
11. Weinshenker, 'Idolatry and Sculpture in *Ancien Régime* France', 495, 496.
12. Jürgen Habermas, *The Structural Transformation of the Public Sphere*, trans. Thomas Burger (Cambridge: Polity, 1989), 26–28.
13. Clay, 'Bouchardon's Statue of Louis XV', 100–101.
14. Burleigh, *Earthly Powers*, 46.
15. Weinshenker, 'Idolatry and Sculpture in *Ancien Régime* France', 501.
16. Morgan, 'The Vicissitudes of Seeing', 171, 175.
17. Simon Schaffer, 'The Devices of Iconoclasm', in Bruno Latour and Peter Weibel (eds.) *Iconoclash: Beyond the Image Wars in Science, Religion, and Art* (London: MIT Press, 2002), 500.
18. Schaffer, 'The Devices of Iconoclasm', 503–504, 507.
19. Burleigh, *Earthly Powers*, 45.
20. Burleigh, *Earthly Powers*, 21–22.
21. Burleigh, *Earthly Powers*, 43.
22. Burleigh, *Earthly Powers*, 82.
23. Benedict Anderson, *Imagined Communities: Reflections on the Origin and Spread of Nationalism* (London: Verso, 2003), 36.
24. Michael Taussig, *Defacement: Public Secrecy and the Labor of the Negative* (Stanford: Stanford University Press, 1999), 3.
25. Idzerda, 'Iconoclasm during the French Revolution', 18.
26. Taussig, *Defacement*, 21.
27. Idzerda, 'Iconoclasm during the French Revolution', 13.

28 Van Kley, *The Religious Origins of the French Revolution*, 367.
29 Idzerda, 'Iconoclasm during the French Revolution', 14.
30 Christopher M. Greene, 'Alexandre Lenoir and the Musée des monuments français during the French Revolution', *French Historical Studies*, 12, no. 2 (1981): 210, 214.
31 Greene, 'Alexandre Lenoir', 216–217.
32 Greene, 'Alexandre Lenoir', 218.
33 Weinshenker, 'Idolatry and Sculpture in *Ancien Régime* France', 494.
34 Clay, 'Bouchardon's Statue of Louis XV', 95.
35 Clay, 'Bouchardon's Statue of Louis XV', 99.
36 Clay, 'Bouchardon's Statue of Louis XV', 110–111.
37 Clay, 'Bouchardon's Statue of Louis XV', 116–117.
38 Richard Clay, 'Smells, Bells and Touch: Iconoclasm in Paris during the French Revolution', *Eighteenth-Century Studies*, 35, no. 4 (2012).
39 C. Edson Armi, 'Report on the Destruction of Romanesque Architecture in Burgundy', *Journal of the Society of Architectural Historians*, 55, no. 3 (1996): 320.
40 Idzerda, 'Iconoclasm during the French Revolution', 21.
41 Idzerda, 'Iconoclasm during the French Revolution', 26. For a fuller study of this connection between iconoclasm and the Enlightenment museum, through the prism of the violent 'self-confidence' of Western modernity, see James Simpson, *Under the Hammer: Iconoclasm in the Anglo-American Tradition* (Oxford: Oxford University Press, 2010).

CHAPTER 4

1 Evelyn Waugh, *Brideshead Revisited: the Sacred and Profane Memories of Captain Charles Ryder* (London: Penguin, 1962), 96.
2 Denis Cosgrove, 'The Myth and the Stones of Venice: An Historical Geography of a Symbolic Landscape', *Journal of Historical Geography*, 8, no. 2 (1982): 147.
3 Cosgrove, 'The Myth and the Stones of Venice', 155.
4 Hugh Honour, *The Companion Guide to Venice* (London: Collins, 1970), 113.
5 Henry James, *Letters from the Palazzo Barbaro*, ed. Rosella Mamoli Zorzi (London: Pushkin, 1998), 27.
6 Leon Edel, Foreword to *Letters from the Palazzo Barbaro*, 13.
7 Henry James, *Italian Hours* (New York: Grove Press, 1979), 54.
8 Henry James, *The American Scene* (New York: Penguin, 1994), 93.
9 James, *Italian Hours*, 1.
10 Mary McCarthy, *The Stones of Florence and Venice Observed* (Harmondsworth: Penguin, 1979), 180.

NOTES

11 Adrian Stokes, 'Venice' (1945), in *The Critical Writings of Adrian Stokes, Vol. II (1937–1958)* (New York: Thames and Hudson, 1978), 112.
12 Ezra Pound, 'Canto XVI' in *The Cantos* (London: Faber and Faber, 1964), 73. I shall henceforth refer to this text by both Canto number and the page number of the Faber 1964 edition – in other words, Canto XVI, page 73 will be cited as *Canto* 16.73.
13 *Canto* 17.80.
14 Rosella Mamoli Zorzi, 'Intertextual Violence: Blood and Crime and Death Renewed in Two Contemporary Novels', in *Venetian Views, Venetian Blinds: English Fantasies of Venice*, ed. Manfred Pfister and Barbara Schaff (Amsterdam: Rodopi, 1999), 225.
15 Zorzi, Introduction to *Letters from the Palazzo Barbaro*, 20.
16 Sergio Perosa, 'Literary Deaths in Venice', in *Venetian Views, Venetian Blinds*, 118.
17 Michael Taussig, 'The Beach (a Fantasy)', *Critical Inquiry*, 26, no. 2 (2000): 266.
18 Henry James, 'The Princess Casamassima', in *Novels 1886–1890: The Princess Casamassima, The Reverberator, The Tragic Muse* (New York: Library of America, 1989), 353–354.
19 Henry James, 'The Aspern Papers', in *Complete Stories: 1884–1891* (New York: Library of America, 1999), 316.
20 Henri Lefebvre uses these words to describe the process of 'the archetypal touristic delusion' in *The Productions of Space*, trans. Donald Nicholson-Smith (Oxford: Blackwell, 1991), 189.
21 James, *Italian Hours*, 8.
22 Waugh, *Brideshead Revisited*, 97.
23 W. J. T. Mitchell, *Iconology: Image, Text, Ideology* (Chicago: University of Chicago Press, 1986), 103, 187.
24 McCarthy, *Venice Observed*, 195.
25 McCarthy, *Venice Observed*, 177.
26 John Ruskin, 'The Quarry', in *The Stones of Venice*, from *Works*, ed. Edward Cook and Alexander Wedderburn (London: George Allen, 1903–1912), vol. I, 17.
27 *Canto* 45. 243, 245.
28 Honour, *The Companion Guide*, 31.
29 Clive Wilmer, 'Sculpture and Economics in Pound and Ruskin', *PN Review 122*, 24, no. 6 (1998): 44.
30 *Canto* 46.244.
31 David-Everett Blythe, 'A Stone of Ruskin's Venice', in *New Approaches to Ruskin: Thirteen Essays*, ed. Robert Hewison (London: Routledge, 1981), 157.
32 *Be thy cross, Oh Christ, the true safety of this place.*
   Around this temple, let the merchant's law be just – his weights true, and his agreements guileless.

33 Blythe, 'A Stone of Ruskin's Venice', 158–59.
34 Blythe, 'A Stone of Ruskin's Venice', 159.
35 Blythe, 'A Stone of Ruskin's Venice', 160.
36 Blythe, 'A Stone of Ruskin's Venice', 169.
37 T.S. Eliot, 'Burbank with a Baedeker: Bleistein with a Cigar', in *Collected Poems 1909–1962* (London: Faber and Faber, 1963), 42–43.
38 F. T. Marinetti, 'The Founding and Manifesto of Futurism', in *Marinetti, Selected Writings*, ed. R.W. Flint, trans. R.W. Flint and Arthur Coppotelli (New York: Farrar, Straus, and Giroux, 1972), 39–44.
39 Alexandra Wilson, 'Torrefranca vs. Puccini: Embodying a decadent Italy', *Cambridge Opera Journal*, 13, no. 1 (2001): 39.
40 Umberto Boccioni, 'Technical Manifesto of Futurist Sculpture' (1912), in *Modern Artists on Art*, ed. Robert L. Herbert (Mineola, N.Y.: Dover, 2000), 46.
41 Boccioni, 'Technical Manifesto of Futurist Sculpture', 50.
42 Antonio Sant'Elia, 'Manifesto of Futurist Architecture' (1914), in *Documents of Twentieth Century Art: Futurist Manifestos*, ed. Umbro Apollonio, trans. Robert Brain, R.W. Flint, J.C. Higgitt, and Caroline Tisdall (New York: Viking, 1973), 169–170.
43 Dorthe Gert Simonsen, 'Accelerating Modernity: Time–Space Compression in the Wake of the Aeroplane', *Journal of Transport History*, 26, no. 2 (2005): 107.
44 Marinetti, 'Against Past-Loving Venice', in *Marinetti: Selected Writings*, 55.
45 Simonsen, 'Accelerating Modernity', 104.
46 Cinzia Sartini Blum, *The Other Modernism: F.T. Marinetti's Futurist Fiction of Power* (Berkeley: University of California Press, 1996), 179, n. 30.
47 Claire Bishop and Boris Groys, 'Bring the Noise', interview on Futurism for *Tate etc. Online*, 2009, http://tinyurl.com/tate-interview-futurism
48 Simonsen, 'Accelerating Modernity', 105.
49 Marinetti, 'Manifesto concerning the Ethiopian Colonial War' (1934), quoted in Walter Benjamin, *The Work of Art in the Age of Mechanical Reproduction* (London: Penguin, 2008), 36–37.
50 Benjamin, *The Work of Art in the Age of Mechanical Reproduction*, 36.
51 Marjorie Perloff, *The Futurist Moment: Avant-garde, Avant guerre, and the Language of Rupture* (Chicago: University of Chicago Press, 2003), 103.
52 Anne Bowler, 'Politics as Art: Italian Futurism and Fascism', *Theory and Society*, 20, no. 6 (1991): 772.
53 Perloff, *The Futurist Moment*, 36.

CHAPTER 5

1. W.G. Sebald, *On the Natural History of Destruction*, trans. Anthea Bell (London: Penguin, 2003), 65.
2. Erich Fromm, *The Anatomy of Human Destructiveness* (London: Pimlico, 1997), 528.
3. Anthony McElligott, *The German Urban Experience, 1900-1945: Modernity and Crisis* (Abingdon: Routledge, 2001), 1.
4. Adolf Hitler, *Mein Kampf*, trans. Ralph Manheim (London: Pimlico, 1997), 136.
5. For a history of bombing, see Sven Lindqvist, *A History of Bombing*, trans. Linda Rugg (New York: The New Press, 2001). See also Tom Vanderbilt, *Survival City: Adventures Among the Ruins of Atomic America* (New York: Princeton Architectural Press, 2002), 53.
6. William H. McNeill, *The Pursuit of Power: Technology, Armed Force, and Society since A.D. 1000* (Oxford: Blackwell, 1983), 306.
7. Hew Strachan, 'Strategic Bombing and the Question of Civilian Casualties up to 1945', in *Firestorm: The Bombing of Dresden, 1945*, ed. Paul Addison and Jeremy A. Crang (London: Pimlico, 2006), 2.
8. Nicola Lambourne, *War Damage in Western Europe: the Destruction of historic Monuments during the Second World War* (Edinburgh: Edinburgh University Press, 2001), 13.
9. Lambourne, *War Damage in Western Europe*, 14.
10. Lambourne, *War Damage in Western Europe*, 22.
11. Jon Calame, 'Post-war Reconstruction: Concerns, Models and Approaches', *Center for Macro Projects and Diplomacy Working Paper Series*, 6 (2005), 1.
12. Calame, 'Post-war Reconstruction', 2.
13. Carl von Clausewitz, *On War*, trans. Michael Howard and Peter Paret (Princeton: Princeton University Press, 1989), 77.
14. Sebald, *On the Natural History of Destruction*, 19.
15. Sebald, *On the Natural History of Destruction*, 20.
16. Thomas Mann, *Doctor Faustus: the Life of the German Composer Adrian Leverkühn, as told by a Friend*, trans. H.T. Lowe-Porter (London: Minerva, 1996), 337.
17. Lambourne, *War Damage in Western Europe*, 1–2.
18. Jaqueline Borin, 'Embers of the Soul: the Destruction of Jewish Books and Libraries in Poland during World War II', *Libraries and Culture*, 28, no. 4 (1993): 456–457.
19. Marek Sroka, 'The University of Cracow Library under Nazi Occupation: 1939–1945', *Libraries and Culture*, 34, no. 1 (1999): 3.
20. Sroka, 'The University of Cracow Library under Nazi Occupation', 12.

21 See, for example, Ulrich Herbert, 'Extermination Policy: New Answers and Questions about the History of the "Holocaust" in German Historiography', and Christoph Dieckmann, 'The War and the Killing of the Lithuanian Jews', both in *National Socialist Extermination Policies: Contemporary German Perspectives and Controversies*, ed. Ulrich Herbert (New York: Berghahn, 2000), and Tobias Jersak, 'Blitzkrieg Revisited: A New Look at Nazi War and Extermination Planning', *The Historical Journal*, 43, no. 2 (2000).
22 Robert Bevan, *The Destruction of Memory: Architecture at War* (London: Reaktion, 2006), 97.
23 Anthony Tung, *Preserving the World's Great Cities: the Destruction and Renewal of the Historic Metropolis* (New York: Three Rivers Press, 2001), 73.
24 Niels Gutschow, *Ordnungswahn: Architekten planen im 'eingedeutschten Osten', 1939–1945* (Gütersloh: Bertelsmann Fachzeitschriften, 2001), 45–46.
25 Marian Marek Drozdowski and Andrzej Zahorski, *Historia Warszawy* (Warsaw: Jeden Swiat Wydawnictwo, 2004), 322.
26 Cited in Irene Tomaszewsi, *Inside a Gestapo Prison: the Letters of Krystyna Wituska, 1942–1944* (Detroit: Wayne State University Press, 2006), xxii.
27 Gerhard Fehl, 'The Nazi Garden City', in *The Garden City: Past, Present, and Future*, ed. Stephen V. Ward (Abingdon: Taylor and Francis, 1992), 88.
28 Fehl, 'The Nazi Garden City', 94. My italics.
29 Richard Grunberger, *A Social History of the Third Reich* (London: Penguin, 1991), 278.
30 Grunberger, *A Social History of the Third Reich*, 280.
31 For details of those deported, see *Księga Pamięci, Transporty Polaków z Warszawy do KL Auschwitz 1940–1944*, published by the Auschwitz Museum in 2000.
32 Borin, 'Embers of the Soul', 447.
33 Lambourne, *War Damage in Western Europe*, 198–199.
34 Sebald, *On the Natural History of Destruction*, 6–7.
35 Cited in James E. Young, 'The Biography of a Memorial Icon: Nathan Rapoport's Warsaw Ghetto Monument', *Representations*, 26 (1989): 82.
36 Jerzy Elzanowski, 'Manufacturing Ruins: Architecture and Representation in Post-catastrophic Warsaw', *The Journal of Architecture*, 15, no. 1 (2010): 73.
37 Calame, 'Post-war Reconstruction', 9.
38 Calame, 'Post-war Reconstruction', 9.
39 Calame, 'Post-war Reconstruction', 13–14.
40 Tung, *Preserving the World's Great Cities*, 84.
41 Elzanowski, 'Manufacturing Ruins', 74.
42 Elzanowski, 'Manufacturing Ruins', 79–80.
43 Alexi Ferster Marmot, 'Urbanism in Warsaw: Solidarity and Beyond', *Places*, 1, no. 2 (1983): 83.

44 Elzanowski, 'Manufacturing Ruins', 71.
45 See Christina Cameron, 'The Context of the World Heritage Convention: Key Decisions and Emerging Concepts', paper given at UNESCO, 25–27, 2009, *Reflections on the Future of the World Heritage Convention*, http://tinyurl.com/cameron-pdf

CHAPTER 6

1 András J. Riedlmayer, 'From the Ashes: The Past and Future of Bosnia's Cultural Heritage', in *Islam and Bosnia: Conflict Resolution and Foreign Policy in Multi-Ethnic States*, ed. Maya Shatzmiller (Montreal: McGill–Queens University Press, 2002), 115.
2 Erica Bouris, *Complex Political Victims* (Bloomfield, C.T.: Kumarian Press, 2007), 101.
3 Samuel Huntington, 'The Erosion of American National Interests', *Foreign Affairs*, 76, no. 5 (1997): 28.
4 P.H. Liotta and Anna Simons, 'Thicker than Water? Kin, Religion, and Conflict in the Balkans', *Parameters*, 23, no. 4 (1998): 12.
5 See *The Desecularization of the World: Resurgent Religion and World Politics*, ed. Peter Berger (Grand Rapids, Mich.: Eerdmans, 1999); the November 2006 edition of *Prospect* entitled 'God Returns to Europe', in particular Eric Kaufmann, 'Breeding for God'; Danilo Breschi, 'A New Humanism in Europe: Between Secularism and the Return of Religion', *Telos*, 2007, http://tinyurl.com/breschi-humanism; *Religion in International Relations: The Return from Exile*, ed. Fabio Petito and Pavlos Hatzopoulos (Basingstoke: Palgrave Macmillan, 2003); and Jürgen Habermas and Joseph Ratzinger, *The Dialectics of Secularization: on Reason and Religion* (San Francisco: Ignatius, 2006).
6 Edin Hajdarpašić, 'Out of the Ruins of the Ottoman Empire: Reflections on the Ottoman Legacy in South-eastern Europe', *Middle Eastern Studies*, 44, no. 5 (2008): 717.
7 For a refutation of the notion of secularization, see John Milbank, *Theology and Social Theory: Beyond Secular Reason* (Oxford: Blackwell, 2006), and Adrian Pabst, 'The Paradox of Faith: Religion beyond Secularization and Desecularization', in *The Deepening Crisis: Governance Challenges after Neoliberalism*, ed. Craig Calhoun and Georgi M. Derlugian (New York: New York University Press, 2011), 162.
8 Hajdarpašić, 'Out of the Ruins of the Ottoman Empire', 718.
9 Noel Malcolm, *Bosnia: A Short History* (London: Macmillan, 1996), 222.
10 Malcolm, *Bosnia*, 222–223.
11 Malcolm, *Bosnia*, 215–217.

12 Viktor Meier, cited in Sabrina P. Ramet, *Thinking about Yugoslavia: Scholarly Debates about the Yugoslav Breakup and the Wars in Bosnia and Kosovo* (Cambridge: Cambridge University Press, 2005), 4.
13 Hajdarpašić, 'Out of the Ruins of the Ottoman Empire', 729–730.
14 Hajdarpašić, 'Out of the Ruins of the Ottoman Empire', 730.
15 Liotta and Simons, 'Kin, Religion, and Conflict in the Balkans'.
16 Vjekoslav Perica, 'The Politics of Ambivalence: Europeanization and the Serbian Orthodox Church', in *Religion in an Expanding Europe*, ed. Timothy A. Byrnes and Peter J. Katzenstein (Cambridge: Cambridge University Press, 2006), 182.
17 Michael Sells, *The Bridge Betrayed: Religion and Genocide in Bosnia* (Berkeley: University of California Press, 1998), 89.
18 Perica, 'The Politics of Ambivalence', 182.
19 Sells, *The Bridge Betrayed*, 89.
20 Michael Sells, 'Religion, History, and Genocide in Bosnia-Herzegovina', in *Religion and Justice in the War over Bosnia*, ed. G. Scott Davis (New York: Routledge, 1997), 24.
21 Sells, 'Religion, History, and Genocide in Bosnia-Herzegovina', 33.
22 Sells, 'Religion, History, and Genocide in Bosnia-Herzegovina', 35.
23 Malcolm, *Bosnia*, 213.
24 Sells, 'Religion, History, and Genocide in Bosnia-Herzegovina', 35.
25 Riedlmayer, 'From the Ashes', 99.
26 Riedlmayer, 'From the Ashes', 113, 115.
27 Martin Coward, 'Urbicide in Bosnia', in *Cities, War, and Terrorism: towards an Urban Geopolitics*, ed. Stephen Graham (Oxford: Blackwell, 2004), 165.
28 Coward, 'Urbicide in Bosnia', 166.
29 Malcolm, *Bosnia*, 246.
30 Sara Fregonese and Ralf Brand, 'Polarization as a Socio-Material Phenomenon: A Bibliographical Review', *Journal of Urban Technology*, 16, no. 2 (2009): 14.
31 See the testimony of 'D.V.' from Emmett, Idaho, in *Children of Atlantis: voices from the former Yugoslavia*, ed. Zdenko Lešić (Budapest: Central European University Press, 1995), 31.
32 Machiel Kiel, 'Un héritage non désiré : le patrimoine architectural islamique ottoman dans l'Europe du Sud-Est, 1370–1912', *Études Balkaniques*, 12 (2005), 26–28.
33 Riedlmayer, 'From the Ashes', 103.
34 Riedlmayer, 'From the Ashes', 118.
35 Human Rights Chamber for Bosnia and Herzegovina, Case no. CH/96/29, 'The Islamic Community in Bosnia and Herzegovina against The Republika Srpska' (1999), 15.
36 'The Islamic Community in Bosnia and Herzegovina against The Republika Srpska', 8.

37 Hajdarpašić, 'Out of the Ruins of the Ottoman Empire', 715.
38 Bosnia and Herzegovina Commission to Preserve National Monuments, *Report no. 08.2-6-533/03-8*, articles II and III, 2003, http://tinyurl.com/ferhadija-commission-report
39 Nadia Copuzzo Derković, 'Dealing with the Past: the Role of Cultural Heritage Preservation and Monuments in a Post-Conflict Society', in *World Heritage and Cultural Diversity*, ed. Marie-Therese Albert and Dieter Offenhäusser (German Commission for UNESCO, 2010), 188.
40 Malcolm, *Bosnia*, 219, 220.
41 Sells, 'Religion, History, and Genocide in Bosnia-Herzegovina', 38.
42 Huntington, *The Clash of Civilizations*, 254.
43 See video uploaded as 'British Mujahideen in Bosnia' on YouTube, http://tinyurl.com/british-fighter-bosnia
44 Riedlmayer, 'From the Ashes', 128.
45 Stephen Schwartz, 'Islamic Fundamentalism in the Balkans', *Partisan Review*, 67, no. 3 (2000), http://tinyurl.com/schwartz-fundamentalism
46 Dan Bilefsky, 'Islamic Revival Tests Bosnia's Secular Cast', in *New York Times*, December 27, 2008.
47 Robert J. Donia, 'Nationalism and Religious Extremism in Bosnia-Herzegovina and Kosovo since 1990', *International Institute for Middle East and Balkan Studies*, 2007, http://tinyurl.com/donia-balkans
48 Stephen Schwartz, 'The Arab Betrayal of Balkan Islam', *Middle East Quarterly*, 9, no. 2 (2002), http://tinyurl.com/schwartz-arab-betrayal

CHAPTER 7

1 Finbarr Barry Flood, 'Between Cult and Culture: Bamiyan, Islamic Iconoclasm, and the Museum', *The Art Bulletin*, 84, no. 4 (2002): 651.
2 Peter Maass, 'The Toppling: how the Media inflated a Minor Moment in a Long War', in *The New Yorker*, January 10, 2011.
3 See Jytte Klausen, 'The Danish Cartoons and Modern Iconoclasm in the Cosmopolitan Muslim Diaspora', *Harvard Middle Eastern and Islamic Review*, 8, no. 1 (2009): 86–118. See also Michael Sells, 'Taliban, Image War, and Iconoclasm', http://tinyurl.com/sells-taliban
4 Flood, 'Between Cult and Culture', 641.
5 The trailer for Frei's 2005 film, *The Giant Buddhas*, shows the attacks from two angles, one close-range and the other from across the valley. It is available online: http://tinyurl.com/frei-buddha. Another film of historical interest is that of Hal, Halla and David Linker's travelogue documentary, *Adventure in Afghanistan: The Wild, the Weird, and the Wonderful* (1973), available through the Smithsonian Institution and the Human Studies Film Archives' series of anthropological films posted on YouTube. It shows the Linkers walking up the cliffside and through a

newly discovered network of passages and caves to stand on one of the Buddhas' heads, from which wall-paintings can be seen on the rock face. It is available online: http://tinyurl.com/linker-buddha

6. Matthew Power, 'Dispatch from Afghanistan', *Slate*, 2004, http://tinyurl.com/power-bamiyan
7. Flood, 'Between Cult and Culture', 643.
8. Flood, 'Between Cult and Culture', 654.
9. Flood, 'Between Cult and Culture', 645.
10. Jamal J. Elias, '(Un)making Idolatry: from Mecca to Bamiyan', *Future Anterior*, 4, no. 2 (2007):14.
11. Elias, '(Un)making Idolatry', 16.
12. Elias, '(Un)making Idolatry', 19.
13. Elias, '(Un)making Idolatry', 20.
14. Elias, '(Un)making Idolatry', 22.
15. These interviews are available on the Internet. For example, see the conversation between Charlie Rose and Sayed Rahmatullah Hashemi in 2001, available on YouTube, http://tinyurl.com/rose-taliban
16. Elias, '(Un)making Idolatry', 23.
17. Flood, 'Between Cult and Culture', 651.
18. Flood, 'Between Cult and Culture', 653.
19. Elias, '(Un)making Idolatry', 14.
20. Cited in Giovanna Borradori, *Philosophy in a Time of Terror: Dialogues with Jürgen Habermas and Jacques Derrida* (Chicago: University of Chicago Press, 2003), 28.
21. 'Saudi Arabia hopes Giant Clock Will Establish "Mecca Time" to Replace GMT', *Agence France Presse*, 8 November 2010.
22. Quoted from the website for the Fairmont Makkah Clock Royal Hotel, http://www.fairmont.com/makkah
23. Quoted from the website for the Fairmont Makkah Clock Royal Hotel.
24. 'Redevelopment Plans: Oxford Business Group talks to Osama al-Bar, Mayor of Mecca', in *Report: Saudi Arabia 2010* (London: Oxford Business Group, 2010), 17.
25. 'Al-Shoala and Emaar sign SR27 billion joint Venture to develop 31 million sq. m. Rawabi Rumah mixed-use Project', in *Al-Bawaba*, 5 October 2008.
26. Hassan M. Fattah, 'The Price of Progress: Transforming Islam's Holiest Site', in *New York Times*, 8 March 2007.
27. On the Turkish minister's comparison of Saudi Arabia's construction of Abraj al-Bait and the Taliban's destruction of the Bamiyan Buddhas, see the report, 'Turkey criticizes Saudi Arabia over Ottoman Fortress Destruction', in *Al-Bawaba*, 9 January 2002.
28. 'Saudis hit back over Mecca Castle', *BBC News*, 9 January 2002.

29 A frustratingly little amount of scholarly material has been published on the construction of Abraj al-Bait, and as a result much of my information comes from research through unverified – and unverifiable – internet sites, most of which are characterized by accusation and anger. This is made more difficult by the fact that, as a non-Muslim, I am unable to visit Mecca myself to confirm the condition of shrines which are said to have been destroyed. However, a list of such sites was provided by the opposition activist Irfan Ahmed al-Alawi, in 'The Destruction of Holy Sites in Mecca and Medina', *Islamica Magazine*, 15 (2007), 71. Accessed 2 September 2009.
30 Muhammad al-Atawneh, *Wahhabi Islam facing the Challenges of Modernity: Dar al-Ifta in the Modern Saudi State* (Leiden: Brill, 2010), 147.
31 Al-Atawneh, *Wahhabi Islam facing the Challenges of Modernity*, 149.
32 Al-Atawneh, *Wahhabi Islam facing the Challenges of Modernity*, 165, 166, 167.
33 Al-Atawneh, *Wahhabi Islam facing the Challenges of Modernity*, 147.
34 Khalid S. al-Dakhil, 'Wahhabism as an Ideology of State Formation', in *Religion and Politics in Saudi Arabia: Wahhabism and the State*, ed. Mohammed Ayoob and Hasan Kosebalaban (Boulder, C.O.: Lynne Rienner, 2008), 24.
35 Al-Dakhil, 'Wahhabism as an Ideology of State Formation', 25.
36 Alexander Knysh, 'A Clear and Present Danger: "Wahhabism" as a Rhetorical Foil', *Die Welt des Islams*, 4, no. 1 (2004): 9, 22.
37 Ziauddin Sardar, 'Rethinking Islam', in *Islam, Postmodernism, and other Futures: a Ziauddin Sardar Reader*, ed. Sohail Inayatullah and Gail Boxwell (London: Pluto, 2003), 32–33.
38 Elias, '(Un)making Idolatry', 26.

CONCLUSION

1 Weber, *The Protestant Ethic*, 114.
2 Fromm, *The Anatomy of Human Destructiveness*, 33.
3 Fromm, *The Anatomy of Human Destructiveness*, 575.
4 Theodor W. Adorno and Max Horkheimer, *Dialectic of Enlightenment*, trans. John Cumming (London: Verso, 1997), 4.
5 Bruno Latour, *We have Never been Modern*, trans. Catherine Porter (Cambridge, Mass.: Harvard University Press, 1993), 62.
6 Asad, *Formations of the Secular*, 62.
7 Milbank, *Theology and Social Theory*, 16.
8 Sebald, *On the Natural History of Destruction*, 65, 18.
9 Sebald, *On the Natural History of Destruction*, 66.
10 Fromm, *The Anatomy of Human Destructiveness*, 459–460.
11 Fromm, *The Anatomy of Human Destructiveness*, 462.

12 Adorno and Horkheimer, *Dialectic of Enlightenment*, 24, 13.
13 Latour, *We have Never been Modern*, 55.
14 Latour, *We have Never been Modern*, 46, 59.
15 Bruno Latour, *Pandora's Hope: Essays on the Reality of Science Studies* (Cambridge, Mass.: Harvard University Press, 1999), 266–267.

Bibliography

INTRODUCTION AND CONCLUSION

ADORNO, Theodor W., and Max Horkheimer. *Dialectic of Enlightenment*. Translated by John Cumming. London: Verso, 1997.

AMIS, Martin. *Koba the Dread: Laughter and the Twenty Million*. London: Jonathan Cape, 2002.

ASAD, Talal. *Formations of the Secular: Christianity, Islam, Modernity*. Stanford: Stanford University Press, 2003.

AUGUSTINE. *Concerning the City of God Against the Pagans*. Translated by Henry Bettenson. London: Penguin, 1972.

BARBER, Charles. *Figure and Likeness: On the Limits of Representation in Byzantine Iconoclasm*. Princeton: Princeton University Press, 2002.

BARTHES, Roland. *Mythologies*. Translated by Annette Lavers. London: Vintage, 2000.

BESANCON, Alain. *The Forbidden Image: An Intellectual History of Iconoclasm*. Translated by Jane Marie Todd. Chicago: University of Chicago Press, 2000.

CHAPMAN, Henry, and Benjamin Geare. 'Palaeoecology and the Perception of prehistoric Landscapes: some Comments on visual Approaches to Phenomenology'. *Antiquity* 74, no. 284 (2000): 316–319.

DAMASCUS, John of. *On Holy Images: Followed by Three Sermons on the Assumption*. Translated by M.H. Allies. London: Thomas Baker, 1899.

DANTO, Arthur C. *Narration and Knowledge*. New York: Columbia University Press, 1985.

DAVIES, J. G. *Pilgrimage Yesterday and Today: Why? Where? How?* London: SCM Press, 1988.

FROMM, Erich. *The Anatomy of Human Destructiveness*. London: Pimlico, 1997.

GAMBONI, Dario. *The Destruction of Art: Iconoclasm and Vandalism since the French Revolution*. Yale: Yale University Press, 1997.

GIRARD, René. *Violence and the Sacred*. Translated by Patrick Gregory. London: Continuum, 2005.

GRABAR, André. *Byzantine Painting*. Translated by Stuart Gilbert. Geneva: Albert Skira, 1953.

HOBBES, Thomas. *Leviathan*. New York: Norton, 1977.

HUFF, Toby, and Wolfgang Schluchter. *Max Weber and Islam*. London, Transaction: 1999.

HUNTINGTON, Samuel P. *The Clash of Civilizations and the Remaking of World Order*. New York: Simon and Schuster, 1997.
JASPERS, Karl. *Leonardo, Descartes, Max Weber: Three Essays*. Translated by Ralph Manheim. London: Routledge, 1964.
JOHN PAUL II. 'Celebration of the Unveiling of the Restoration of Michelangelo's Frescoes in the Sistine Chapel'. *Vatican Homilies* 1994. http://tinyurl.com/john-paul-michelangelo
———. 'Letter to Artists', *Vatican Letters* 1999. http://tinyurl.com/john-paul-artists
JULIUS, Anthony. *Idolizing Pictures: Idolatry, Iconoclasm, and Jewish Art*. London: Thames and Hudson, 2001.
LATOUR, Bruno. *We have Never been Modern*. Translated by Catherine Porter. Cambridge, Massachusetts: Harvard University Press, 1993.
———. *Pandora's Hope: Essays on the Reality of Science Studies*. Cambridge, Massachusetts: Harvard University Press, 1999.
———, and Peter Weibel (eds.). *Iconoclash: Beyond the Image Wars in Science, Religion, and Art*. Cambridge, Massachusetts: MIT Press, 2002.
LUPTON, J.H. *St. John of Damascus*. London: Society for Promoting Christian Knowledge, 1882.
MCCLANAN, Anne (ed.). *Negating the Image: Case Studies in Iconoclasm*. London: Ashgate, 2006.
MILBANK, John, Graham Ward, and Edith Wyschogrod. *Theological Perspectives on God and Beauty*. London: Continuum, 2003.
———. *Theology and Social Theory: Beyond Secular Reason*. Oxford: Blackwell, 2006.
MIRANDOLA, Giovanni Pico della. *On the Dignity of Man*. Translated by Charles Glenn Wallis. Indianapolis: Hackett, 1998.
MORGAN, David. 'The Vicissitudes of Seeing: Iconoclasm and Idolatry'. *Religion* 33, no. 2 (2003): 170–180.
MUMFORD, Lewis. *The City in History: Its Origins, Its Transformations, and Its Prospects*. London: Secker and Warburg, 1961.
NOWELL, Gregory. 'Hyper-Conservative Modernization: The United States, Saudi Arabia, and Poland'. Paper presented at the International Studies Association, Montreal, 17 March 2004.
OUSPENSKY, Léonide. *La Théologie de l'Icône dans l'Église Orthodoxe*. Paris: Les Éditions du Cerf, 1980.
PABST, Adrian. 'The Paradox of Faith: Religion beyond Secularization and Desecularization'. In *The Deepening Crisis: Governance Challenges after Neoliberalism*. Edited by Craig Calhoun and Georgi M. Derlugian. New York: New York University Press, 2011.
PARTRIDGE, Loren. *Michelangelo: The Last Judgement – A Glorious Restoration*. New York: Harry N. Abrams, 2000.
PETERS, F.E. *Judaism, Christianity, and Islam: The Classic Texts and their Interpretation*. Princeton: Princeton University Press, 1990.
RACKHAM, Oliver. *The History of the Countryside: the Classic History of Britain's Landscape, Flora, and Fauna*. London: Phoenix, 2000.

RAMBELLI, Fabio, and Eric Reinders. *Buddhism and Iconoclasm in East Asia: A History*. London: Continuum, 2012.

RÉAU, Louis. *Histoire du vandalisme: les monuments détruits de l'art français*. Paris: Laffont, 1994.

RYE, Walter. *A History of Norfolk*. London: Elliot Stock, 1885.

SAUSSURE, Ferdinand de. *Cours de linguistique générale*. Paris: Payot, 1916.

SEBALD, W.G. *On the Natural History of Destruction*. Translated by Anthea Bell. London: Penguin, 2004.

SKINNER, Quentin. *The Foundations of Modern Political Thought. Volume One: The Renaissance*. Cambridge: Cambridge University Press, 1978.

SUMPTION, Jonathan. *Pilgrimage: An Image of Mediaeval Religion*. London: Faber and Faber, 2002.

TREVOR-ROPER, Hugh. *The Last Days of Hitler*. London: Macmillan, 1995.

TURNER, Bryan S. *Weber and Islam*. London: Routledge, 1998.

TURNER, Denys. *Faith, Reason, and the Existence of God*. Cambridge: Cambridge University Press, 2004.

WEBER, Max. *The Sociology of Religion*. Translated by Ephraim Fischoff. London: Methuen, 1965.

———. *Economy and Society: an Outline of Interpretive Sociology*. Translated by Ephraim Fischoff. Berkeley: University of California Press, 1979.

———. *Political Writings*. Edited by Peter Lassman and Ronald Speirs. Cambridge: Cambridge University Press, 1994.

———. *The Protestant Ethic and the Spirit of Capitalism*. Translated by Talcott Parsons. London: Routledge, 2001.

WILSON, Ian. *The Turin Shroud*. London: Penguin, 1979.

CHAPTER 1

BAINTON, Roland H. 'Interpretations of the Reformation'. In *The Reformation: Basic Interpretations*. Edited by Lewis W. Spitz. Toronto: D. C. Heath, 1972.

BONJOUR, Edgar. *A Short History of Switzerland*. Oxford: Clarendon, 1952.

BOUWSMA, William J. *John Calvin: A Sixteenth-Century Portrait*. New York: Oxford University Press, 1988.

BREEN, Quirinus. *John Calvin: A Study in French Humanism*. North Haven: Archon, 1968.

BRIÇONNET, Guillaume, and Marguerite D'Angouleme, *Correspondance (1521-1524). Vol. 1, Années 1521-1522*. Geneva: Droz, 1975.

CALVIN, John. *Commentary on the Book of Psalms*. Translated by James Anderson. Edinburgh: Calvin Translation Society, 1845–49.

———. 'Vita Calvini'. In *Ioannis Calvini Opera quae supersunt omnia, vol. 23*. Edited by G. Baum, E. Cunitz, and E. Reuss. Braunschweig: C.A. Schwetschke und Sohn, 1863–1900.

———. *Commentaries*. Edited by Joseph Haroutunian. London: SCM Press, 1958.

———. *Commentary on the Gospel according to St. John. 1–10.* Translated by T.H.L. Parker. Edinburgh: Oliver and Boyd, 1959.
———. *Institutes of the Christian Religion.* Translated by Henry Beveridge. London: James Clarke and Co., 1962.
———. *Letters of John Calvin selected from the Bonnet Edition.* Edinburgh: The Banner of Truth Trust, 1980.
CHAMBERS, D. S. *Popes, Cardinals, and War: The Military Church in Renaissance and Early Modern Europe.* London: I.B.Tauris, 2006.
COLEMAN, Simon, and John Elsner. *Pilgrimage Past and Present: Sacred Travel and Sacred Space in the World Religions.* London: British Museum Press, 1995.
CREW, P.M. *Calvinist Preaching and Iconoclasm in the Netherlands, 1544–1569.* Cambridge: Cambridge University Press, 1978.
EIRE, Carlos. *War Against the Idols: The Reformation of Worship from Erasmus to Calvin.* Cambridge: Cambridge University Press, 1989.
ELTON, G.R. *Reformation Europe 1517–1559.* London: Collins, 1964.
FROMMENT, Antoine. *Les actes et gestes merveilleux de la cité de Genève nouvellement convertie à l'Evangille, faictz du temps de leur Reformation et comment ils l'ont receue, redigez par escript en fourme de Chroniques, Annales ou Hystoyres commençant l'an MDXXXII.* Geneva: Jules Guillaume Fick, 1854.
GINZBURG, Carlos. *The Cheese and the Worms: The Cosmos of a Sixteenth-Century Miller.* London: Penguin, 1992.
GORDON, Bruce. *The Swiss Reformation.* Manchester: Manchester University Press, 2002.
GORSKI, Philip S. *The Disciplinary Revolution: Calvinism and the Rise of the State in Early Modern Europe.* Chicago: Chicago University Press, 2003.
GREENBLATT, Stephen. *Renaissance Self-Fashioning: From More to Shakespeare.* Chicago: University of Chicago Press, 1984.
GRELL, Ole Peter. 'Merchants and Ministers: the Foundation of International Calvinism'. In *Calvinism in Europe, 1540–1620.* Edited by Andrew Pettegree, Alastair Duke, and Gillian Lewis. Cambridge: Cambridge University Press, 1994.
HEYER, Henri. *Guillaume Farel: An Introduction to his Theology.* Translated by Blair Reynolds. Lewiston: Mellen, 1990.
HÖPFL, Harro. *The Christian Polity of John Calvin.* Cambridge: Cambridge University Press, 1982.
———. *Luther and Calvin on Secular Authority.* Cambridge: Cambridge University Press, 2005.
KNOWLES, David. *Bare Ruined Choirs: The Dissolution of the English Monasteries.* Cambridge: Cambridge University Press, 1976.
MCGRATH, Alister E. *A Life of John Calvin: A Study in the Shaping of Western Culture.* Oxford: Blackwell, 1990.
MCNEILL, John T. *The History and Character of Calvinism.* New York: Oxford University Press, 1954.

MANGRUM, Bryan D., and Giuseppe Scavizzi (eds.), *A Reformation Debate: Karlstadt, Emser, and Eck on Sacred Images. Three Treatises in Translation*. Toronto: Dovehouse Editions, 1991.

MONTER, E. William. *Studies in Genevan Government, 1536–1605*. Geneva: Droz, 1964.

———. 'Historical Demography and Religious History in Sixteenth-Century Geneva'. *Journal of Interdisciplinary History* 9, no. 3 (1979): 399–427.

MULLER, Richard A. 'John Calvin and later Calvinism: the Identity of the Reformed tradition'. In *The Cambridge Companion to Reformation Theology*. Edited by David Bagchi and David C. Steinmetz. Cambridge: Cambridge University Press, 2004.

MURDOCK, Graeme. *Beyond Calvin: The Intellectual, Political and Cultural World of Europe's Reformed Churches*. London: Palgrave, 2004.

NAPHY, William G. 'Calvin's Geneva'. In *The Cambridge Companion to John Calvin*. Edited by Donald K. McKim, Cambridge: Cambridge University Press, 2004.

NICHOLLS, David. 'Heresy and Protestantism, 1520–1542: Questions of Perception and Communication'. *French History* 10, no. 2 (1996): 182–205.

PARKER, T. H. L. *John Calvin: A Biography*. London: J. M. Dent, 1975.

PRESTWICH, Menna (ed.). *International Calvinism 1541–1715*. Oxford: Clarendon, 1985.

RÉMOND, Florimond de. *L'Histoire de la naissance, progrèz et décadence de l'hérésie de ce siècle*. Paris: Guillaume de La Noue, 1605.

STEINMETZ, David C. 'The Theology of John Calvin'. In *The Cambridge Companion to Reformation Theology*. Edited by David Bagchi and David C. Steinmetz. Cambridge: Cambridge University Press, 2004.

STEVENSON, William R. Jnr.. 'Calvin and Political Issues'. In *The Cambridge Companion to John Calvin*. Edited by Donald K. McKim. Cambridge: Cambridge University Press, 2004.

VALERI, Mark. 'Religion, Discipline, and the Economy in Calvin's Geneva'. *Sixteenth Century Journal* 28, no. 1 (1997): 123–142.

WANDEL, Lee Palmer. *The Eucharist in the Reformation: Incarnation and Liturgy*. Cambridge: Cambridge University Press, 2006.

ZWINGLI, Ulrich. *Commentary on True and False Religion*. Oslo: Labyrinth Press, 1981.

CHAPTERS 2 AND 7

AL-ABBASI, Ali Bey. *Travels of Ali Bey in Morocco, Tripoli, Cyprus, Egypt, Arabia, Syria and Turkey, between the Years 1803 and 1807, written by Himself*. London: Longman, Hurst, Rees, Orme, and Brown, 1816.

AL-ALAWI, Irfan Ahmed. 'The Destruction of Holy Sites in Mecca and Medina'. *Islamica Magazine* 15 (2007).

AL-ANSARY, A.R. *Qaryat al-Fau*. Riyadh: University of Riyadh, 1981.

ASAD, Muhammad. *The Road to Mecca*. London: Muslim Academic Trust, 1998.
AL-ATAWNEH, Muhammad. *Wahhabi Islam facing the Challenges of Modernity: Dar al-Ifta in the Modern Saudi State*. Leiden: Brill, 2010.
AL-AZMEH, Aziz. *Islam and Modernities*. London: Verso, 1993.
———. *Muslim Kingship: Power and the Sacred in Muslim, Christian, and Pagan Polities*. London: I.B.Tauris, 1997.
AL-BAGHDADI, Ibrahim Fasih al-Haydari. *Unwan al-majd fi tarikh Baghdad wa-l-basra wa-najd*. Baghdad: Dar Manshurat al-Basri, 1962.
BARI, Muhammad. 'The Early Wahhabis and the Sharifs of Makkah'. *Journal of The Pakistan Historical Society* 3, no. 2 (1955): 91–104.
IBN BISHR, Uthman. *Unwan al-Majd fi Tarikh Najd*. Riyadh: Matbuat Darat al-Malik Abd al-Aziz, 1982.
BORRADORI, Giovanna. *Philosophy in a Time of Terror: Dialogues with Jürgen Habermas and Jacques Derrida*. Chicago: University of Chicago Press, 2003.
BRYDGES, H.J. *An Account of the Transactions of his Majesty's Mission to the Court of Persia, in the years 1807–1811 ... to which is appended, A Brief History of the Wahauby*. London: J. Bohn, 1834.
BURCKHARDT, Jean Louis. *Travels in Arabia, comprehending an Account of those Territories in Hedjaz which the Muhammadans regard as Sacred*. London: H. Colburn, 1829.
———. 'Materials for a History of the Wahábys'. In *Notes on the Bedouins and Wahábys*. Reading: Garnet, 1992 (1830).
COOK, Michael. 'On the Origins of Wahhabism'. *Journal of the Royal Asiatic Society* 2, no. 2 (1992): 191–202.
CORANCEZ, Louis Alexandre Olivier de. *The History of the Wahabis from their Origin until the end of 1809*. Translated by Eric Tabet. Reading: Garnet, 1995.
AL-DAKHIL, Khalid S. 'Wahhabism as an Ideology of State Formation'. In *Religion and Politics in Saudi Arabia: Wahhabism and the State*. Edited by Mohammed Ayoob and Hasan Kosebalaban. Boulder, C.O.: Lynne Rienner, 2008.
DALLAL, Ahmad. 'The Origins and Objectives of Islamic Revivalist Thought, 1750–1850'. *Journal of the American Oriental Society* 113, no. 3 (1993): 341–359.
DELONG-BAS, Natana J. *Wahhabi Islam: from Revival and Reform to global Jihad*. London: I.B.Tauris, 2007.
DRESCH, Paul. 'Arabia to the End of the First World War'. In *The New Cambridge History of Islam. Vol 5: The Islamic World in the Age of Western Dominance*. Edited by F.H. Robinson. Cambridge: Cambridge University Press, 2010.
ELIAS, Jamal J. '(Un)making Idolatry: from Mecca to Bamiyan'. *Future Anterior* 4, no. 2 (2007): 12–29.
FAHD, Toufic. *Le Panthéon de l'Arabie occidentale avant l'Hégire*. Paris: Paul Guethner, 1968.
FAROQHI, Suraiya. *Pilgrims and Sultans: The Hajj under the Ottomans, 1517–1683*. London: I.B.Tauris, 1994.

AL-FARSY, Fouad. *Saudi Arabia: A Case-Study in Development*. London: Kegan Paul International, 1982.

FATTAH, Hassan. 'The Price of Progress: Transforming Islam's Holiest Site'. *New York Times*, 8 March 2007.

FLOOD, Finbarr Barry. 'Between Cult and Culture: Bamiyan, Islamic Iconoclasm, and the Museum'. *The Art Bulletin* 84, no. 4 (2002): 641–659.

GEAVES, Ron. *Aspects of Islam*. London: Ashgate, 2005.

GELLNER, Ernest. *Muslim Society*. Cambridge: Cambridge University Press, 1981.

IBN GHANNAM, Husayn. *Tarikh Najd*. Beirut: Dar al-Shuruq, 1994.

GOLDHIZER, Ignac. *Muslim Studies (Muhammedanische Studien)*. Translated by C.R. Barber and S.M. Stern. Chicago, Albany: Aldine, 1966.

GOLDRUP, Lawrence Paul. *Saudi Arabia: 1902–1932: The Development of a Wahhabi Society*. Unpublished Doctoral Dissertation. University of California, Los Angeles, 1971.

HOURANI, Albert. *A History of the Arab Peoples*. London: Faber, 2002.

IBN HUMAYD, Muhammad ibn Abdallah. *Al-Suhub al-wabila ala daraih al-hanabila*. Edited by Bakr Abdallah Abu Zayd and Abd al-Rahman ibn Sulayman al-Uthaymin. Beirut: Muassasat al-Risala, 1996.

HUNTER, W.W. *The Indian Musalmans: Are they Bound in Conscience to Rebel against the Queen?* London: Trubner, 1871.

KEDDIE, Nikki R. 'The Revolt of Islam, 1700 to 1993: Comparative Considerations and Relations to Imperialism'. *Comparative Studies in Society and History* 36, no. 3 (1994): 463–487.

KING, G. R. D. 'Islam, Iconoclasm, and the Declaration of Doctrine'. *Bulletin of the School of Oriental and African Studies* 48, no. 2 (1985): 267–277.

KLAUSEN, Jytte. 'The Danish Cartoons and Modern Iconoclasm in the Cosmopolitan Muslim Diaspora'. *Harvard Middle Eastern and Islamic Review* 8, no. 1 (2009): 86–118.

KNYSH, Alexander. 'The Cult of Saints in Hadramawt: An Overview'. In *New Arabian Studies, Vol 1*. Edited by R.B. Serjeant, R.W. Bidwell, and G. Rex Smith. Exeter: University of Exeter Press, 1993.

———. 'A Clear and Present Danger: "Wahhabism" as a Rhetorical Foil'. *Die Welt des Islams* 4, no. 1 (2004): 3–26.

KOSTINER, Joseph. 'Transforming Dualities: Tribe and State Formation in Saudi Arabia'. In *Tribes and State Formation in the Middle East*. Edited by Philip S. Khoury and Joseph Kostiner. London: I.B.Tauris, 1992.

LAPIDUS, Ira M. 'The Evolution of Muslim Urban Society'. *Comparative Studies in Society and History* 15, no. 1 (1973): 21–50.

MAASS, Peter. 'The Toppling: how the Media inflated a Minor Moment in a Long War'. *The New Yorker*, 10 January 2011.

MESSICK, Brinkley. *The Calligraphic State: Textual Domination and History in a Muslim Society*. Berkeley: University of California Press, 1993.

POWER, Matthew. 'Dispatch from Afghanistan'. *Slate*, 2004. http://tinyurl.com/power-bamiyan

AL-QUSAIBI, Ghazi bin Abdulrahman. 'Saudi Arabian Myths', 2002. http://tinyurl.com/saudi-myths.

AL-RASHEED, Madawi. 'Durable and non-durable Dynasties: The Rashidis and Saudis in Central Arabia'. *British Journal of Middle Eastern Studies* 19, no. 2 (1992):144–158.

———. *A History of Saudi Arabia*. Cambridge: Cambridge University Press: 2002.

SAID, Edward W. *Orientalism*. London: Penguin, 2003.

SARDAR, Ziauddin. *Islam, Postmodernism, and other Futures: a Ziauddin Sardar Reader*. Edited by Sohail Inayatullah and Gail Boxwell. London: Pluto, 2003.

SAUNDERS, Daniel. *A Journal of the Travels and Sufferings of Daniel Saunders, Jun, Mariner on board the ship Commerce, of Boston, SAMUEL JOHNSON, Commander, which was cast away near Cape Moribot, on the coast of Arabia, July 10, 1792*. Hudson, NY: Ashbel Stoddard, 1805.

SELLS, Michael. 'Taliban, Image War, and Iconoclasm'. Accessed 6 July 2010. http://tinyurl.com/sells-taliban

SNOUK, Hurgronje C. *Mekka in the Latter Part of the 19th Century: Daily Life, Customs, and Learning of the Muslims of the East-Indian Archipelago*. Leiden: Brill, 1931.

TEITELBAUM, Joshua. *The Rise and Fall of the Hashemite Kingdom*. London: Hurst and Co., 2001.

AL-TORKI, S., and D. Cole. *Arabian Oasis City: The Transformation of Unayzah*. Austin: University of Texas Press, 1989.

TRABOULSI, Samer. 'An Early Refutation of Muhammed ibn Abd al-Wahhab's Reformist Views'. *Die Welt des Islams* 42, no. 3 (2002): 373–415.

TROELLER, Gary. *The Birth of Saudi Arabia*. London: Routledge, 1976.

VASSILIEV, Alexei. *The History of Saudi Arabia*. London: Saqi, 1998.

VOLL, John. 'Muhammed Hayya al-Sindi and Muhammed ibn Abd al-Wahhab: An Analysis of an Intellectual Group in Eighteenth-Century Madina'. *Bulletin of the School of Oriental and African Studies* 38, no. 1 (1975): 32–39.

AL-WAHHAB, Muhammad ibn Abd. *Muallafat al-Shaykh al-Imam Muhammad ibn Abd al-Wahhab, vol. 1*. Riyadh: Jamiat al-Imam Muhammad bin Saud al-Islamiyah, 1977.

———. *Three Essays on Tawhid*. Edited by Ismail Raji al-Faruqi. Philadelphia: North American Trust Publications, 1979.

———. *Kitab al-Tawhid*. Edited by Allamah Abd al-Rahman al-Sadi. Birmingham: al-Hidaayah, 2003.

———. *Kitab Kashf al-Shubuhat*, Edited by Abu Ammar Yasir Qadhi. Birmingham: al-Hidaayah, 2003.

ZDANOWSKI, Jerzy. 'Military Organization of the Wahhabi Amirates (1750–1932)'. In *New Arabian Studies, vol. 2*. Edited by R.L Bidwell, J.R. Smart, and G. Rex Smith. Exeter: University of Exeter Press, 1993.

'Turkey criticizes Saudi Arabia over Ottoman Fortress Destruction'. *Al-Bawaba*, 9 January 2002.

'Saudis hit back over Mecca Castle', *BBC News*, 9 January 2002.
'Al-Shoala and Emaar sign SR27 billion joint Venture to develop 31 million sq. m. Rawabi Rumah mixed-use Project'. *Al-Bawaba*, 5 October 2008.
'Saudi Arabia hopes Giant Clock Will Establish "Mecca Time" to Replace GMT'. *Agence France Presse*, 8 November 2010.
'Redevelopment Plans: Oxford Business Group talks to Osama al-Bar, Mayor of Mecca'. In *Report: Saudi Arabia 2010*. London: Oxford Business Group, 2010.

CHAPTERS 3 AND 4

ANDERSON, Benedict. *Imagined Communities: Reflections on the Origin and Spread of Nationalism*. London: Verso, 2003.
ARMI, C. Edson. 'Report on the Destruction of Romanesque Architecture in Burgundy'. *Journal of the Society of Architectural Historians* 55, no. 3 (1996): 300–327.
BELLOC, Hilaire. *The French Revolution*. London: Butterworth, 1941.
BENJAMIN, Walter. *The Work of Art in the Age of Mechanical Reproduction*. London: Penguin, 2008.
BISHOP, Claire, and Boris Groys. 'Bring the Noise'. *Tate etc. Online*, 2009, http://tinyurl.com/tate-interview-futurism
BLUM, Cinzia Sartini. *The Other Modernism: F.T. Marinetti's Futurist Fiction of Power*. Berkeley: University of California Press, 1996.
BOCCIONI, Umberto. 'Technical Manifesto of Futurist Sculpture'. In *Modern Artists on Art*. Edited by Robert L. Herbert. Mineola, N.Y.: Dover, 2000.
BOWLER, Anne. 'Politics as Art: Italian Futurism and Fascism'. *Theory and Society* 20, no. 6 (1991): 763–794.
BURLEIGH, Michael. *Earthly Powers: The Conflict between Religion and Politics from the French Revolution to the Great War*. London: Harper, 2006.
CLAY, Richard. 'Bouchardon's Statue of Louis XV: Iconoclasm and the Transformation of Signs'. In *Iconoclasm: Contested Objects, Contested Terms*. Edited by Stacy Boldrick and Richard Clay. London: Ashgate, 2007.
———. 'Smells, Bells and Touch: Iconoclasm in Paris during the French Revolution'. *Eighteenth-Century Studies* 35, no. 4 (2012): 521 – 533.
COSGROVE, Denis. 'The Myth and the Stones of Venice: An Historical Geography of a Symbolic Landscape'. *Journal of Historical Geography* 8, no. 2 (1982): 145–169.
ELIOT, T.S. *Collected Poems 1909–1962*. London: Faber and Faber, 1963.
GREENE, Christopher M. 'Alexandre Lenoir and the Musée des monuments français during the French Revolution'. *French Historical Studies* 12, no. 2 (1981): 200–222.
HABERMAS, Jürgen. *The Structural Transformation of the Public Sphere*. Translated by Thomas Burger. Cambridge: Polity, 1989.
HEWISON, Robert (ed.). *New Approaches to Ruskin: Thirteen Essays*. London: Routledge, 1981.

HONOUR, Hugh. *The Companion Guide to Venice*. London: Collins, 1970.
IDZERDA, Stanley J. 'Iconoclasm during the French Revolution'. *American Historical Review* 60, no. 1 (1954): 13–26.
JAMES, Henry. *Italian Hours*. New York: Grove Press, 1979.
———. 'The Princess Casamassima'. In *Novels 1886–1890: The Princess Casamassima, The Reverberator, The Tragic Muse*. New York: Library of America, 1989.
———. *The American Scene*. New York: Penguin, 1994.
———. *Letters from the Palazzo Barbaro*. Edited by Rosella Mamoli Zorzi. London: Pushkin, 1998.
———. 'The Aspern Papers'. In *Complete Stories: 1884–1891*. New York: Library of America, 1999.
VAN KLEY, Dale K. *The Religious Origins of the French Revolution: from Calvin to the Civil Constitution, 1560–1791*. New Haven: Yale University Press, 1996.
LEFEBVRE, Henri. *The Productions of Space*. Translated by Donald Nicholson-Smith. Oxford: Blackwell, 1991.
MCCARTHY, Mary. *The Stones of Florence and Venice Observed*. Harmondsworth: Penguin, 1979.
MCFETRIDGE, Nathaniel S. *Calvinism in History*. Edmonton: Still Waters, 1989.
MARINETTI, F.T. *Selected Writings*. Edited by R.W. Flint, translated by R.W. Flint and Arthur Coppotelli. New York: Farrar, Straus, and Giroux, 1972.
MITCHELL, W. J. T. *Iconology: Image, Text, Ideology*. Chicago: University of Chicago Press, 1986.
PERLOFF, Marjorie. *The Futurist Moment: Avant-garde, Avant guerre, and the Language of Rupture*. Chicago: University of Chicago Press, 2003.
PEROSA, Sergio. 'Literary Deaths in Venice'. In *Venetian Views, Venetian Blinds: English Fantasies of Venice*. Edited by Manfred Pfister and Barbara Schaff. Amsterdam: Rodopi, 1999.
POUND, Ezra. *The Cantos*. London: Faber and Faber, 1964.
RUSKIN, John. 'The Stones of Venice'. In *Works, vol. 1*. Edited by Edward Cook and Alexander Wedderburn. London: George Allen, 1903–1912.
SANT'ELIA, Antonio. 'Manifesto of Futurist Architecture'. In *Documents of Twentieth Century Art: Futurist Manifestos*. Edited by Umbro Apollonio, translated by Robert Brain, R.W. Flint, J.C. Higgitt, and Caroline Tisdall. New York: Viking, 1973.
SIMONSEN, Dorthe Gert. 'Accelerating Modernity: Time–Space Compression in the Wake of the Aeroplane'. *Journal of Transport History* 26, no. 2 (2005): 98–117.
SIMPSON, James. *Under the Hammer: Iconoclasm in the Anglo-American Tradition*. Oxford: Oxford University Press, 2010.
STOKES, Adrian. 'Venice'. In *The Critical Writings of Adrian Stokes, Vol. II (1937–1958)*. New York: Thames and Hudson, 1978.
TAUSSIG, Michael. *Defacement: Public Secrecy and the Labor of the Negative*. Stanford: Stanford University Press, 1999.

———. 'The Beach (a Fantasy)'. *Critical Inquiry* 26, no. 2 (2000): 248–278.
WAUGH, Evelyn. *Brideshead Revisited: the Sacred and Profane Memories of Captain Charles Ryder*. London: Penguin, 1962.
WEINSHENKER, Anne Betty. 'Idolatry and Sculpture in Ancien Régime France'. *Eighteenth-Century Studies* 38, no. 3 (2005): 485–507.
WILMER, Clive. 'Sculpture and Economics in Pound and Ruskin'. *P.N Review 122* 24, no. 6 (1998): 43–49.
WILSON, Alexandra. 'Torrefranca vs. Puccini: Embodying a decadent Italy'. *Cambridge Opera Journal* 13, no. 1 (2001): 29–53.
ZORZI, Rosella Mamoli. 'Intertextual Venice: Blood and Crime and Death renewed in two contemporary Novels'. In *Venetian Views, Venetian Blinds: English Fantasies of Venice*. Edited by Manfred Pfister and Barbara Schaff. Amsterdam: Rodopi, 1999.

CHAPTERS 5 AND 6

ADDISON, Paul, and Jeremy A. Crang (eds.). *Firestorm: The Bombing of Dresden, 1945*. London: Pimlico, 2006.
BERGER, Peter. *The Desecularization of the World: Resurgent Religion and World Politics*. Grand Rapids, Michigan: Eerdmans, 1999.
BILEFSKY, Dan. 'Islamic Revival Tests Bosnia's Secular Cast'. *New York Times*, December 27, 2008.
BORIN, Jacqueline. 'Embers of the Soul: the Destruction of Jewish Books and Libraries in Poland during World War II'. *Libraries and Culture* 28, no. 4 (1993): 445–460.
BOURIS, Erica. *Complex Political Victims*. Bloomfield, Connecticut: Kumarian Press, 2007.
BRESCHI, Danilo. 'A New Humanism in Europe: Between Secularism and the Return of Religion'. *Telos*, 2007, http://tinyurl.com/breschi-humanism
CALAME, Jon. 'Post-war Reconstruction: Concerns, Models and Approaches'. Center for Macro Projects and Diplomacy Working Paper, Series 6, 2005.
CAMERON, Christina. 'The Context of the World Heritage Convention: Key Decisions and Emerging Concepts'. Paper given at UNESCO, 25–27, 2009, *Reflections on the Future of the World Heritage Convention*, http://tinyurl.com/cameron-pdf
VON CLAUSEWITZ, Carl. *On War*. Translated by Michael Howard and Peter Paret. Princeton: Princeton University Press, 1989.
COWARD, Martin. 'Urbicide in Bosnia'. In *Cities, War, and Terrorism: towards an Urban Geopolitics*. Edited by Stephen Graham. Oxford: Blackwell, 2004.
DERKOVIĆ, Nadia Copuzzo. 'Dealing with the Past: the Role of Cultural Heritage Preservation and Monuments in a Post-Conflict Society'. In *World Heritage and Cultural Diversity*. Edited by Marie-Therese Albert and Dieter Offenhäusser. German Commission for UNESCO, 2010.

DONIA, Robert J. 'Nationalism and Religious Extremism in Bosnia-Herzegovina and Kosovo since 1990'. *International Institute for Middle East and Balkan Studies*, 2007, http://tinyurl.com/donia-balkans

DROZDOWSKI, Marian Marek, and Andrzej Zahorski. *Historia Warszawy*. Warsaw: Jeden Swiat Wydawnictwo, 2004.

ELZANOWSKI, Jerzy. 'Manufacturing Ruins: Architecture and Representation in Post-catastrophic Warsaw'. *The Journal of Architecture* 15, no. 1 (2010): 71–86.

FREGONESE, Sara, and Ralf Brand, 'Polarization as a Socio-Material Phenomenon: A Bibliographical Review'. *Journal of Urban Technology* 16, no. 2 (2009): 9–33.

GRUNBERGER, Richard. *A Social History of the Third Reich*. London: Penguin, 1991.

GUTSCHOW, Niels. *Ordnungswahn: Architekten planen im 'eingedeutschten Osten', 1939–1945*. Gütersloh: Bertelsmann Fachzeitschriften, 2001.

HABERMAS, Jürgen, and Joseph Ratzinger. *The Dialectics of Secularization: on Reason and Religion*. San Francisco: Ignatius, 2006.

HAJDARPAŠIĆ, Edin. 'Out of the Ruins of the Ottoman Empire: Reflections on the Ottoman Legacy in South-eastern Europe'. *Middle Eastern Studies* 44, no. 5 (2008): 715–734.

HERBERT, Ulrich (ed.). *National Socialist Extermination Policies: Contemporary German Perspectives and Controversies*. New York: Berghahn, 2000.

HITLER, Adolf. *Mein Kampf*. Translated by Ralph Manheim. London: Pimlico, 1997.

HUNTINGTON, Samuel. 'The Erosion of American National Interests'. *Foreign Affairs* 76, no. 5 (1997): 28–49.

JERSAK, Tobias. 'Blitzkrieg Revisited: A New Look at Nazi War and Extermination Planning'. *The Historical Journal* 43, no. 2 (2000): 565–582.

KIEL, Machiel. 'Un héritage non désiré : le patrimoine architectural islamique ottoman dans l'Europe du Sud-Est, 1370–1912'. *Études Balkaniques* 12 (2005): 15–82.

LAMBOURNE, Nicola. *War Damage in Western Europe: the Destruction of historic Monuments during the Second World War*. Edinburgh: Edinburgh University Press, 2001.

LEŠIĆ, Zdenko (ed.). *Children of Atlantis: voices from the former Yugoslavia*. Budapest: Central European University Press, 1995.

LINDQVIST, Sven. *A History of Bombing*. Translated by Linda Rugg. New York: The New Press, 2001.

LIOTTA, P.H., and Anna Simons. 'Thicker than Water? Kin, Religion, and Conflict in the Balkans'. *Parameters* 23, no. 4 (1998): 11–27.

MCELLIGOTT, Anthony. *The German Urban Experience, 1900-1945: Modernity and Crisis*. Abingdon: Routledge, 2001.

MCNEILL, William H. *The Pursuit of Power: Technology, Armed Force, and Society since A.D. 1000*. Oxford: Blackwell, 1983.

MALCOLM, Noel. *Bosnia: A Short History*. London: Macmillan, 1996.

MANN, Thomas. *Doctor Faustus: the Life of the German Composer Adrian Leverkühn, as told by a Friend*. Translated by H.T. Lowe-Porter. London: Minerva, 1996.
MARMOT, Alexi Ferster. 'Urbanism in Warsaw: Solidarity and Beyond'. *Places* 1, no. 2 (1983): 78–83.
PERICA, Vjekoslav. 'The Politics of Ambivalence: Europeanization and the Serbian Orthodox Church'. In *Religion in an Expanding Europe*. Edited by Timothy A. Byrnes and Peter J. Katzenstein. Cambridge: Cambridge University Press, 2006.
PETITO, Fabio, and Pavlos Hatzopoulos (eds.). *Religion in International Relations: The Return from Exile*. Basingstoke: Palgrave Macmillan, 2003.
RAMET, Sabrina P. *Thinking about Yugoslavia: Scholarly Debates about the Yugoslav Breakup and the Wars in Bosnia and Kosovo*. Cambridge: Cambridge University Press, 2005.
RIEDLMAYER, András J. 'From the Ashes: The Past and Future of Bosnia's Cultural Heritage'. In *Islam and Bosnia: Conflict Resolution and Foreign Policy in Multi-Ethnic States*. Edited by Maya Shatzmiller. Montreal: McGill–Queens University Press, 2002.
SCHWARTZ, Stephen. 'Islamic Fundamentalism in the Balkans'. *Partisan Review* 67, no. 3 (2000): 421–427.
———. 'The Arab Betrayal of Balkan Islam'. *Middle East Quarterly* 9, no. 2 (2002): 43–52.
SELLS, Michael. 'Religion, History, and Genocide in Bosnia-Herzegovina'. In *Religion and Justice in the War over Bosnia*. Edited by G. Scott Davis. New York: Routledge, 1997.
———. *The Bridge Betrayed: Religion and Genocide in Bosnia*. Berkeley: University of California Press, 1998.
SROKA, Marek. 'The University of Cracow Library under Nazi Occupation: 1939–1945'. *Libraries and Culture* 34, no. 1 (1999): 1–17.
TOMASZEWSI, Irene. *Inside a Gestapo Prison: the Letters of Krystyna Wituska, 1942–1944*. Detroit: Wayne State University Press, 2006.
TUNG, Anthony. *Preserving the World's Great Cities: the Destruction and Renewal of the Historic Metropolis*. New York: Three Rivers Press, 2001.
VANDERBILT, Tom. *Survival City: Adventures Among the Ruins of Atomic America*. New York: Princeton Architectural Press, 2002.
WARD, Stephen V. (ed.). *The Garden City: Past, Present, and Future*. Abingdon: Taylor and Francis, 1992.
YOUNG, James E. 'The Biography of a Memorial Icon: Nathan Rapoport's Warsaw Ghetto Monument', *Representations* 26 (1989): 69–106.

Human Rights Chamber for Bosnia and Herzegovina. 'The Islamic Community in Bosnia and Herzegovina against The Republika Srpska'. *Case no. CH/96/29* (1999).
Bosnia and Herzegovina Commission to Preserve National Monuments. *Report no. 08.2-6-533/03-8* (2003), http://tinyurl.com/ferhadija-commission-report

Index of Key Names

Abraham/Ibrahim, 4, 6-8, 33, 46, 70-72, 75, 92
Abraj al-Bait. *See* Mecca
Adorno, Theodor, 182, 184
al-Diriyyah, 16, 62, 64, 75-76, 79, 82-84
Aquinas, Thomas, 12
Assad, Bashar al, xiii
Augustine of Hippo, 9, 38

Bamiyan, the Buddhas of, xi, 158, 166–172, 175, 180–181
Banja Luka
    attack on the Ferhadija mosque, 156–159, 165
Belloc, Hilaire, 100
Benjamin, Walter, 118, 126
Berger, John, xiv
Boccioni, Umberto, 123–126
Bosnia-Herzegovina
    attacks on religious buildings, 1, 148, 152
    political identity of, 148–151, 154
    reconstruction of mosques, 157, 159–165
    religious identity of, 148–154, 158
    'Wahhabi' identity of, 160–165
Bouchardon, Edmé, 19, 109–110
Brydges, Sir Harford, 80
Bullinger, Henry, 53

Calvin, John
    and 'Calvinist' iconoclasm, 54, 57–59
    comparison with Muhammad ibn Abd al-Wahhab, 16–17, 75-77, 92–93
    connection between iconoclasm and political obedience, 41, 43, 46–51, 58
    influence on the French Revolution, 98–103, 105, 107
    move to Geneva, 15, 28, 30–31, 44–45
    theory of idols, 32–36
    theory of the Image of God and the Word of God, 39–41, 50
    theory of social governance, 43–54, 100
    theory of the 'True Church', 33–34, 41–43, 46
    theory of the 'True God', 33, 35, 37–41
Charlie Hebdo, xi, xiv, 167, 172, 180
Clausewitz, Carl von, 132
Cluny, Abbey of, 19, 98, 111

Danto, Arthur, 15, 44
David, Jacques-Louis, 112
Dresden, attack on, 128–129, 132–134

Eliot, T.S., 121–122
Erasmus, Desiderius, 39–40

Farel, Guillaume, 24–31, 43–44, 51–58

Index of Key Names

Ferhadija mosque. *See* Banja Luka
Fromm, Erich, 128, 182, 184
Fromment, Antoine, 24–28, 43, 56

Gellner, Ernest, 85
Geneva
   attack on the Cathedral of Saint Pierre, 2, 25–27, 58
   demography of, 43–44, 52–58
   government of, 28–29, 51–53, 55–56
   monuments to iconoclasm, 15, 23–24
   as the 'New Jerusalem', 43
   relationship to neighbours, 27–29
Golden Calf, the, *See* Moses/Musa

Habermas, Jürgen, 102, 110, 172
Hajj, the, 62, 65–66, 73, 77–82, 85, 87, 90, 170, 173–178
Harris, Arthur 'Bomber', 133
Hatra, x, xiii
Haussmann, Baron Georges-Eugène, 114, 131
Henri-Lévy, Bernard, xii
Hijaz, 17, 62–66, 68–70, 76–84, 88–90, 175
Himmler, Heinrich, 136
Hitler, Adolf, 128–129, 134–136
Hobbes, Thomas, 4, 104
Horkheimer, Max, 182, 184
Howard, Ebenezer, 137

Ibn Ghannam, Hussain, 66, 69, 78, 80, 81
Ibn Saud, King Abdulaziz, 76, 82–83, 87–91
Iraq, attacks on religious sites, x, xii, xiv, 1, 166–167
ISIS, x, xii–xiv, 167, 172, 181, 185
Izetbegović, Alija, 150, 160–161

James, Henry, 115–116, 118–119, 125
John of Damascus, 10–11, 34

John Paul II, Pope
   rejection of idolatry, 9
   theory of apostolic succession, 12
   theory of icon, 9–10

Karlstadt, Andreas, 13, 31
Krakow, attack on, 133–134

Laden, Osama bin, 168, 175, 190n.49
Latour, Bruno
   theory of 'iconoclash', 18–19, 183
Lazar, Prince of Serbia, 152–154
Le Corbusier, 183
Lenin, Vladimir, 1, 105
Lenoir, Alexandre, 108–109
Ludendorff, Erich, 130–132

Mann, Thomas, 117–118, 133
Marinetti, Filippo Tommaso, 122–126
Marx, Karl, 18, 102, 119, 182
Mecca
   attacks on shrines and tombs, 1, 16–17, 74–75, 77–82, 88, 175–176
   construction of Abraj al-Bait, 2, 167, 173–176, 179
   site of the *Hajj*, 8, 65, 77–80, 173–176
Medina, 16, 19, 61–62, 67–68, 80–81, 165, 175
Michelangelo, 9, 12, 123
Milošević, Slobodan, 150–154
Moses/Musa
   convenant, 4, 10, 33, 45, 177
   reaction to the golden calf, 4–6
Mosul, x, xiii

Najd
   demography of, 62–65, 82
   political society of, 66, 77, 82–83, 84–91

Newton, Isaac, 103
Niceron, Jean-François, 104
Nimrud, x, xiii–xiv, 185

Omar, Mullah, 168, 171

Paris
  attacks on art and statues,
    104–110
  political development of
    museums, 108,
    111–112, 131
Pound, Ezra, 117, 119–122, 125
Poussin, Nicolas, 101

Réau, Louis, 106, 181
Reims Cathedral, attack on,
    130–131
Riyadh, urban development of,
    16–17, 82, 84–89, 173, 175,
    178
Robert, Hubert, 106–107, 116
Rousseau, Jean-Jacques, 100,
    104–105
Ruskin, John, 111, 115, 117–118,
    120–121

Said, Edward, 63
St. Denis, attack on the Basilica of,
    98, 101, 104–109
Sant'Elia, Antonio, 124
Saudi Arabia, state formation, 77,
    82–92, 173, 176–178
Shylock, 120, 121
Sindi, Muhammad Hayya al, 68
Sistine Chapel, the, 9–10
Skinner, Quentin, 15, 19, 91, 182
Speer, Albert, 128
Strasbourg Cathedral, attack on,
    131

UNESCO, 73, 114, 145, 159, 163,
    170, 175

Venice
  as a corrupted city, 116–119,
    121–122
  iconoclastic rhetoric against,
    122–125
  as the ideal city, 115
  and ruination, 115, 120, 125
  and usury, 119–122, 125
Viollet-le-Duc, Eugène, 111
Voltaire, François-Marie Arouet,
    102, 104

Wahhab, Muhammad ibn Abd al
  biographical accounts of, 66–70
  comparison with John Calvin,
    16–17, 75–77, 92–93
  contemporary European views of,
    67, 78–80
  intellectual influences on, 67–69
  political alliance with the al-
    Sauds, 16, 62, 68, 77, 85
  theory of idolatry, 16, 61, 71–73
  theory of monotheism, 16, 61,
    70–72
  and 'Wahhabi' iconoclasm,
    16–18, 61–62, 68, 72–73,
    75–78, 80–81, 175
Warsaw
  destruction of, 130, 133–138
  New German City of (Pabst
    Plan), 136–138
  reconstruction of, 140–145
Waugh, Evelyn, 119
Weber, Max
  methodology of religious studies,
    18, 94
  theory of civil society, 85
  theory of Islam, 18
  theory of officialdom, 1
World Trade Center, xi–xii, 18, 158,
    166, 172, 179–180

Zachwatowicz, Jan, 144–145

James Noyes holds a doctorate in Religious Studies from the University of Cambridge. He has taught on religion, culture and conflict at the Paris Institute of Political Studies (Sciences Po) in France, and works as a policy advisor on these matters in the UK.

'The span of Noyes's tour d'horizon is impressive… the book's major achievement is to show how central politics has been in the history of iconoclasm, thereby making a crucial contribution to the body of recent landmark publications in this field… highly relevant to readers with a more general interest in modern political history. Moving beyond the old master-narratives of modernity and secularization, it sheds new light on the relation between the sacred, political and material worlds in the modern age.'

David Motadel, *Times Literary Supplement*

'Usually, iconoclasm has been seen as a sub-plot in modern history. James Noyes suggests that it may be the main plot – linking together aspects of Islam, the Reformation and modern secular revolutions. In this light, modernity itself appears much more as the bearer of a negative, destructive impulse hidden behind various schemas of reform and projects of progress. So the reader is led by careful scholarly and analytic paths to a dark and subversive conclusion.'

John Milbank, Professor in Religion, Politics and Ethics, University of Nottingham

'This erudite, interesting, and highly readable book makes an important connection between the struggle for political power and iconoclastic religious extremism. It artfully shows that the radical rejection of religious images and icons is a challenge to orthodox authority and a basis for political power. Finding striking similarities between Protestant Calvinism and Islamic Wahhabism, it demonstrates that these historical examples are related to the rise of the modern state, and have a direct link to contemporary movements of religious activism. This book will be much discussed: it will impress both historians and policy-makers, and be an eye-opener to those who follow global religious and political trends in the contemporary era.'

Mark Juergensmeyer, Director, Orfalea Center for Global & International Studies, University of California, Santa Barbara, and author of *Terror in the Mind of God: The Global Rise of Religious Violence*

'*The Politics of Iconoclasm* is an achievement – original and thought provoking. Beginning with chapters on the formative histories of "Calvinism" and "Wahhabism" and their connections with image-breaking and state-building, James Noyes goes on to explore surprising connections between violence and religious-political thought through a number of historical case studies – including acts of symbolic destruction in the French Revolution, the calculated destruction of European cities during World War II, and the recent destruction and rebuilding of parts of Mecca in modern style. Noyes invites the reader to consider "iconoclasm" not simply as a label for fanaticism, but as the deliberate breaking of physical objects (images, buildings, shrines) that are mediated theologically, and carried out as acts of self-formation in the creation and assertion of modern state power. This is a remarkably suggestive book: careful in assembling its sources and yet engagingly written and argued.'

Talal Asad, Distinguished Professor of
Anthropology, City University of New York
(CUNY) Graduate Center

www.ingramcontent.com/pod-product-compliance
Lightning Source LLC
Chambersburg PA
CBHW071836230426